Lecture Notes in Computer Science 15153

Founding Editors

Gerhard Goos
Juris Hartmanis

AF817255

Editorial Board Members

Elisa Bertino, *Purdue University, West Lafayette, IN, USA*
Wen Gao, *Peking University, Beijing, China*
Bernhard Steffen, *TU Dortmund University, Dortmund, Germany*
Moti Yung, *Columbia University, New York, NY, USA*

The series Lecture Notes in Computer Science (LNCS), including its subseries Lecture Notes in Artificial Intelligence (LNAI) and Lecture Notes in Bioinformatics (LNBI), has established itself as a medium for the publication of new developments in computer science and information technology research, teaching, and education.

LNCS enjoys close cooperation with the computer science R & D community, the series counts many renowned academics among its volume editors and paper authors, and collaborates with prestigious societies. Its mission is to serve this international community by providing an invaluable service, mainly focused on the publication of conference and workshop proceedings and postproceedings. LNCS commenced publication in 1973.

Marieke Huisman · Falk Howar
Editors

Tests and Proofs

18th International Conference, TAP 2024
Milan, Italy, September 9–10, 2024
Proceedings

Springer

Editors
Marieke Huisman
University of Twente
Enschede, The Netherlands

Falk Howar
TU Dortmund University
Dortmund, Nordrhein-Westfalen, Germany

ISSN 0302-9743 ISSN 1611-3349 (electronic)
Lecture Notes in Computer Science
ISBN 978-3-031-72043-7 ISBN 978-3-031-72044-4 (eBook)
https://doi.org/10.1007/978-3-031-72044-4

© The Editor(s) (if applicable) and The Author(s), under exclusive license
to Springer Nature Switzerland AG 2025

This work is subject to copyright. All rights are solely and exclusively licensed by the Publisher, whether the whole or part of the material is concerned, specifically the rights of translation, reprinting, reuse of illustrations, recitation, broadcasting, reproduction on microfilms or in any other physical way, and transmission or information storage and retrieval, electronic adaptation, computer software, or by similar or dissimilar methodology now known or hereafter developed.
The use of general descriptive names, registered names, trademarks, service marks, etc. in this publication does not imply, even in the absence of a specific statement, that such names are exempt from the relevant protective laws and regulations and therefore free for general use.
The publisher, the authors and the editors are safe to assume that the advice and information in this book are believed to be true and accurate at the date of publication. Neither the publisher nor the authors or the editors give a warranty, expressed or implied, with respect to the material contained herein or for any errors or omissions that may have been made. The publisher remains neutral with regard to jurisdictional claims in published maps and institutional affiliations.

This Springer imprint is published by the registered company Springer Nature Switzerland AG
The registered company address is: Gewerbestrasse 11, 6330 Cham, Switzerland

If disposing of this product, please recycle the paper.

Preface

It is a pleasure for us to introduce the articles that were presented at the 18th International Conference on Tests and Proofs (TAP). TAP 2024 took place in Milan, Italy, on September 9 and 10, 2024 as part of the Formal Methods symposium (FM 2024), which included four more co-located conferences besides TAP: FMICS (Formal Methods in Industrial Critical Systems), LOPSTR (International Symposium on Logic-based Program Synthesis and Transformation), PPDP (International Symposium on Principles and Practice of Declarative Programming), and FACS (International Conference on Formal Aspects of Component Software.

TAP's scope encompasses many aspects of verification technology, including foundational work, tool development, and empirical research. Topics of interest center around the combination of static techniques such as proving and dynamic techniques such as testing. We solicited papers on new techniques combining static and dynamic analysis techniques, as well as case studies that were analysed using a mixture of different techniques.

TAP 2024 featured two invited talks. One invited talk was given by Rosemary Monahan, Maynooth University, Ireland, on *Formalising Requirements for Systems Verification*, and was shared with the other co-located FM events. The other invited talk was given by Rüdiger Ehlers, Clausthal University of Technology, Germany, on *Efficient Temporal Logic Runtime Monitoring for Tiny Systems*. This volume includes 8 regular papers that were presented in the research track, out of which 7 were regular papers and 1 was a short paper, one extended abstract, and one invited paper for the invited talks. In total TAP 2024 received 15 submissions, including 1 submitted abstract that was withdrawn before a full submission was made. One submission was desk-rejected as it was out of scope for TAP. All papers were reviewed by at least three reviewers following a single-blind review process conducted by TAP's 2024 Program Committee and external sub-reviewers.

TAP provided a (lightweight) artifact evaluation. Authors of accepted papers were invited to submit artifacts. Four artifacts were submitted for review. TAP 2024 awarded EAPLS badges to artifacts. All artifacts received an 'Artifact Available' badge, one additionally received an 'Artifact Functional' badge, and two were awarded an 'Artifact Reusable' badge.

We thank all the authors for their work and their interest in TAP 2024, as well as the PC members and sub-reviewers for their very thorough reviews and insightful remarks that have greatly helped to improve the quality of the papers that are presented in this volume. We also thank our artifact reviewers, who in a very short period managed to do a quick but thorough evaluation of the submitted artifacts. We also extend our thanks to the TAP steering committee for all their support in preparing the conference, as well as to the organizers of FM 2024 for all support with the practical organisation issues.

July 2024

Falk Howar
Marieke Huisman

Organization

Program Committee

Wolfgang Ahrendt	Chalmers University of Technology, Sweden
Oana Andrei	University of Glasgow, UK
Catherine Dubois	ENSIIE-Samovar, France
Rüdiger Ehlers	Clausthal University of Technology, Germany
Marie Farrell	University of Manchester, UK
María del Mar Gallardo	University of Málaga, Spain
Fatemeh Ghassemi	University of Tehran, Iran
Falk Howar (Chair)	TU Dortmund University, Germany
Marieke Huisman (Chair)	University of Twente, Netherlands
Reiner Hähnle	TU Darmstadt, Germany
Marie-Christine Jakobs	Ludwig-Maximilians-Universität München, Germany
Jan Kofroň	Charles University, Czechia
Nikolai Kosmatov	Thales Research & Technology, France
Florian Lorber	Silicon Austria Labs, Austria
Anastasia Mavridou	KBR/NASA Ames Research Center, USA
Luigia Petre	Åbo Akademi University, Finland
Virgile Prevosto	Université Paris-Saclay, France
Daniel Ratiu	Autonomous Intelligent Driving, Germany
Cristina Seceleanu	Mälardalen University, Sweden
Jan Strejček	Masaryk University, Czechia
Mattias Ulbrich	Karlsruhe Institute of Technology, Germany
Neil Walkinshaw	University of Sheffield, UK
Heike Wehrheim	University of Oldenburg, Germany

Steering Committee

Wolfgang Ahrendt	Chalmers University of Technology, Sweden
Bernhard K. Aichernig	Graz University of Technology, Austria
Jasmin Blanchette	LMU, Germany
Achim D. Brucker	University of Exeter, UK
Catherine Dubois	École Nationale Supérieure d'Informatique pour l'Industrie et l'Entreprise, France

Nikolai Kosmatov Thales Research and Technology, France
Burkhart Wolff Université Paris-Saclay, France

Additional Reviewers

Richard Bubel
Jan Haltermann
Ayrat Khalimov
Romain Pascual

Artifact Reviewers

Simon Dierl
Robert Rubbens
Richard Stewing
Robert Mensing
Dominik Schmid
Philip Tasche

Invited Talk

Formalising Requirements for Verification

Rosemary Monahan

Maynooth University, Maynooth, Ireland

The verification of software systems often relies on a combination of formal methods, testing and simulation based approaches. Knowing what to specify for verification cannot be achieved without clear, unambiguous descriptions of the system requirements. This makes detailed requirements elicitation and formalisation a crucial step in the process. Tools such as NASA's Formal Requirements Elicitation Tool (FRET) have been developed to bridge the gap between natural language requirements and the logics normally used for formal specification [3]. We have used FRET to formalise natural language requirements, enabling the use of mathematically-based techniques to guarantee that the system obeys certain properties. These formalised requirements subsequently guide the systems verification using a combination of paradigms, providing for system-level modelling and verification using model checkers and deductive verifiers. Our use cases include an aircraft engine controller [2] and a mechanical lung ventilator [1].

Our experience confirms FRET's suitability as a framework for the elicitation and understanding of requirements and for providing traceability from requirements to specification. We discuss our approach to providing traceability from natural-language requirements to a formal design model, using the FRETISH structured requirements language as an intermediate step. We reflect on the requirements that we could and could not formalise with FRET, those that required further details for formalisation, and those that provided a link between formal requirements and formal specifications. In addition to providing requirements traceability, we have provided extensions to FRET with adaptations of software code refactorings for requirements, making requirements more manageable. We support this in Mu-FRET[1], a version of FRET which enables refactoring of requirements and proof that the refactored requirements have the same behaviour as the original requirements.

References

1. Farrell, M., Luckcuck, M., Monahan, R., Reynolds, C., Sheridan, O.: Fretting and formal modelling: a mechanical lung ventilator. In Bonfanti, S., Gargantini, A., Leuschel, M., Riccobene, E., Scandurra, P. (eds.) Rigorous State-Based Methods. ABZ 2024. Lecture Notes in Computer Science, vol. 14759, pp. 360–383. Springer, Cham (2024). https://doi.org/10.1007/978-3-031-63790-2_28

[1] https://github.com/valu3s-mu/mu-fret

2. Farrell, M., Luckcuck, M., Sheridan, O., Monahan, R.: FRETting about requirements: formalised requirements for an aircraft engine controller. In: Gervasi, V., Vogelsang, A. (eds.) Requirements Engineering: Foundation for Software Quality. REFSQ 2022. Lecture Notes in Computer Science, vol. 13216, pp. 96–111. Springer, Springer, Cham (2022). https://doi.org/10.1007/978-3-030-98464-9_9
3. Giannakopoulou, D., Pressburger, T., Mavridou, A., Schumann, J.: Automated formalization of structured natural language requirements. Inf. Softw. Technol. **137**, 106590 (2021)

Contents

Invited Talks

Efficient Temporal Logic Runtime Monitoring for Tiny Systems 3
Rüdiger Ehlers

Quality of Tests and Proofs

Is MCDC Really Better? Lessons from Combining Tests and Proofs 25
Li Huang, Bertrand Meyer, and Manuel Oriol

Refining CEGAR-Based Test-Case Generation with Feasibility Annotations 45
Max Barth and Marie-Christine Jakobs

No Smoke Without Fire: Detecting Specification Inconsistencies with Frama-C/WP 65
Allan Blanchard, Loïc Correnson, Adel Djoudi, and Nikolai Kosmatov

Testing and Proving Advanced Properties

Runtime Verification for High-Level Security Properties: Case Study on the TPM Software Stack 87
Yani Ziani, Nikolai Kosmatov, Frédéric Loulergue, and Daniel Gracia Pérez

Cyclone: A New Tool for Verifying/Testing Graph-Based Structures: Tool Paper 107
Hao Wu, Thomas Flinkow, and Dominique Méry

Applications of Tests and Proofs

Model-Based Testing of Quantum Computations 127
Malte Lochau and Ina Schaefer

AFFINITREE: A Compositional Framework for Formal Analysis and Explanation of Deep Neural Networks 148
Maximilian Schlüter and Bernhard Steffen

Exploring Loose Coupling of Slicing with Dynamic Symbolic Execution on the JVM 168
Malte Mues, Julian Rüschoff, and Ben Hermann

Author Index 177

Invited Talks

Efficient Temporal Logic Runtime Monitoring for Tiny Systems

Rüdiger Ehlers(✉)

Clausthal University of Technology, Clausthal-Zellerfeld, Germany
ruediger.ehlers@tu-clausthal.de

Abstract. While the theory and practice of runtime monitoring are overall well developed, in embedded systems, runtime monitoring is not as common as one would expect. Especially small-scale embedded systems, which are found in many household devices, are often somewhat safety-critical and could benefit from the possibility to detect software or hardware defects that cannot be uncovered with verification alone. While monitoring frameworks such as RTLola and Copilot are available to address this problem, employing them leads to a gap between verification and runtime monitoring by these frameworks having specialized specification languages for monitoring, and what can be expressed in them is incomparable to the capabilities of the temporal logics traditionally employed in formal verification.

This paper discusses how (linear) temporal logic runtime monitoring for small-scale embedded systems can be made more efficient and attractive to the embedded systems practitioner. This includes identifying why monitoring for traditional temporal logics is somewhat inefficient in software, how this problem can be addressed in a low-cost way, and how runtime monitors can become a more useful component of an embedded system. By providing a way to translate a specification to monitor code that also tracks the reason for a specification violation, the overall approach discussed in the paper makes spending developer time on writing a relatively precise specification of a system to build attractive, which also helps paving the way to make formal verification for small-scale embedded systems more common.

1 Introduction

Many real-world systems are too complex to verify directly. They have too many states, so that we cannot simply build a transition system representation of them and compare it against some specification. This problem is addressed by several different approaches in formal methods. They key activity in some of them is abstracting the design under concern to something more manageable, either by means of a carefully made abstraction, or by learning such an abstraction and using the result as a model.

Not all systems lend themselves to obtaining such an abstraction, however, and in such a case, we have to deal with a relatively complex system. This is especially the case when the environment of a system is not fully modeled, but

© The Author(s), under exclusive license to Springer Nature Switzerland AG 2025
M. Huisman and F. Howar (Eds.): TAP 2024, LNCS 15153, pp. 3–21, 2025.
https://doi.org/10.1007/978-3-031-72044-4_1

the environment behavior is crucial for the correctness of a system. In such a case, we have to trade being able to detect every error (right away) against being able to analyze a complex system without abstraction, which means observing system behavior and *testing* or *monitoring* it for correctness. In this case, the system is used in a black-box or gray-box manner without the need for an abstraction. We can however still utilize a formal specification, so that we can reason formally about *an* execution of a system, but not its set of executions.

Testing and monitoring differ by scope and how a system is used. In the former case, a system (under test) is employed in a testing environment, which allows to focus on individual aspects of its operation and to observe the system's behavior in carefully crafted situations, such as boundary cases. Furthermore, in testing, relatively expensive analysis techniques can be used for analyzing the behavior of the system under test, and testing setups can be augmented with components for tracking the precise nature of a specification violation, which helps with finding the cause of a specification violation in case it occurs.

Monitoring, on the other hand, is a related but independent activity. Monitoring means to assess the correctness of the system's behavior by observing its behavior and raising an alarm whenever a violation of the specification is witnessed. Monitoring can be used in the scope of testing but is not bound to it – an efficient monitor can be deployed in the field along with the system whose correctness we are interested in, so that even violations of properties of interest that were not found during testing due to missing test scenarios can be uncovered. In the case of embedded systems, monitoring also allows to identify erroneous behavior due to hardware defects (e.g., in sensors or actuators) for which the system's behavior was not formally verified. The output of a monitor can furthermore be used to influence the system's operation itself, such as by the system shutting down in an orderly manner in case of a specification violation.

The possibilities to also detect specification violations due to unmodelled causes (such as hardware defects) and to allow the system to react to violations are unique properties of monitoring among the different approaches to proving the correctness of a system. Especially for embedded systems of a smaller scale, monitoring is attractive, as the interaction of such systems with the physical environment and their hardware-specific software implementations reduce the possible degree of test automation (when compared to pure software-based systems). Small-scale embedded systems do not have layers of abstraction that allow to test their software independent of the hardware. Many required properties of embedded systems can be represented using *temporal logics*, and approaches to temporal logic runtime monitoring have been developed that yield monitors that can be integrated into embedded systems.

For instance, Havelund and Rosu [21] showed how to translate a linear past time temporal logic formula into C code that monitors the satisfaction of the formula when calling the monitor update/step function whenever the propositions occurring in the formula receive new values. The C code is relatively cumbersome to execute due to having many bitwise operations that each take at least one clock cycle for a microcontroller. This can be avoided by having the monitor run on a *field-programmable gate array (FPGA)*, where bitwise operations can execute in parallel and when monitoring the input/output behavior of an existing system, the FPGA can simply be connected to input and output to perform the monitoring process [27]. This approach has the drawback that FPGAs are normally more expensive than the microcontrollers they monitor, which causes the approach to have a relatively high cost.

While most embedded systems are closed-source and hence statistics on the adoption of runtime monitoring in embedded systems are difficult to give, it can still be observed that both in research as well as at industry trade shows, runtime monitoring for small-scale embedded systems is seldom a topic that is widely discussed (unlike, e.g., security for embedded systems), despite many runtime monitoring approaches already being available. This is rather unfortunate, as it has been noted that a show-stopper to the wider adoption of formal methods in industry is the need to train engineers in writing and working with formal specifications [32]. With its unique properties, runtime monitoring could be a wedge in the door toward greater adoption of formal methods in the embedded systems industry, which would then also help with paving the way for proof-based formal methods (such as the combination of learning a system model from traces and verifying this model against the specification [36]).

In recent years, runtime monitoring frameworks such as Copilot [28] and RTLola [18] entered the scene, which take runtime monitoring to the next level by allowing to provide a stream-based specification of the properties to be monitored and having compilation workflows to either C code or FPGA implementations. They feature operations over stream data as first-class citizens, which makes expressing complex properties over data feasible. As such, they make monitoring more attractive, but come with the draw-back that the domain-specific monitoring languages are less expressive in the temporal behavior of systems than classical temporal logics such as linear temporal logic (LTL, [29]). Also, employing monitoring-specific specification languages causes a divide between runtime monitoring and formal verification (before the deployment of a system), which is undesirable for establishing more rigorous specification engineering practices in industry. Arguably, even the existing work on monitoring linear past time temporal logic formulas can be considered to be part of such a division, as formal verification is frequently done with temporal operators that look into the future.

So why is it that runtime monitoring with classical (future-time) temporal logics appears to be under-explored in industry given its benefits? We argue that there are still two problems that need to be solved to make runtime monitoring for low-cost embedded systems useful. On the one hand, monitors are surprisingly *costly*: the amount of computation time of a microcontroller spent monitoring in software can easily grow larger than the computation time needed for the core functionality. Conversely, when offloading the monitoring task to an FPGA, this extra chip can easily be more expensive than the microcontroller for the core functionality. On the other hand, for a monitor to be useful, detecting violations needs to be useful. Without diagnostic information on *how* and *why* a violation occurred, a reported error is hardly useful for improving the design of a system, which is often the reason for applying formal methods in the first place.

We show in the following how both problems can at least be partially addressed in a way suitable for very small embedded systems with computing hardware costs of less than 2 Euros. Starting from linear temporal logic as specification formalism, we summarize some previously known concepts for the computation of an online runtime monitor for embedded systems and show what makes the resulting monitors difficult to apply on small-scale embedded systems. To address these issues, we present a novel microcontroller temporal logic runtime monitoring component that is easy to integrate into future microcontrollers for safety-critical systems, and for which a prototype has already been produced in silicon. To address the need for the monitor supporting the debugging of real-world systems, we also show how the problem of automatically capturing debug information with temporal logic runtime monitors can be addressed in a way that is reasonable under very tight storage space constraints for trace information, as commonly the case in tiny embedded systems.

2 Related Work

With the focus of this paper on showing why temporal logic monitoring is difficult on small-scale embedded systems and discussing what can be done about it, the amount of related work is too big to discuss it in a comprehensive way. Rather, a (small) selection of existing results that are particularly related to the following discussion are mentioned below. Runtime monitoring is a core concept of the research field of *runtime verification*, for which an introductory textbook exists [3], as well as a dedicated conference series (RV).

Temporal logics such as linear temporal logic (LTL, [29]) are well-established for the specification of desired system behavior. LTL reasons over infinite traces, while in runtime monitoring, we can only observe *finite prefixes* of a trace. Apart from defining special LTL semantics for runtime monitoring that reason over finite traces [6,20], one can solve this problem by defining monitoring as the problem of continuously checking if the trace of the system observed so far can be *extended* to one that satisfies the specification. Doing so lets the LTL semantics for model checking and runtime monitoring coincide. We call a prefix trace of a system a *bad prefix* if it cannot be extended to a trace satisfying the specification. Monitoring in this semantics amounts to checking if a bad prefix has been observed, and hence only the *safety hull* of a property under concern can be monitored, with relatively few exceptions [16].

Kupferman and Vardi described how to monitor the safety hull of an LTL property, where the monitor is a finite-state machine of size at most doubly-exponential in the length of the LTL property [22]. The monitor is structured in a way amenable to symbolic implementations, which enables, for instance, a compact encoding of the monitor as a circuit. Such an encoding can be compiled to a circuit for monitoring and this circuit can be implemented in a *field-programmable gate array* (FPGA). Due to the fact that FPGAs offer highly parallel computing in real-time, they are used in many monitoring approaches (e.g., [8,27,30]). The application of FPGAs for monitoring requires that the FPGA is physically connected to the signals to be monitored and at the same time using FPGAs adds to the cost of a system. Also, when the monitored signals change too fast for the synthesized FPGA implementation to process, only sampling-based runtime monitoring [10] can be applied.

For embedded systems that employ microcontrollers, the cost of an FPGA for monitoring can easily exceed the cost of the system to be monitored. Deploying a monitor on the microcontroller itself is a more reasonable alternative. It involves *instrumenting* [11] the microcontroller code to be monitored so that the monitor gets informed of events of relevance to the satisfaction of the specification.

For complex embedded systems that run a real-time operating system, evaluating the stream of events for whether it represents a bad prefix can be done in a separate thread that is regularly scheduled by the real-time operating system [26]. Not all microcontrollers in embedded systems run real-time operating systems, though. Especially when their purpose does not require communication between different software components and when they need to react quickly to events, scheduling real-time tasks can complicate a design rather than simplifying it. Rather, many simpler embedded systems are programmed "bare metal", which gives the system engineer full control over the microcontroller timing. This observation advocates for integrating the monitor code directly into the monitored code itself so that it runs *synchronously* with the code to be executed [4].

Either way, monitoring needs to be efficient as the overhead of runtime monitoring for temporal logics can be substantial. Symbolic implementations of automata for the evaluation of logical formulas, as used in FPGA-based monitoring, are difficult to translate to efficient microcontroller code as a lot of "bit fiddling" code needs to be used then (see, e.g., [21]), which leads to a high number of clock cycles of overhead to the instrumented instructions.

The detection of a specification violation can be used in multiple ways. Apart from switching the monitored system to a *fail-safe mode*, detecting a violation is the starting point to finding out *why* the system behaved incorrectly. For instance, Wang et al. [39] presented an approach based on causality analysis, in which the component responsible for the violation within a bigger system is identified. Finding this component has also been studied outside of the area of runtime verification (see, e.g., [5] and the references therein).

In a sense, approaches that identify components that behave incorrectly are however only the second step to analyzing specification violations. Especially for more complex specifications, finding out *how* a specification was violated is a useful first step. This can for instance be done by highlighting which parts of the trace contribute to the violation of the specification. Beer et al. [9] employ causality to find the important time point/proposition combinations in counterexamples. They show that determining the minimal number of combinations needed to explain a violation is NP-hard, but give a polynomial-time heuristic. The approach is however not applicable to online monitoring as it requires the complete trace for the analysis. Ferrère et al. [19] provide an alternative approach that is not based on causality, but is also suitable for metric time logic and the explanation of violations in infinite (lasso-shaped) traces. The development of a corresponding online monitoring approach was left for future work.

The idea to perform runtime monitoring in hardware in order to reduce the computational cost of runtime monitoring is not restricted to the use of FPGAs [27,33]. Walters et al. [38] discuss this idea for supervising a microcontroller, however without a temporal logic specification. Reinmacher et al. [31] propose the development of a programmable runtime verification component, but focus on describing the concept rather than refining it to an implementation of such a component.

3 Linear Temporal Logic Runtime Monitoring on Small-Scale Systems – Step By Step

To illustrate why a straight-forward application of classical temporal logic runtime monitoring results yields monitors that are relatively inefficient, we illustrate how they work on an example. The example is then used as motivation for discussing refinements of the approach.

Full-length monitor code for the example in the following is available from [17]. We consider a couple of monitor code variants and report on code sizes and computation times for a 32-bit F446RE microcontroller by ST Microelectronics, which features an ARM Cortex M4 processor core, 512 kilobytes of program memory (Flash) and 128 kilobytes of RAM. While it is not actually a tiny system, its processor core has a useful extra feature, namely a clock cycle counter, which we employ for comparing the computation times of different monitors. Computation times for the monitor are taken on an example trace of length 7.

Linear Temporal Logic: We start with a specification in Linear Temporal Logic (LTL, [29]), which is a logic over infinite words $w \in (2^{\mathsf{AP}})^\omega$ of which each character assigns values to a finite set of atomic propositions AP. A word either satisfies an LTL formula or not. In the latter case, we say that the formula is *violated.* Linear temporal logic extends Boolean logic by the temporal operators G ("globally"), F ("eventually"), X ("next"), $\mathcal{U}$ ("until"), and $\mathcal{R}$ ("release"). We refer the reader to [22,29] for a formal definition of LTL.

For the example in the following, we consider monitoring a simple traffic light at an intersection, which is safety-critical and has temporal requirements. The traffic light has remotely controlled override signals for ambulance vans. To keep the example simple, we assume that the system is clocked with a clock rate of one execution step per second. For every direction, the traffic light has red, yellow and green light bulbs, and we assume that the signals shown on opposite sides of the intersection are always the same. The traffic light controller has to satisfy four properties:

1. Whenever one of the traffic lights shows yellow, it shows red next. Whenever a traffic light shows red+yellow, green follows next.

2. After a traffic light shows green, it has to show yellow or green next. Similarly, after a red light in any direction, the respective traffic light has to show red or red+yellow next.
3. Only in one direction at a time, the traffic lights may have a yellow or green light bulb lit.
4. In each direction, an ambulance van override signal can be issued, and if it keeps being issued for 10 s, the traffic light for the respective direction has to show green after the 10 s and stay green until the signal is turned off again.

The specification has the interesting property that no system can satisfy it along all possible executions. Ambulance van override signals can be given for two directions at the same time, and then the traffic light controller would need to give two green signals in different directions at the same time, which violates the third property. However, this case may not occur in practice, for instance by the receiver for the ambulance override signals only allowing one such signal at a time, and unlike in formal verification, we do not have to model this environment aspect to avoid that the employed verification approach spuriously detects the specification to be violated.

To formalize the specification in linear temporal logic, we first need to define a set of atomic propositions for the system. For simplicity, we assume a four-way intersection with traffic lights that always have the same bulbs lit in opposite directions, without separate signaling for cars that wish to turn left. We use $r_1, r_2, y_1, y_2, g_1, g_2$ as the propositions for the red, yellow, and green signals for the two relevant directions, respectively, and the two additional propositions a_1, a_2 for the ambulance override signals in these directions. The specification parts from above can be encoded into LTL as follows:

1. $\bigwedge_{i \in \{1,2\}} \mathsf{G}(\neg r_1 \wedge y_i \rightarrow \mathsf{X}(\neg y_i \wedge r_i)) \wedge \mathsf{G}(r_i \wedge y_i \rightarrow \mathsf{X} g_i)$
2. $\bigwedge_{i \in \{1,2\}} \mathsf{G}(g_i \rightarrow \mathsf{X}(g_i \vee y_i)) \wedge \mathsf{G}(r_i \rightarrow \mathsf{X}(r_i \vee \neg r_i \wedge y_i))$
3. $\mathsf{G}\neg((y_1 \vee g_1) \wedge (y_2 \vee g_2))$
4. $\bigwedge_{i \in \{1,2\}} \mathsf{G}(a_i \rightarrow \underbrace{\mathsf{X}(\neg a_i \vee \mathsf{X}(\neg a_i \vee}_{10 \text{ times}} \ldots (g_i \mathcal{U} \neg a_i) \ldots)))$

Note that not all aspects of the system's operation have been formalized, such as that if a traffic light has its green bulb lit, its other light bulbs have to be switched off. For runtime monitoring, which we want to formalize next, it is not necessary to include all such aspects.

Runtime Monitoring of LTL: Runtime monitoring is the process of observing the execution of a (reactive) system and continuously checking whether the trace so far already violates a given specification. Early guaranteed satisfaction is not considered in this paper. *Reactive systems*, which continuously interact with their environment, do not terminate and their execution can be written as an infinite *trace* in which each *trace element* provides information about the current input/output and the state of the system. For many monitoring tasks, the trace can be abstracted into a form in which each trace element is an assignment to a set of Boolean variables AP, which enables the use of LTL to specify desired system properties. Linear temporal logic is defined on traces of infinite length, and hence whether a specification is violated is not directly defined for a finite trace prefix that can be observed at runtime. To avoid introducing a special semantics for LTL over finite traces, it is common to monitor for *bad prefixes* of an trace. Formally, given an infinite word $w = w_0 w_1 \ldots \in (2^{\mathsf{AP}})^\omega$, a bad prefix $w_0 w_1 \ldots w_i$ of w (for some $i \in \mathbb{N}$) has the property that for every $w' \in (2^{\mathsf{AP}})^\omega$, we have that $w_0 \ldots w_i w'$ violates the specification.

For the traffic light specification that we formalized above, an example bad prefix is $\{r_1, r_2\}\,\{r_1, y_2\}\,\{r_1, g_2\}\,\{g_1, r_2\}$, as here, a sudden switch from green to red occurs for the second direction, which violates specification part number 2 above.

So how can we construct software components of embedded systems from LTL specifications that allow us to detect bad prefixes of the system's execution? Kupferman and Vardi [22] describe an automata-theoretic way for doing so that is based on *Büchi automata.*

Büchi Automata: A Büchi automaton is a tuple $\mathcal{A} = (Q, \Sigma, \delta, Q_0, F)$ with a finite set of states Q, an alphabet Σ (which will be a set of valuations of an atomic proposition set AP in this paper), a transition relation $\delta \subseteq Q \times \Sigma \times Q$, a set of initial states $Q_0 \subseteq Q$, and a set of accepting states F. Büchi automata operate on infinite words $w = w_0 w_1 \ldots \in \Sigma^\omega$. We say that an infinite sequence $\pi = \pi_0 \pi_1 \ldots \in Q^\omega$ is a run of $\mathcal{A}$ on w if $\pi_0 \in Q_0$ and for all $i \in \mathbb{N}$, we have $(\pi_i, w_i, \pi_{i+1}) \in \delta$. We say that π is accepting if some state in F occurs infinitely often along π, and the word w is *accepted* by $\mathcal{A}$ if there exists some accepting run for w and $\mathcal{A}$. The words accepted by an automaton form its *language*. We extend the notion of a run of a Büchi automaton to finite words in the straight-forward way, but note that it does not make sense to talk about the acceptance of such a run.

It is known how to translate a linear temporal logic formula to a Büchi automaton of size exponential in the size of the LTL formula [37]. In this context, the set of words satisfying the LTL property is the language of the Büchi automaton. For the specification given above (where we take the conjunction of the specification parts as the overall specification), we can obtain an equivalent Büchi automaton with 2904 states when using the LTL-to-Büchi translation that is part of the `spot` framework [13] (of which we use version 2.12 in this paper).

Runtime Monitoring with Büchi Automata – First Version: A Büchi automaton for a specification can be used to detect bad prefixes of the specification. For a first approach, we first need to prune all states from a Büchi automaton $\mathcal{A}$ that cannot occur along an accepting run of a word [12], which is a standard optimization step of LTL-to-Büchi translators anyway [34]. Afterwards, we have that a prefix word $w = w_0 w_1 \ldots w_n$ is a bad prefix for the language of a Büchi automaton $\mathcal{A}$ if and only if there is no finite run of $\mathcal{A}$ for w [2]. To see this, consider that there is such a finite run π. Then it can be extended to an accepting run for some infinite extension of w (as π can be the beginning of an accepting run as otherwise the state that is last in π would have been pruned away). On

```
/* State storage information */
uint8_t inState0 = 1;
uint8_t inState1 = 0;
...
uint8_t inState2903 = 0;

/* Monitor step/update function */
int monitor(uint8_t r1,uint8_t y1,uint8_t g1,uint8_t r2,uint8_t y2,uint8_t g2,
  uint8_t a1,uint8_t a2) {
  uint8_t nextState0 = 0;
  ...
  uint8_t nextState2903 = 0;
  if (inState0){
    if (!g1&&!y1&&!g2&&!y2&&!a1&&!a2&&!r1&&!r2) nextState0 = 1;
    if (!g1&&!y1&&!g2&&!y2&&!a1&&!a2&&!r1&&r2) nextState1 = 1;
  ...
  if (inState2903){
    if (g1&&!y1&&!g2&&!y2&&!a1&&!a2&&r1&&r2) nextState75 = 1;
    if (g1&&!y1&&!g2&&!y2&&a1&&!a2&&r1&&r2) nextState2679 = 1;
  }
  inState0 = nextState0;
  ...
  inState2903 = nextState2903;
  if (inState0) return 0;
  ...
  if (inState2903) return 0;
  return 1; /* Reporting a violation */
}
```

Fig. 1. Some excerpts of a runtime monitor code based on a single Büchi automaton

the other hand, if there is no such finite run π, then there is no infinite run for any infinite extension of w, which makes w a bad prefix.

This observation allows to perform runtime monitoring in a simple way: while observing the behavior of the system, a monitor can read the proposition valuations step-by-step and keep track of in which Büchi automaton states a run for the prefix trace observed so far can be. Once this state set becomes empty, a bad prefix has been observed, and the monitor can flag an alarm. We can compile a Büchi automaton to monitoring code that computes the next state set from the previous state set and the atomic propositions. To do so effectively, we group transitions by their predecessor and successor states and compile the set of characters for which some transition in the group can be taken into some symbolic expression.

For our running example, the Büchi automaton for the conjunction of the four properties has 2904 states. Figure 1 shows a part of the resulting monitor code for our example, which overall has 98303 source code lines. The source code file is too large to compile to ARM with the GNU C compiler version 7.2.1 (which runs out of memory on a 32 GB RAM computer), both with code optimization turned on or off.

Runtime Monitoring with Büchi Automata – Deterministic Approach: The program code shown in Fig. 1 shows a problem with the simple approach to runtime monitoring described above, namely that the generated code is quite inefficient. Since code blocks for different predecessor states of the automaton's transitions need to be executed for each step of the monitor, the computation time of a monitor step is quite long.

A simple way to address this problem is to treat the pruned Büchi automaton as a non-deterministic safety automaton (so that every state is accepting) and to determinize this automaton [7,35]. Every state in the determinized automaton is then labeled by the set of states in the original automaton in which a run can be in. Whenever the state labeled by the empty set is reached in a run of the determinized automaton, this constitutes having read a bad prefix.

In our running example, determinization (and performing exact automaton minimization of the result) actually decreases the number of states to 2816. For tracking the state, only a single integer variable needs to be stored in the microcontroller's RAM. The GNU C compiler again fails to compile the resulting monitor code due to running out of memory when code optimization is turned on. Without code optimization, the resulting code size for our example is 2434380 bytes, which is too large for small and medium-sized microcontrollers.

Runtime Monitoring with Büchi Automata – Fragmenting the Specification: A way to generate smaller monitoring code is to build four separate monitors for each of the four properties in the running example, and monitoring them separately. This means that we build non-deterministic Büchi automata for each of them and generate the same type of code as for the first monitor version, once for each automaton. If and when at runtime, any component monitor reports a violation, the joint monitor reports a violation.

This approach leads to more compact monitor code, requiring only 27024 bytes of code size, which now fits the program memory of the example microcontroller. The four Büchi automata built for this monitor have 147 states overall. On the short example trace, we find that the code needs 2907 clock cycles on average per monitor step for its execution.

Runtime Monitoring with Universal Automata: The observation from the previous variant, namely that the monitor became smaller after translating the specification parts to automata separately, leads to the question of how far the idea can be pushed. Is there perhaps a way to decompose the specification into many very small conjuncts? On an automata-theoretic level, this question has a positive answer in the form of *universal automata* [23]. In a nutshell, the idea in universal automata over infinite words is that *every* infinite run of the automaton for a word needs to be accepting for the word to be accepted by the automaton.

In fact, every LTL property can be translated to an equivalent *universal co-Büchi* automaton for the specification. The co-Büchi acceptance condition in this context defines that runs for which states in the automaton's F set (which are then called the *rejecting states*) are visited only finitely often are accepting. Universal co-Büchi automata for a specification consisting of many conjuncts often look more structured than non-deterministic Büchi automata for the same language, as the different states in such automata keep track of different requirements on the rest of the word in order for it to be accepted. A sub-class of universal co-Büchi word automata are *universal very weak automata*,

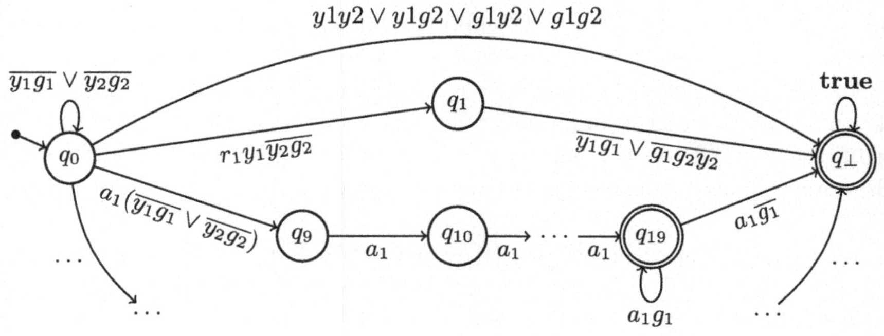

Fig. 2. A part of the universal co-Büchi automaton for the specification of the running example. Rejecting states are doubly-circled. It can be observed that some transition labels are needlessly complicated as the focus of the LTL-to-Büchi translator is on minimizing the number of states rather than the simplifying the transition labels.

which capture exactly those temporal properties that are expressible in LTL as well as computation tree logic (CTL) with universal path quantifiers, where in the latter case, we consider the satisfaction of the property along all paths of a computation tree [25]. In fact, the specification from above falls into this class, and there exists a specialized translation procedure from a subset of LTL into universal very weak automata [1].

Since when working with universal automata, the automaton rejects a word if *any* trace violates the specification, we need to modify what the monitor code does. We still need to track in which states a run of the automaton can be. However, to detect bad prefixes with universal automata, we need to check if for the respective current state combination Q', every suffix word has a rejecting run from *one* of the states in Q'. For a given universal automaton, finding these state combinations is a model checking problem that can be solved upfront when generating the monitor. However, when the specification is simple enough, these state combinations are often exactly the ones containing a state that has an empty language, i.e., one for which when changing the initial states of the automaton to only that state, the language of the automaton becomes empty. A simplification at the cost of completeness (i.e., we may miss violations in some cases) is to refine the monitoring problem to be detecting if some run of the universal automaton has already reached such a state with an empty language.

Our specification in the running example translates to a universal very weak automaton using `spot` 2.12 even without the specialized translation procedure from [1] and is simple enough so that detecting a bad prefix by checking if the state with the empty language has been reached is sound and complete. A part of the universal automaton is shown in Fig. 2, and the complete automaton has 30 states.

The resulting monitor code needs 3136 bytes of program memory and takes 549 clock cycles on average to execute per monitor step. We note that the program code is small enough to fit into the program memory of low-cost microcontrollers, which typically have 16–128 kilobytes of this memory type. A particular advantage of monitoring with universal automata is that the monitor code size does not grow superlinearly with the number of monitored properties. In case the main functionality of the microcontroller needs most of the program memory, we can prioritize the properties to monitor in order to fill the remaining memory with monitor code for a selection of the properties.

4 Keeping Track of Specification Violation Reasons

For the example in the previous section (for which all details and the translation procedures to monitors are available in [17]), we used results from the literature, namely on runtime monitoring using non-deterministic Büchi automata [12], deterministic automata [35], and on universal co-Büchi automata, where in the last of these cases, we adapted the monitoring approach from [12] to account for the complemented branching and acceptance conditions. The Python script for compiling the monitors in all considered variants only has 435 lines of code, showing that monitors of all considered types can easily be built.

While the monitors are already usable for embedded systems (when adding calls to the monitor step function in the main program code manually), they leave room for improvement in several directions, of which we want to address two in this paper.

First of all, what happens if there is a violation? The monitor detects this, and the embedded system implementation can then react to the violation, for instance by shutting down the system's service. For systems in a prototyping stage and systems that can report specification violations back to the manufacturer, recording the reason for a violation would also be useful, so that after a violation, debugging and continuous engineering activities can be supported with a suitable starting point. Recording complete execution traces is however out of question, as microcontroller memory is extremely limited.

We propose an alternative approach that makes use of the structure of universal very weak automata, as we have in the running example above. An automaton is said to be very weak (or *1-weak*) if all loops along the transitions in the automaton are self-loops [25]. For universal such automata, the different possible paths that runs can take through the automaton constitute different ways of violating the specification, where a path defines the states along a run without state repetitions. For instance, the path $q_0 \rightarrow q_1 \rightarrow q_\perp$ in the automaton in Fig. 2 represents the case that after red+yellow is shown for the traffic light in direction 1, green is not shown right afterwards (where the actual transition conditions happen to be more complex in the automaton so that this path cannot be taken when certain other specification violations happen at the same time). Similarly, a path from q_0 to $q_\perp$ via $q_9 \rightarrow \ldots \rightarrow q_{19}$ constitutes a specification violation by the ambulance van override signal not working correctly. In this case, however, the number of trace characters between leaving q_0 and entering $q_\perp$ along a run is not bounded, as the run may stay in q_{19} arbitrarily long.

Given that an embedded system has little memory, which information about a trace should be recorded? Surely, the concrete path from q_0 to $q_\perp$ should be recorded in order to explain *how* the specification was violated. The fact that in universal very weak automata, there are only finitely many different paths makes this possible. But we can actually record more: whenever a run moves forward along a path in the automaton, it intuitively moves *closer* towards violating the property (if the respective run ever reaches $q_\bot$). The values of the propositions along such transitions closer to $q_\bot$ then provide evidence on *why* the specification violation occurred.

For instance, when recording the proposition values for a violation along the path $q_0 \rightarrow q_1 \rightarrow q_\bot$, the values of a_1 and a_2 tell the system engineer whether an ambulance van override signal was involved in the violation or not, which helps pinpointing the cause of the violation. Similarly, if a violation via the path $q_0 \rightarrow q_9 \rightarrow \ldots \rightarrow q_{19} \rightarrow q_\bot$ is found and the proposition values along a violating run are recorded whenever the run switches states, the recorded information shows the (observable) traffic light states before stabilizing the green light for direction 1, and additionally how this stabilization was broken.

On a technical level, recording the proposition valuations along a path can be implemented by augmenting the monitor code variables tracking for each automaton state if a run can be in the state with a trace recording buffer. The buffer information needs to contain the prefix path and the proposition valuations for this prefix path. Whenever there exist multiple prefix runs leading to a state, an arbitrary of these is used for the stored buffer information.

While the choice to track proposition valuations when switching states in the universal automaton is a heuristic, and hence not always the most useful trace parts are recorded in this way, this heuristic has the advantage that the needed buffer sizes can be computed upfront and are constant, and we track proposition valuations at well-defined time points that have a clear reason for being *potentially* interesting, without a need for the engineer to specify a violation analysis strategy. In the example specification from above, we would need 130 extra bytes of RAM for storing the trace information for all states as well as persistent storage of 12 bytes for storing the trace information of an actual specification violation for later retrieval by the application engineer. This is even small enough for the low amount of EEPROM memory that low-cost microcontrollers have (such as the 512 bytes of EEPROM of the low-power STM32L010RB microcontroller by ST Microelectronics).

Finally, we note that if the specification automaton is not actually very weak, we can record the proposition valuations of a run at the time points at which it switches between strongly connected components of the automaton. Furthermore, it needs to be noted that if the universal automaton has bad prefixes along which a state with an empty language is not reached for some run, no violation reason can be recorded for such a case.

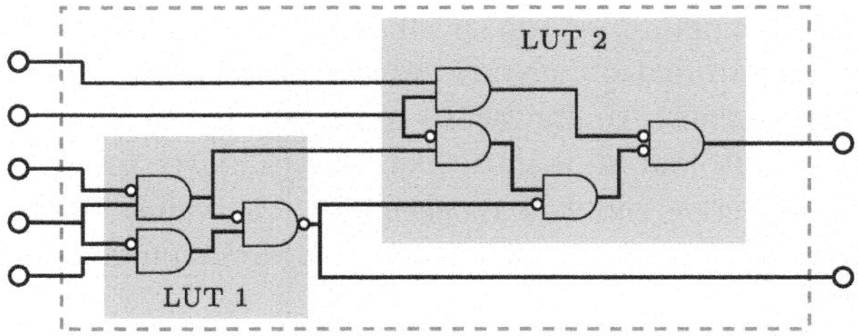

Fig. 3. Graphical depiction of the idea to map circuit elements to lookup tables (LUTs). The example circuit does not originate from an actual monitoring problem.

5 A Specialized Microcontroller Component for Temporal Logic Runtime Monitoring

The monitor based on universal automata built in Sect. 3 needs 549 clock cycles on average per monitor step on the example trace. While this is substantially less than for the other monitor types that we looked at, the number of cycles is still relatively large, and for simple applications, the overall monitoring overhead can easily exceed the number of clock cycles used for the core functionality of the system. This is caused by the many Boolean operations performed on the proposition values, for which even an optimizing compiler can only cache a few. Each such Boolean operation needs at least one clock cycle (as simple microcontrollers cannot parallelize basic operations).

This efficiency problem can be addressed by *hardware support* for temporal logic monitoring. Microcontrollers often have many components apart from a processor core and memory, and they communicate via one or more shared busses, to which a runtime monitoring component could be connected. As a proof of concept, we implemented such a component. The component was also accepted for fabrication with the Google-sponsored *Open MPW* program [15], and we describe its main ideas in the following.

The starting point of our monitoring component is the observation that monitor program code, such as the one in Fig. 1, can be represented as a *combinatorial circuit*, which takes as input the current proposition valuation and the previous values of the single-bit variables representing in which states a run of the universal automaton can be, and outputs the next values of these state variables (of which one represents if a violation has been observed so far). The circuit can be minimized based on the reachable state combinations in the automaton as *careset*, for instance with the approach by Lee et al. [24]. A number of flip-flops looping back the state variables then complement the combinatorial circuit to a runtime monitor.

In order to simulate the behavior of such a combinatorial circuit, we do not have to perform the Boolean operations in a sequential way. Rather, we can group multiple circuit gates together and compute their output values simulataneously by *table lookups*. Figure 3 depicts the idea. We split simulating the circuit into a sequence of table lookups, each using one or more input bits and producing one

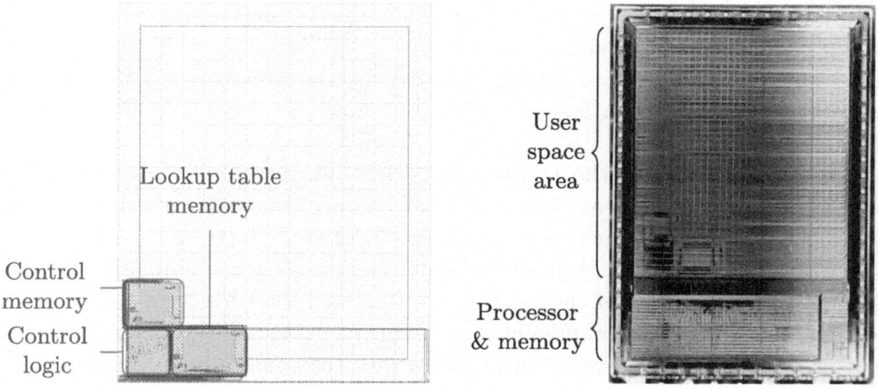

Fig. 4. The temporal logic runtime monitoring component in hardware. The left hand-side shows the utilization of the user space area on the Caravel SoC, where the runtime monitoring component only needs a small part of it. The right-hand side shows a photo of the manufactured system on chip, which includes the user space area at the top.

or more output bits. At the end of a sequence of table lookups, we obtain the new values for the state variables.

The runtime monitoring component, available under an open source license from https://github.com/progirep/temporal_runtime_monitor_for_caravel, was designed to interface to the *Wishbone* bus of a *Caravel* System-on-chip (SoC) [14]. New proposition values can be provided to the component by a single 32-bit write access to the bus, and the component computes the result of the monitor step function while the processor core can already continue with its main functionality computation. The component has a 64-bit main state register that is continuously updated with each table lookup. Every table lookup takes 8 clock cycles, in which the following actions are performed:

1. A state register bit selection for the input to the lookup table as well as a lookup table starting address are read from a 1 kilobyte large *control memory* block.
2. The state register bits selected are extracted from the state register using a *bit extract* [40] operation.
3. Using the extracted bits as table row selection and the lookup table starting address, the table lookup is performed.
4. Another bit mask is read from the control memory, and the state register bits are compressed using another bit extract operation on the bit mask. The result of the table lookup from the previous step is then added to the state register content.

We implemented the component with 2 kilobyte lookup table memory, and it was manufactured in a 130 nm feature size IC production process. The right-hand side of Fig. 4 shows the resulting chip, consisting of the SoC processor and memory at the bottom and a user space area for the added functionality of the SoC at the top. The user space area measures approximately 10 square millimeters, and only a small part of it was actually needed for the monitoring component. A design drawing of the user space area is also shown on the left-hand side of the figure.

A control register of the component stores information on the number of propositions used as well as the number of lookup tables. The component also allows write access to its memories to fill the them with the configuration needed to monitor for the specification of interest. An open-source compiler for encoding a circuit and a split of the circuit into lookup tables into the configuration encoding needed by the component is available at https://github.com/progirep/monitor_compiler_for_caraval_monitor. How to automatically optimize such a split based on a given monitoring circuit is left for future work. For the specification from the running example, a manual split into 7 lookup tables yields an encoding that needs 1504 bytes of lookup table memory and 144 bytes of control memory. As the monitoring component needs 8 clock cycles per lookup table (plus 8 cycles to filter the final state register content to those bits needed for its next step), a monitoring step of this component takes fewer than the 549 cycles needed by the software monitor based on a universal automaton.

We experimentally validated that the component actually works in silicon, except that the memory blocks, which were taken off-the-shelf, are unable to hold their values. When running the component with the randomly initialized but stable values of the memories, the results match those from a high-level simulation run on the memory contents read out from the component, indicating that when replacing the memory blocks or otherwise improving the stability of their operation, we obtain a working temporal logic runtime monitoring microcontroller component.

In its current version, the runtime monitoring component does not feature the specification violation information tracking approach from Sect. 4. The component is however not actually restricted to runtime monitoring, but can also be used for other computations that map nicely to simulating a sequential circuit.

6 Conclusion

In this paper, we gave a quick run-through of some existing results on compiling temporal logic specifications to runtime monitoring code. The focus was on using future-time temporal logic, as common in verification, while targeting tiny systems (i.e., embedded systems with a low-cost microcontroller). It should be noted that there is a large volume of related work that could not be discussed, such as for instance on offline runtime monitoring, multi-valued semantics for monitoring, automatic code instrumentation for monitoring, and runtime monitoring in a separate thread in more complex embedded systems.

In our run-through, we focused on closing the gap between formal verification and runtime monitoring by employing a specification formalism that is common in formal verification for runtime monitoring as well. We discussed two ways for making runtime monitoring more useful, hopefully encouraging system designers to write formal specifications more often. In particular, we showed how tiny systems can record information about a specification violation without the engineer having to declare which trace information is to be recorded. Furthermore, we described an in-silicon temporal logic runtime monitoring component that can be integrated into future microcontrollers for light-weight monitoring.

Multiple directions of future work can be identified from the discussions and results in this paper. For instance, general purpose tools for encoding computation that is easy to represent as a circuit to efficient program code to be executed by regular processors can make runtime monitoring on such processors more efficient. Then, automaton minimization approaches that reduce the sizes of transition labels of universal co-Büchi automata can also make monitors built from them more efficient to execute. For runtime monitoring in hardware, an approach for optimally partitioning a combinatorial circuit into a sequence of lookup tables is also needed. Finally, a monitoring approach that uses regular linear time temporal logic for specifications while adding a monitoring-specific formalism that allows the engineer to define which runtime information is most useful for debugging specification violations may make runtime monitoring more attractive for debugging the early versions of embedded systems in the field.

Acknowledgements. The author thanks Google for sponsoring the Open MPW program [15], in which the monitoring component described in Sect. 5 was manufactured, and Dr. Ivan Xavier Torres Cordova for taking the photo in Fig. 4.

References

1. Adabala, K., Ehlers, R.: A fragment of linear temporal logic for universal very weak automata. In: Lahiri, S.K., Wang, C. (eds.) ATVA 2018. LNCS, vol. 11138, pp. 335–351. Springer, Cham (2018). https://doi.org/10.1007/978-3-030-01090-4_20
2. Alpern, B., Schneider, F.B.: Recognizing safety and liveness. Distrib. Comput. **2**(3), 117–126 (1987)
3. Bartocci, E., Falcone, Y. (eds.): Lectures on Runtime Verification - Introductory and Advanced Topics. Lecture Notes in Computer Science, vol. 10457. Springer, Cham (2018). https://doi.org/10.1007/978-3-319-75632-5
4. Bartocci, E., Falcone, Y., Francalanza, A., Reger, G.: Introduction to runtime verification. In: Bartocci, E., Falcone, Y. (eds.) Lectures on Runtime Verification. LNCS, vol. 10457, pp. 1–33. Springer, Cham (2018). https://doi.org/10.1007/978-3-319-75632-5_1
5. Bartocci, E., Manjunath, N., Mariani, L., Mateis, C., Ničković, D.: Automatic failure explanation in CPS models. In: Ölveczky, P.C., Salaün, G. (eds.) SEFM 2019. LNCS, vol. 11724, pp. 69–86. Springer, Cham (2019). https://doi.org/10.1007/978-3-030-30446-1_4
6. Bauer, A., Leucker, M., Schallhart, C.: Comparing LTL semantics for runtime verification. J. Log. Comput. **20**(3), 651–674 (2010)
7. Bauer, A., Leucker, M., Schallhart, C.: Runtime verification for LTL and TLTL. ACM Trans. Softw. Eng. Methodol. **20**(4), 14:1–14:64 (2011)

8. Baumeister, J., Finkbeiner, B., Schwenger, M., Torfah, H.: FPGA stream-monitoring of real-time properties. ACM Trans. Embed. Comput. Syst. **18**(5s), 88:1–88:24 (2019)
9. Beer, I., Ben-David, S., Chockler, H., Orni, A., Trefler, R.J.: Explaining counterexamples using causality. Formal Methods Syst. Des. **40**(1), 20–40 (2012)
10. Bonakdarpour, B., Navabpour, S., Fischmeister, S.: Sampling-based runtime verification. In: Butler, M., Schulte, W. (eds.) FM 2011. LNCS, vol. 6664, pp. 88–102. Springer, Heidelberg (2011). https://doi.org/10.1007/978-3-642-21437-0_9
11. Chen, F., Roşu, G.: Java-MOP: a monitoring oriented programming environment for Java. In: Halbwachs, N., Zuck, L.D. (eds.) TACAS 2005. LNCS, vol. 3440, pp. 546–550. Springer, Heidelberg (2005). https://doi.org/10.1007/978-3-540-31980-1_36
12. d'Amorim, M., Roşu, G.: Efficient monitoring of ω-languages. In: Etessami, K., Rajamani, S.K. (eds.) CAV 2005. LNCS, vol. 3576, pp. 364–378. Springer, Heidelberg (2005). https://doi.org/10.1007/11513988_36
13. Duret-Lutz, A., et al.: From spot 2.0 to spot 2.10: what's new? In: Shoham, S., Vizel, Y. (eds.) CAV 2022. LNCS, vol. 13372, pp. 174–187. Springer, Cham (2022). https://doi.org/10.1007/978-3-031-13188-2_9
14. Efabless Corporation: Caravel system on chip (2021). https://github.com/efabless/caravel
15. Efabless Corporation: The open MPW program (2022). https://efabless.com/open_shuttle_program
16. Ehlers, R., Finkbeiner, B.: Monitoring realizability. In: Khurshid, S., Sen, K. (eds.) RV 2011. LNCS, vol. 7186, pp. 427–441. Springer, Heidelberg (2012). https://doi.org/10.1007/978-3-642-29860-8_34
17. Ehlers, R.: Runtime monitoring example data/TAP 2024 (2024). https://doi.org/10.5281/zenodo.12789827
18. Faymonville, P., et al.: StreamLAB: stream-based monitoring of cyber-physical systems. In: Dillig, I., Tasiran, S. (eds.) CAV 2019. LNCS, vol. 11561, pp. 421–431. Springer, Cham (2019). https://doi.org/10.1007/978-3-030-25540-4_24
19. Ferrère, T., Maler, O., Ničković, D.: Trace diagnostics using temporal implicants. In: Finkbeiner, B., Pu, G., Zhang, L. (eds.) ATVA 2015. LNCS, vol. 9364, pp. 241–258. Springer, Cham (2015). https://doi.org/10.1007/978-3-319-24953-7_20
20. Havelund, K., Rosu, G.: Monitoring Java programs with Java PathExplorer. Electron. Notes Theor. Comput. Sci. **55**(2), 200–217 (2001)
21. Havelund, K., Roşu, G.: Synthesizing monitors for safety properties. In: Katoen, J.-P., Stevens, P. (eds.) TACAS 2002. LNCS, vol. 2280, pp. 342–356. Springer, Heidelberg (2002). https://doi.org/10.1007/3-540-46002-0_24
22. Kupferman, O., Vardi, M.Y.: Model checking of safety properties. Formal Methods Syst. Des. **19**(3), 291–314 (2001)
23. Kupferman, O., Vardi, M.Y.: Safraless decision procedures. In: 46th Annual IEEE Symposium on Foundations of Computer Science (FOCS), pp. 531–542. IEEE (2005)
24. Lee, S.Y., Riener, H., De Micheli, G.: External don't cares in logic synthesis. In: Drechsler, R., Huhn, S. (eds.) Advanced Boolean Techniques, pp. 33–47. Springer, Cham (2023). https://doi.org/10.1007/978-3-031-28916-3_3
25. Maidl, M.: The common fragment of CTL and LTL. In: 41st Annual Symposium on Foundations of Computer Science (FOCS), pp. 643–652 (2000)

26. Medhat, R., Kumar, D., Bonakdarpour, B., Fischmeister, S.: Sacrificing a little space can significantly improve monitoring of time-sensitive cyber-physical systems. In: ACM/IEEE International Conference on Cyber-Physical Systems (ICCPS), pp. 115–126 (2014)
27. Moosbrugger, P., Rozier, K.Y., Schumann, J.: R2U2: monitoring and diagnosis of security threats for unmanned aerial systems. Formal Methods Syst. Des. **51**(1), 31–61 (2017)
28. Pike, L., Wegmann, N., Niller, S., Goodloe, A.: Copilot: monitoring embedded systems. Innov. Syst. Softw. Eng. **9**(4), 235–255 (2013)
29. Pnueli, A.: The temporal logic of programs. In: 18th Annual Symposium on Foundations of Computer Science, pp. 46–57 (1977)
30. Reinbacher, T., Brauer, J., Horauer, M., Steininger, A., Kowalewski, S.: Past time LTL runtime verification for microcontroller binary code. In: Salaün, G., Schätz, B. (eds.) FMICS 2011. LNCS, vol. 6959, pp. 37–51. Springer, Heidelberg (2011). https://doi.org/10.1007/978-3-642-24431-5_5
31. Reinbacher, T., Horauer, M., Steininger, A.: A runtime verification unit for microcontrollers. In: Proceedings of the 2012 System, Software, SoC and Silicon Debug Conference, pp. 1–6 (2012)
32. Snook, C.F.: Exploring the barriers to formal specification. Ph.D. thesis, University of Southampton, UK (2001). https://ethos.bl.uk/OrderDetails.do?uin=uk.bl.ethos.268626
33. Solet, D., Béchennec, J., Briday, M., Faucou, S., Pillement, S.: Hardware runtime verification of embedded software in SoPC. In: 11th IEEE Symposium on Industrial Embedded Systems (SIES), pp. 171–176. IEEE (2016)
34. Somenzi, F., Bloem, R.: Efficient Büchi automata from LTL formulae. In: Emerson, E.A., Sistla, A.P. (eds.) CAV 2000. LNCS, vol. 1855, pp. 248–263. Springer, Heidelberg (2000). https://doi.org/10.1007/10722167_21
35. Tabakov, D., Rozier, K.Y., Vardi, M.Y.: Optimized temporal monitors for SystemC. Formal Methods Syst. Des. **41**(3), 236–268 (2012)
36. Vaandrager, F.W.: Model learning. Commun. ACM **60**(2), 86–95 (2017)
37. Vardi, M.Y., Wolper, P.: Reasoning about infinite computations. Inf. Comput. **115**(1), 1–37 (1994)
38. Walters, G., King, E., Kessinger, R., Fryer, R.: Processor design and implementation for real-time testing of embedded systems. In: 17th DASC. AIAA/IEEE/SAE Digital Avionics Systems Conference, vol. 1, pp. B44–1. IEEE (1998)
39. Wang, S., Geoffroy, Y., Gössler, G., Sokolsky, O., Lee, I.: A hybrid approach to causality analysis. In: Bartocci, E., Majumdar, R. (eds.) RV 2015. LNCS, vol. 9333, pp. 250–265. Springer, Cham (2015). https://doi.org/10.1007/978-3-319-23820-3_16
40. Wolf, C.X.: Reference hardware implementations of bit extract/deposit instructions (2017). https://github.com/cliffordwolf/bextdep

Quality of Tests and Proofs

Is MCDC Really Better? Lessons from Combining Tests and Proofs

Li Huang[1,2(✉)], Bertrand Meyer[1,2,3], and Manuel Oriol[1,2]

[1] Constructor Institute, Schaffhausen, Switzerland
{li.huang,bm,mo}@constructor.org
[2] Constructor University, Bremen, Germany
[3] Eiffel Software, Santa Barbara, CA, USA
https://constructor.org, https://constructor.university,
https://eiffel.com

Abstract. MCDC, for "Modified Condition/Decision Coverage", is a test coverage criterion recommended in several important industrial software safety standards. The intuition behind MCDC is that it should be more effective than industry's default coverage criterion, branch coverage, since it uses a finer-grain decomposition of program conditions.

Manually generating MCDC-compliant test suites is, however, tedious and error-prone; there is, as a result, little empirical evidence of whether that intuition holds up in practice. Does MCDC really provide enough of an advantage over branch coverage to justify the extra work and longer test runs?

To help answer this question, the present work takes advantage of verification technology that combines tests and proofs, based on the AutoProof program verifier.

For each decision point in the program, the approach proceeds in four steps. First, compute a set of conditions that satisfy MCDC. Then, inject into the program, for each combination, an incorrect instruction (a "seeded contradiction" in the terminology of previous work). Next, apply the prover to verify the instrumented program; the prover naturally fails, but in the process it produces a set of *counterexamples* covering all the combinations. Finally, turn this result into a directly usable test suite—guaranteed by construction to satisfy the MCDC criterion.

The results, on a significant set of example programs, yield insights on how MCDC coverage compares to branch coverage and adaptive random testing when trying to detect faults.

Keywords: Testing · Coverage · MCDC · Software verification · Eiffel

1 Overview

The "MCDC" test coverage criterion[1] has gained practical importance from its inclusion as either required or recommended in industry standards [16,23,36],

[1] Also written MC/DC. We follow the slash-less moniker recommended by Ammann and Offutt [1], themselves following Chilenski [10].

© The Author(s), under exclusive license to Springer Nature Switzerland AG 2025
M. Huisman and F. Howar (Eds.): TAP 2024, LNCS 15153, pp. 25–44, 2025.
https://doi.org/10.1007/978-3-031-72044-4_2

particularly in aerospace. Surprisingly little support exists, however, for MCDC: on the theoretical side, few results have been formally established on its actual benefits over simpler coverage measures; and few tools are available to achieve high MCDC coverage. The present work, taking advantage of a test infrastructure based on program-proving technology, sheds some light on the merits of MCDC and provides automatic tools to generate test suites satisfying MCDC.

The rest of this overview provides a reminder of the role of coverage measures (Subsect. 1.1) and defines MCDC (Subsect. 1.2). Subsequent sections are organized as follows. Section 2 presents the technology base, the AutoProof program verification environment, that made the present work possible. Section 3 explains how to use that technology base to generate test suites satisfying MCDC. Section 4 describes the results of applying these ideas and tools to a number of representative examples. Section 5 compares the approach to previously published work. Section 6 assesses the limits of the work and threats to its validity. Section 7 draws a number of lessons regarding the value of MCDC, its practical applicability, and prospects for further work.

1.1 Coverage Measures

In spite of advances in static software verification techniques, including program proofs, testing remains the dominant form of software quality assurance. Even though Edsger Dijkstra famously pointed out more than five decades ago that tests "*can only show the presence of errors, never their absence*" [14], industry continues to use tests as the principal technique of quality assurance. In particular, it relies on a numerical measure: test *coverage*, assessing the extent to which a test suite exercises every possibility of a program's execution. It is common for companies to require a minimum coverage value before shipping a product.

Rather than a single metric, test coverage actually denotes a family of criteria assessing the exhaustiveness of a test campaign. (Ammann and Offut [1,2] provide a detailed survey.) The most commonly used measure is *branch coverage*, the percentage of program branches (edges in the program's flow graph) the tests have exercised. A test suite "achieves branch coverage" if that percentage is 100% (excluding unreachable branches). A typical rule-of-thumb in industry is that shipping a product requires 80% branch coverage, although in practice some organizations satisfy themselves with thresholds as low as 30%.

Branch coverage and other coverage measures, are imperfect proxies; studies (e.g. [11]) have shown that in long test runs the number of faults detected, a more directly relevant witness of software quality, may continue to increase long after branch coverage has reached its peak. Branch coverage continues to be popular, however, since it is an intuitive concept and can be measured using relatively simple program instrumentation. When taken as a binary rather than numerical criterion, branch coverage is also called **decision coverage** (DC). Can more sophisticated coverage criteria do better?

1.2 The Need for MCDC

One of the proposed replacements for decision coverage, MCDC (the focus of this article) has gained practical importance because a number of software quality standards specify it (see Sect. 5). The acronym means "Modified Condition/Decision Coverage". MCDC addresses an obvious limitation of pure DC. Assume that the program contains a decision point, for example a conditional instruction

```
if dec then instruction end
```

If the boolean expression `dec` (the "decision") is a simple condition `b`, which could be a simple boolean-valued expression `x` > `y` or just a boolean variable, achieving DC means that the test suite must contain at least one test under which `b` has value `T` (True) and another under which it has value `F` (False). This property justifies the name "Decision Coverage": the test suite will lead to two separate decisions in the test run—executing `instruction`, and not executing it.

The need for a finer criterion arises when the decision `dec` is no longer an atomic boolean property but a composite boolean expression, using the boolean operators $\wedge$, $\vee$ and $\neg$[2]. An example is

a ∧ b ∧ c

Here DC only needs two tests, one making the overall condition true and one making it false. It suffices for example to have one with `a` = `b` = `c` = `True` and the other with `a` = `b` = `c` = `False`. This coarse choice ignores some of the individual contributions of the operands `a`, `b` and `c`.

One criterion that does take all these contributions into account is **condition coverage** (CC), also called combinatorial coverage, which exercises all their possible combinations. In this example CC would force us to consider 8 combinations of the three operands' values. In the general case, achieving CC triggers a combinatorial explosion, since it requires producing 2^n different tests for an expression of n operands[3]

The MCDC (Modified Condition/Decision Coverage) criterion provides an intermediate solution between those two extremes: DC, too coarse, and CC, leading to combinatorial explosion. The idea is to retain from CC only those tests in which flipping a condition leads to a different result. MCDC can indeed be considered an optimization of CC, removing any redundant tests, in a sense of redundancy defined in Sect. 1.3.

Definitions of MCDC in the literature are not always clear. For example numerous presentations (e.g. [41], p. 9) state that in MCDC "*Every Boolean expression in the program will need to evaluate to both True and False*"; since an expression can evaluate to only one of True and False, the reader must understand that these two values occur in different test runs, but this point should

---

[2] Representing respectively "and", "or" and "not". See below about other operators and constants.

[3] The total number of cases to consider is not the full 2^n in the presence of "semi-strict" or "short-circuit" operators, such as **and then** in Eiffel and && in C++, which do not require evaluating the second operand when the first one determines the result. They only marginally affect the discussion and will be ignored in the theoretical discussion, although our implementation handles them correctly.

be made clear. Discussions of MCDC similarly state that (here in the words of the same reference, a few lines before the previous extract) "*each condition in a decision has been shown to independently affect that decision's outcome*" without explaining how this determination is made: by static analysis? By testing? Asking these questions is not nitpicking since the ambiguous phrasings lead to the result (again in the words of that same reference, page 8!) that "*Many interpretations exist for a coverage criterion satisfying the intent of MCDC*".

Even after such ambiguities are corrected, there is no agreement on the substance. For example, one of the most respected references on testing and coverage criteria did not include MCDC explicitly in its first edition [2] and in its second edition explicitly deprecates the use of this name, mentioning it only in connection with another Active Clause Coverage ("*ACC is almost identical to the way early papers describing another technique called MCDC*"[4]). Even if (as these authors assert) a more systematic terminology would be preferable, we have to continue using "MCDC" because of the wide use of this name, codified, as noted, in important industry standards. A precise definition follows.

1.3 Precise Definition and Properties of MCDC

The goal of the definition below is not to be fully general (that would require an extensive analysis, synthesizing and updating existing references [1,2,41]) but simply to provide a clear framework for the present work. In particular, the definition makes a number of simplifying assumptions (although the tools themselves can handle more general cases):

- The basis for the discussion is a condition `dec` called the "**decision**", made of **individual conditions**, whose individual values determine the value of `dec`, called the **result**.
- It assumes a property of the decision: `dec` must be what in logic is called a **contingent** boolean expression, meaning that neither `dec` nor any of its subexpressions is a tautology (true for all values of individual conditions, as with $\texttt{a} \vee \neg\texttt{a}$) or a contradiction (always false, as with $\texttt{a} \wedge \neg\texttt{a}$). Without this requirement—which the literature often does not mention—it is impossible to obtain both a test that satisfies a condition and one that does not.
- The decision is obtained from individual conditions through the application of three available boolean operators: $\wedge$ (and), $\vee$ (or) and $\neg$ (not). Other operators such as "implies" and "exclusive or", as well as the boolean constants `True` and `False`, can be deduced from them through the usual definitions.
- We ignore the "semistrict" or "short-circuit" operators such as **and then** and **or else** in Eiffel and Ada, and && and || in C-based languages, which are not commutative as they ignore their second operand, avoiding its possibly failed evaluation if the first operand suffices to give the result (for example, $\texttt{x} \neq \texttt{0} \wedge \texttt{1} / \texttt{x} = \texttt{y}$ may fail to evaluate properly if $\texttt{x} = \texttt{0}$, whereas $\texttt{x} \neq \texttt{0}$ **and then** $\texttt{1} / \texttt{x} = \texttt{y}$ is always defined, with value `False` if $\texttt{x} = \texttt{0}$).

[4] Page 182 of the cited book, which also mentions MCDC in its bibliographic notes, pages 231-232.

- MCDC has several variants. The definition covers the strongest interpretation of MCDC, "Unique-Cause MCDC", the version required by the DO-178B standard [15]. The implementation presented in the following sections also applies to this variant. For weaker forms, such as Masking MCDC or Unique-Cause + Masking MCDC [10], the methodology is similar and the implementation can be easily adapted.

The notion of test itself requires a definition (not necessarily the most general but adapted to the needs of the present discussion).

Definition 1. *A **test** for a decision is a particular combination of the values of its individual conditions.*

(This notion is the same as "boolean vector" in [41].) We may express a test by the values of the operands, followed by "|" and the result. For example `TTT| T` is a test for the decision `a and b and c`, making `a`, `b` and `c` all true with result `T`.

Definition 2. *A **test suite** for a decision `dec` is a set of tests for it.*

An example is the 8-element test suite, for the decision `a` ∧ `b` ∧ `c`, containing all combinations of values for `a`, `b` and `c`. In expressing a test suite, we may for reference identify each test by a number, writing this example as {1:TTT|T, 2:FTT|F, 3:TFT|F, 4:FFT|F, 5:TTF|F, 6:FTF|F, 7:TFF|F, 8:FFF|F}.

Definition 3. ***Flipping** An individual condition `c` in a test means producing a new test by replacing the value of `c` by `T` if it was `F` and conversely, leaving the other conditions unchanged.*

We say that two tests are "flipped" if one is a result of flipping an individual condition `c` in the other. (More specifically, they are "flipped *for* `c`".)

Definition 4. *A test suite `S` for a decision `dec` satisfies **DC (Decision Coverage)** if it contains two tests with different results.*

For example, again using the decision `a` ∧ `b` ∧ `c`, the following test suite satisfies DC since it has two tests with different results: {1:TTT|T, 2:FTT|F}.

Definition 5. *A test suite `S` for a decision `dec` satisfies **CC (Condition Coverage)** (also "combinatorial coverage") if it contains all possible tests for `dec`.*

The test suite satisfying CC for `a` ∧ `b` ∧ `c` was given above: {1:TTT|T, 2:FTT|F, 3:TFT|F, 4:FFT|F, 5:TTF|F, 6:FTF|F, 7:TFF|F, 8:FFF|F}.

A test suite satisfying CC for a decision made of `n` clauses, each possibly negated, combined by ∧ and ∨, has a maximum of 2^n tests. (The maximum is not necessarily reached if the clauses are not independent: for example, `c` ∧ `c` has only two tests).

Under the assumption that the decision is contingent as defined above, combinatorial coverage implies decision coverage.

Definition 6. *A test suite for a decision* `dec` *satisfies* ***IC (Individual Condition coverage)*** *for an individual condition* `c` *if it contains two tests that only differ by their values for* `c`*, and have different results. Note that IC (satisfied for any individual condition* `c`*) trivially implies DC.*

Theorem 1. *A test suite satisfying CC satisfies IC for any condition* `c`*.*

The proof relies on the assumption that the decision and its subexpressions are contingent. By induction on the structure of the decision: for a single condition, the two criteria are equivalent. For a decision of the form `e` ∧ `f`, where both parts satisfy the theorem, if `c` occurs in only one of the two, say `e`, we can combine the two IC-compliant tests for `e` (one yielding true and the other false) with a test for `f` of result True (which exists since `f` is contingent). Theorem 1 holds as the combined test suite is a subset of the CC-compliant test suite for `e` ∧ `f`. If `c` appears on both sides, using the induction hypothesis, we combine test suites that are IC-compliant for `c` on both sides, one with value true and one with value false. The reasoning is similar for an expression whose top-level operator is ∨. (For ¬ e it suffices to apply the reasoning to `e`.)

Definition 7. *A test suite* `S` *for a decision* `dec` *satisfies MCDC (Modified Condition/Decision Coverage) if it satisfies IC for every individual condition of* `dec`*.*

In the same example `a` ∧ `b` ∧ `c`, the test suite {1:TTT|T, 2:FTT|F, 3:TFT|F, 4:TTF|F} satisfies MCDC. IC is ensured, for `a`, by tests 1 and 2; for `b`, by 1 and 3; for `c`, by 1 and 4. The following concept captures the value of MCDC over CC.

Definition 8. *A test* `t` *in a test suite* `S` *is* ***MCDC-redundant for an individual condition*** `c` *if* `S` *also contains the test flipped from* `t`*, with the same result. It is* ***MCDC-redundant*** *if it is redundant for all individual conditions.*

For MCDC, if we have two such tests, we can remove either of them:

Theorem 2. *If a test suite* `S` *satisfies MCDC, so does* `S`*' obtained by removing from* `S` *an MCDC-redundant test.*

Proof. For every condition `c`, `S` satisfies IC for `c`, meaning that it contains a test `t` and another $\mathtt{t}_d$ flipped from `t` for `c`, with a *different* result. Removing a flipped test $\mathtt{t}_s$ with the *same* result does not affect that property since it leaves $\mathtt{t}_d$. Note that $\mathtt{t}_d$ will usually be different for the same `t` and different `c`.

This theorem provides the basis for a practical generation of MCDC-compliant test suites: start from the CC suite, with its up to 2^n elements, and remove redundant elements. The optimization can bring the size of the test suite down to the theoretical minimum $n + 1$.

2 Technology Base

The present work is part of a general effort to combine static and dynamic approaches to software verification, by applying program proving techniques to the generation of test suites.

2.1 The AutoProof Environment

The approach relies on the AutoProof environment [3,40], which proves the correctness of contract-equipped Eiffel programs [30–32] against their contracts.

The proof machinery relies on Boogie prover [28], using Dijkstra's weakest-precondition calculus [14] and internally based on an SMT solver, currently Z3 [5,13]. Boogie, when attempting to prove a program translated from Eiffel, produces verification conditions for the SMT solver. A characteristic of this style of proof is that it relies on a *disproof* of the *opposite* property: the SMT solver tries to construct at least one counterexample, violating the desired result. If it cannot find one, the proof is successful. This observation yields fruitful techniques for combining proofs and tests.

2.2 Seeding Contradiction for Test Generation

The technique for generating MCDC-satisfying test suite extends the "Seeding Contradiction (SC)" [21]. The idea of SC is to inject faulty assertions (*contradictions*) at the program points of interest in the original program, and use the general *Failed Proofs to Failing Tests* (FP-FT) approach [19,20] to derive test inputs from counterexamples. Running the program with the test inputs then exercises the program points of the seeded contradictions.

Consider for example a small routine with a single conditional instruction in Fig. 1(a); `x` is an integer attribute of the enclosing class. To generate a test that exercises `Block 1`, we can "seed" an incorrect instruction `check False end` at the beginning of the block, as highlighted in Fig. 1(b). Here "`check C end`" instruction (`assert C` in some other notations [27]) states that the programmer expects condition `C` to hold at the corresponding program point. As the program is now incorrect, AutoProof fails to prove the routine and produces a counterexample for the seeded assertion. Applying FP-FT turns the counterexample into a runnable test, guaranteed to exercise `Block 1`.

```
simple (a: INTEGER)
    do
        if a > 0 then
            x := 1 -- Block 1
        else
            x := 2
        end
    end
```

(a) Original version

```
simple (a: INTEGER)
    do
        if a > 0 then
            check False end
            x := 1 -- Block 1
        else
            x := 2
        end
    end
```

(b) Seeded version

Fig. 1. Seeding contradiction to generate a test covering `Block 1`

2.3 SC for Achieving Branch Coverage

100% branch coverage requires the test suite to execute at least once every branch in the program's control flow. We call a test suite that has the full branch coverage a *branch-compliant* test suite.

Figure 2 shows an example program of how to apply SC to generate a branch-compliant test suite. The original program, as shown in Fig. 2(a), has five *leaf* branches, corresponding to the five blocks that have no embedded conditionals. To generate tests that cover those branches, we can submit to the prover a seeded version of the program in Fig. 2(b), where each leaf branch is instrumented by a contradiction clause. Applying FP-FT with the seeded program will produce five tests, one for each branch.

Here the contradiction uses a conditional form: `if bn = i then check False end end`, where `bn` is an argument that represents "block number", ranging from 1 to N (number of leaf blocks), and i is the number assigned to the corresponding block. The reason of using the conditional form instead of the ordinary form (`check False end`) is to solve the unreachability issue (the detailed explanation is in [21]): if we insert `check False end` into each of the branches, the prover determines that the last two branches (Branch 4, 5) are unreachable, as the program will terminate at one of the three `check False end` clauses of the first conditional. As a result, we only obtain tests covering only the first three branches (Branch 1, 2, 3), not the last two branches as needed.

```
if a > 0 then
    x := 1          -- Leaf Branch 1
else
    if a > −10 then
        x := 2      -- Leaf Branch 2
    else
        x := 3      -- Leaf Branch 3
    end
end
if a^2 > a then
    x := 4          -- Leaf Branch 4
end                 -- Leaf Branch 5
                    (implicit else branch)
```

(a) Original version

```
bn := "Value chosen non−deterministically between 0 and N"
if a > 0 then
    if bn = 1 then check False end end
    x := 1
else
    if a > −10 then
        if bn = 2 then check False end end
        x := 2
    else
        if bn = 3 then check False end end
        x := 3
    end
end
if a^2 > a then
    if bn = 4 then check False end end
    x := 4
else
    if bn = 5 then check False end end
end
```

(b) Seeded version

Fig. 2. Seeding contradictions to generate a test suite satisfying branch coverage

3 Seeding Contradiction for Achieving MCDC

This section first presents an overview of the SC approach to generating tests satisfying MCDC, followed by the details of its implementation in AutoProof.

3.1 Approach

Consider the program in Fig. 3(a), which has a single decision `a>0 and b≤10 or c = 1`. We may use the seeding-contradiction technique to attempt to compute with AutoProof a test suite for the decision that satisfies MCDC.

The technique constructs conditional instructions, each of which uses one of the possible condition combinations. Figure 3(c) shows an example seeded program: four new conditionals, complying with the four conditions in Fig. 3(b), replace the original `if` instruction; each conditional contains a seeded contradiction. The result is a set of tests satisfying the given conditions. Running the FP-FT feature in AutoProof with this seeded program results in four tests, which satisfy the conditions of the four vectors and consequently the MCDC criterion.

```
simple (a, b, c: INTEGER)
    do
        if a > 0 and b ≤ 10 or c = 1 then
            x := 1
        else
            x := 2
        end
    end
```

(a) Original version

	a > 0	b ≤ 10	c = 1	a > 0 and b ≤ 10 or c = 1
Test 1	T	T	F	T
Test 2	F	T	F	F
Test 3	T	F	F	F
Test 4	F	T	T	T

(b) Test vectors satisfying MC/DC

```
simple (a, b, c: INTEGER)
    do
        if a > 0 and b ≤ 10 and not (c = 1) then -- TTF
            if bn = 1 then check False end end
            x := 1
        end

        if not (a > 0) and b ≤ 10 and not (c = 1) then -- FTF
            if bn = 2 then check False end end
            x := 2
        end

        if a > 0 and not (b ≤ 10) and not (c = 1) then -- TFF
            if bn = 3 then check False end end
            x := 2
        end

        if not (a > 0) and b ≤ 10 and c = 1 then -- FTT
            if bn = 4 then check False end end
            x := 1
        end
    end
```

(c) Seeded version

Fig. 3. Seeding contradictions to generate test suite satisfying MCDC

3.2 Implementation

The generation of MCDC-compliant test suites is a new option of AutoProof. As noted in Sect. 1.3, it covers the "unique-cause" MCDC variant. The implementation consists of four steps: (1) Generate test vectors that satisfy MCDC; (2) Transform test vectors into conditionals; (3) Seed contradictions for the new conditionals; (4) Apply FP-FT to generate tests for the seeded program.

The generation of test vectors relies on an abstract representation of the expression, called Abstract Condition Tree (ACT), which only retains the logical structures (relations between logical operators and conditions) of an expression. Figure 4(a) shows an example of the ACT for the expression `a > 0 and b < 10 or c = 1`: the three leaf nodes, $c1$, $c2$ and $c3$, represent the three conditions `a > 0`, `b < 10` and `c = 1`, respectively; the two non-lgfeaf nodes, correspond to the logical operators, `and` and `or`.

The implementation traverses the Abstract Syntax Tree (AST) of the program. Whenever it encounters a node of boolean expression (decision), it transforms the subtree of that node into an ACT. It uses those ACTs to compute

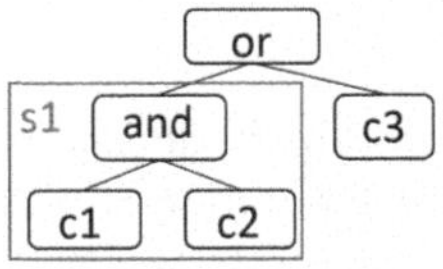

(a) Abstract condition tree

c1	c2	c3	D
T	T	F	T
F	T	F	F

(b) Independent pair for c1

Fig. 4. Generation of an independent pair for condition $c1$

MCDC-satisfying vectors for each decision. Algorithm 1 summarizes the process. It visits each of the condition nodes `leaf` (line 3) and tries to find an independence pair for the condition: starting from `leaf`, it selects the value (`True` or `False`) for its sibling based on the type of their parent (line 8–13), which represents the logical operator that connect `leaf` and its sibling.
For example when `leaf` is $c1$, the value of its sibling $c2$ should be selected in a way such that $c1$ can determine the value of the expression `c1 and c2` (represented by the subtree `s1` in Fig. 4(a)). In this case, the algorithm sets the expected value of $c2$ to `True`. Similarly, as the parent of `s1` is `or`, to allow `s1` to determine the value of the expression `s1 or c3`, the expected value of $c3$ should be `False`.

If the sibling of `leaf`, say `sib`, is not a condition but a node that represents a subexpression of some conditions, the algorithm traverses the subtree to choose the values for its children recursively. The selection of values for children uses a set of predefined combinations to make sure that their values are consistent—the values of children should be selected in such a way that the parent node is evaluated as its expected value. For example, if `sib` is an "`and`" node, whose expected value is `True`, then both its children nodes will be selected as `True`, to make sure that the subexpression represented by `sib` evaluates to `True`. The algorithm continues to visit the parent of `leaf` and repeats the process until it reaches the root of the tree. It then traverses over the list of conditions and uses their values to form a test vector (lines 17–26). The value of the currently processed leaf node (indicated by `pos`) is set as `True` by default.

For example, traversal over the values of three conditions results in a vector `TTF|T` (Fig. 4(b)). Finally, it generates the complement vector for the current condition by flipping the value of the condition (lines 27–33). Flipping the value of first condition of `TTF|T` results in its complement vector `FTF|F`. Those two vectors constitute an independent pair for the first condition.

Redundant tests will not be added, to ensure minimality of the test suite size.

Algorithm 1 Generate a MC/DC-adequate set of test vectors for a decision

```
Input L: a list of leaf nodes of an ACT
Output T: a set of test vectors
across L as leaf loop
   pos := pos + 1
   from node := leaf
   until not (node.has_parent)                  -- Loop until reaching the root
   loop
     op := node.parent.operator
     if op = || or op = ==> then
         node.sibling.set_expected_value (False)
     elseif op = && or op = == or op = ≠ then
         node.sibling.set_expected_value (True)
     end
      node := node.parent
   end
         -- Traverse all leaf nodes to get a test vector
   from i := 1
   until i > L.count
   loop
     if i /= pos then
         test_vector.append (leaf_nodes [i].expected_value)
     else
         test_vector.append (True)
     end
      i := i + 1
   end
         -- Flip the value to get the complement vector
   if not T.has(test_vector) then
      T.extend (test_vector)
      c_test_vector := test_vector.flip_at (pos)
     if not T.has(c_test_vector) then
        T.extend (c_test_vector)
     end
  end
end
```

4 Evaluation

To assess the cost and effectiveness of the SC-based approach, two points of comparison are Branch-SC [21], which uses SC for generating test suite satisfying branch coverage (as described in Sect. 2.3), and AutoTest, the test generation tool for Eiffel using Adaptive Random Testing, specifically ARTOO [12]). The objective is to answer the following questions:

- RQ1. What are the costS, in terms of the size of test suites and test generation time, of Branch-SC and MCDC-SC? Is the overhead induced by MCDC-SC testing compared to Branch-SC at an acceptable level?
- RQ2. How effective are the test suites generated by Branch-SC and MCDC-SC in detecting faults?
- RQ3. Given a certain limit on the number of tests or test generation time, what is the respective performance of the three tools, MCDC-SC, Branch-SC and ARTOO, in terms of fault detection?

4.1 Experimental Setup

All sessions run on a computer with a 2.1 GHz Intel 12-Core processor and 32 GB of memory, in Windows 11 and using Microsoft .NET 7.0.203. Versions of the software used are: EiffelStudio 22.05 (used through AutoProof and AutoTest); Boogie 2.11.10; Z3 solver 4.8.14. The experiment has two parts: (1) evaluate Branch-SC against MCDC-SC; (2) evaluate Branch-SC, MCDC-SC, and ARTOO. In the first part, RQ1 is answered by using both Branch-SC and MCDC-SC on the same programs and comparing the generated test suites as well as the time to generate them.

RQ2 and RQ3 are then evaluated by using mutation testing to assess the quality of the generated test suites on a list of 21 programs adapted from examples in the AutoProof tutorial[5], benchmarks of previous literature, and software verification competitions [7,26,33,34,43]. Table 1 lists the characteristics of the examples, including number of lines of code (LOC), number of decisions, conditions and mutants. The programs and results of the experiment are available at: https://github.com/huangl223/mcdc-sc.

Table 1. Metrics of Examples

Example	LOC	#Decisions	#Conditions	#Mutants
Account	198	3	3	14
Binary search	66	3	4	15
Prime numbers	119	5	6	20
Factorial	58	2	2	11
Smallest	36	3	3	14
Arithmetic	189	11	13	31
Heater	89	3	3	8
Lamp	92	5	5	13
Linear search	69	2	4	11
Recursive binary search	79	4	4	11
Max in array	49	2	2	5
Square root	53	3	4	9
Sum and max	52	2	2	8
Two way max	50	2	2	7
LCM (Least Common Multiple)	93	6	10	32
GCD (Greatest Common Divisor)	117	5	7	20
Prime check	48	2	3	14
Inverse	40	3	4	15
Find first zero	43	3	4	14
Timer	448	21	21	67
Queue	239	10	12	103
Total	**2227**	**104**	**127**	**442**

[5] http://autoproof.sit.org/autoproof/tutorial.

We create faulty variants (mutants) of each example by randomly introducing faults into the correct implementation. The classes of seeded faults consist of: changes of arithmetic operators ($+, -, /, *, mod$), relational operator ($=, <, >, \leq, \geq$), and logical operators ($\texttt{and}, \texttt{or}, \texttt{xor}$); introducing the Boolean operator `not` to a predicate; changing of an integer expression by adding or subtracting 1; removing an instruction (a function call or an assignment) in the body.

4.2 MCDC-SC Versus Branch-SC

To answer RQ1, we use MCDC-SC and Branch-SC to generate test suites, with different random seeds in different runs. Each tool runs 100 times, producing 100 test suites. Table 2 lists the average performance of each tool over these runs, including time and test suite size. In general, MCDC-SC test suites are larger than the Branch-SC test suites, requiring 86% more tests on average. For 13 out of the 21 examples, the size of the MCDC-compliant test suite is no greater than n + 1 (for n conditions); the size of the test suites for 6 other examples is close to n + 1 (containing 1 or 2 more tests).

Generating an MCDC-compliant test suite (a single run of MCDC-SC) requires 1.96 s, which is about 2.15 times of the time cost of producing a branch-compliant test suite (0.91 s).

Table 2. Efficiency of test generation by MCDC-SC and Branch-SC

Example	Avg. Tests		Avg. Time (s)	
	Branch-SC	MCDC-SC	Branch-SC	MCDC-SC
Account	4	6	0.323	0.381
Binary search	3	7	0.419	0.302
Prime numbers	6	12	2.934	7.426
Factorial	3	5	0.209	0.305
Smallest	4	6	0.190	0.395
Arithmetic	19	31	0.956	0.723
Heater	4	6	0.192	0.133
Lamp	6	9	0.251	0.281
Linear search	2	8	0.140	0.325
Recursive binary search	6	8	0.440	0.693
Max in array	2	4	0.159	0.248
Square root	3	6	0.259	0.230
Sum and max	2	4	0.630	0.796
Two way max	2	4	0.379	0.745
LCM (Least Common Multiple)	5	18	0.745	0.094
GCD (Greatest Common Divisor)	4	9	2.221	16.148
Prime check	2	4	0.141	0.141
Inverse	4	7	0.281	0.224
Find first zero	4	7	0.165	0.432
Timer	23	43	6.26	9.06
Queue	14	23	1.81	2.14
Total	122	229	19.104	41.222

The results show that even if the program has the same number of decisions and conditions (each decision has exactly one condition), the sizes of the MCDC-SC and Branch-SC test suites can be different. This is due to the following reasons: as Branch-SC suites are always optimal—they only contain tests for leaf branches (as shown in Fig. 2), which are sufficient to cover all branches in the control flow. The size of a MCDC-SC test suite might not be directly related to the number of decisions. Unlike branch coverage, which only considers decisions in the conditionals that divide the control flow, MCDC considers all boolean expressions appearing in the program, including expressions in the assignment statements such as `a := b and c`.

Although MCDC-SC is more expensive than Branch-SC, the overhead is still acceptable. The time cost and test suites' size of MCDC-SC are still within the same scale as Branch-SC (the difference is less than 10 times). The time cost is still relatively small compared to the performance of other test generation tools: as reported in a previous study [21], to generate a test suite that satisfies branch coverage, IntelliTest [39] (a symbolic execution test-generation tool for .NET) and AutoTest cost about 50 and 500 times more than Branch-SC.

To answer RQ2, we assess the effectiveness of MCDC-SC and compare it with Branch-SC. We run the generated test suites on the set of mutants and collect the failures detected during test execution. The test execution uses AutoTest, which performs run-time assertion checking, using contracts as *test oracles*. In this case, the effectiveness of a test suite is measured by the number of failures (contract violations) detected during test execution. Identification of the uniqueness of a failure uses its enclosing mutant and violated contract. Note that as a fault injected in the program might result in violation of multiple contracts, the number of failures can be larger than the number of mutants.

Table 3. Effectiveness of MCDC-SC and Branch-SC

Example	Min		Max		Mean	
	Branch-SC	MCDC-SC	Branch-SC	MCDC-SC	Branch-SC	MCDC-SC
Account	7	7	10	11	8.64	9.39
Binary search	12	17	22	25	17.64	21.34
Prime numbers	14	19	19	21	18.64	20.56
Factorial	10	10	21	22	16.26	16.42
Smallest	9	9	12	12	10.38	10.7
Arithmetic	41	44	48	49	45.03	45.9
Heater	6	6	11	11	7.55	7.74
Lamp	11	11	12	12	11.92	11.96
Linear search	5	10	11	14	9.33	12.03
Recursive binary search	6	5	11	9	8.99	7.66
Max in array	3	3	6	6	5.02	4.61
Square root	8	8	15	16	11.71	12.73
Sum and max	5	8	9	12	8.78	9.62
Two way max	5	5	10	9	7.14	7.28
LCM (Least Common Multiple)	18	17	34	35	25.98	28.52
GCD (Greatest Common Divisor)	11	22	28	27	23.63	25.47
Prime check	4	10	11	10	7.63	10
Inverse	15	14	16	16	15.02	15.03
Find first zero	6	6	6	11	6	6.28
Timer	58	59	70	70	63.89	63.85
Queue	29	31	228	231	146.74	187.04
Total	283	351	610	629	475.92	534.13

Three metrics enable to measure the fault detection capabilities (Table 3) aggregated over 100 test suites generated: (1) Min: the minimum number of detected failures, which indicates the fault detection capabilities in the *worst case*, (2) Max: the maximum number of detected failures, which indicates the fault detection capabilities in the *best case*, and (3) Mean: the average number of detected failures, which represents the *overall* performance.

The result shows that in worst cases MCDC-SC outperforms Branch-SC and detects 24% more failures. For best cases, there is no significant difference: MCDC-SC only detects about 3% more failures than Branch-SC. For average performance, MCDC-SC has an 12.2% (2.77 more failures) advantage over Branch-SC. The advantage is enlarged for the examples with composite decisions: for the 12 examples with at least one composite decision (number of conditions larger than number of decisions), MCDC-SC detects 4.79 (14.6%) more failures than Branch-SC; for the 9 examples that only have simple decisions (each decision has exactly one condition), MCDC-SC only has a marginal advantage of 0.8% detected failures over Branch-SC.

4.3 MCDC-SC Versus Branch-SC and Adaptive Random Testing

To answer RQ3, we compare the performance of the three test generation tools by collecting the number of cumulative failures detected on all mutants within a certain limit: 180000 (roughly the test suite's size of 100 runs of Branch-SC) for test suites' size and 3 h for execution time. Figure 5 displays the results.

In general, both MCDC-SC and Branch-SC outperform AutoTest significantly, and MCDC-SC outperforms Branch-SC slightly. When running the tools to generate 180000 tests, MCDC-SC is able to detect 719 unique failures, which outperforms Branch-SC and AutoTest by 6% (41 failures) and 88% (338 failures) respectively. When running each tool for a 3-hour session, MCDC-SC is able to detect 726 failures, which is 11.2% (82 failures) and 189% (475 failures) more than Branch-SC and AutoTest.

Unlike AutoTest, which produces and exercises one single test at a time, a run of MCDC-SC or Branch-SC produces a test suite that contains multiple tests, which are then reused for all mutants. This leads to the non-consecutive curves of MCDC-SC and Branch-SC. The abrupt jumps at their beginnings indicate the failures detected by the test suites resulting from the first run of Branch-SC and MCDC-SC, which respectively produce 4511 and 8189 tests for all the 442 mutants. The result indicates that those test suites generated at the first run are already good enough to detect most of the failures—79.6% for Branch-SC and 91.6% for MCDC-SC over the maximum number of cumulative failures.

These results show that MCDC-SC is significantly better at finding faults than Branch-SC and ARTOO. This suggests a more general result: MCDC is better at detecting faults than both branch coverage-only and ART.

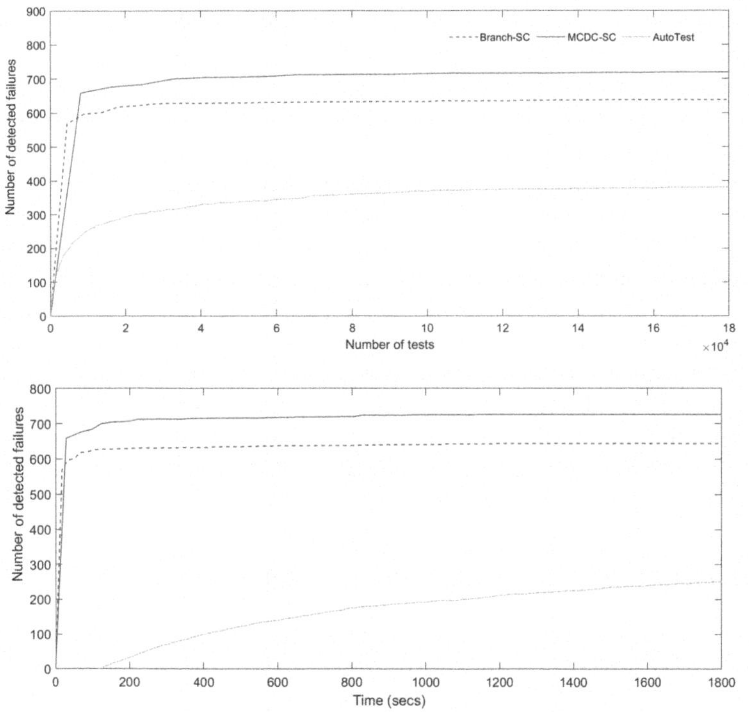

Fig. 5. Number of cumulative failures detected by different test generation tools

5 Related Work

MCDC [9] was originally defined to test safety-critical applications that require the highest level of safety and is originally mentioned in DO-178B [36], a standard for commercial avionics systems. Subsequently it became part other standards such as IEC 61508 [22], a standard for safety-critical electrical systems, and ISO 26262-3 [23], a standard reference for functional safety of cars. The US Department of Transportation also devoted an important report to MCDC [41]. Even if hundreds of systems have now been tested using MCDC—and very few experienced software bugs—it is interesting to see that the main justifications are mathematical and not empirical [9,41]. A few empirical studies exist, such as the one by Dupuy and Leveson [17], which states that 40% of the testing effort was spent on satisfying MCDC.

Some proposed extensions of MCDC (such as RCDC) [35,42] include further testing constraints. While some of these derivations seem to yield better results than MCDC, they have not yet been adopted by the safety community and hence are not considered in the present work. As measuring MCDC is already challenging (few commercial systems are evaluating the compliance to MCDC.[6]) and this is still the object of fairly recent publications [37].

[6] such as RapiCover —https://www.rapitasystems.com/products/rapicover—and LDRA—https://ldra.com/capabilities/code-coverage-analysis.

Several automated execution methodologies and test generation techniques to achieve or enhance MCDC rely on various techniques: Genetic Algorithms (GA) [4], Symbolic execution [18], SAT-solving [25,44], Model Checking [38]. The SAT-solving approaches [25,44] reduce the problem of generating MCDC-satisfying test suite into SAT problem and applies SAT-solver to generate test suites, with the particular objective to find the minimal test suite that satisfy MCDC. Their experimental results show that most of the generated test suites have the size of n+1 tests, which is aligned with the results of our study.

A model-checking approach [38] applies a similar idea to ours for generating MCDC-satisfying test suite from counterexamples: it expresses structural coverage criteria as properties in temporal logic, uses model checkers to produce counterexamples for the negation of those properties, and transforms the counterexamples into test cases. Contrary to the approach presented in the present article, it requires extracting abstract models from program source code, while the present test generation approach directly uses the code.

The LTest tool [29] provides the supports for test generation of C program satisfying various criteria, including MCDC. LTest annotates the C programs with labels that express the objectives of MCDC and generates tests with Dynamic Symbolic Execution. Mathieu et al. [8] proposed a constraint-based approach for generating MCDC-compliant test suite for programs written in the functional programming language Focalize. They expressed the constraints of MCDC as preconditions, translates the program into an equivalent constraint logical program and utilizes constraint solving on the logical program to produce expected test inputs.

6 Limitations and Threats to Validity

Measurement of fault detection capabilities in our study uses randomly seeded faults, rather than existing real faults. Although a 2014 study [24] show that artificial faults could be a good substitute for real faults, it is still possible that experimenting with real faults would lead to different results. Another obvious limitation is that the selected programs are small; it will be useful to extend the technique to larger ones.

7 Conclusions and Future Work

In spite of its inclusion in important industry and government standards, MCDC still has a somewhat sulfurous reputation in some circles and has been the object of controversy, including virulent critiques [6]. The lack of definitive answers has been due in part to the lack of tools to generate MCDC-compliant test suites automatically from the code. The present study makes an objective (if still partial) analysis possible. It suggests in particular, as a clear result, that in spite of the criticism MCDC beats branch coverage and adaptive random testing in working towards one of the primary goals of looking for better testing techniques: uncovering more bugs.

This result is all the more remarkable that—as noted in the previous section about limitations—the programs covered is small. Large-scale industrial programs can be expected to use more complex conditions (the original MCDC paper even suggests, although without concrete evidence, that aerospace programs can have more than 15 and up to 30 conditions!). Clearly, the more complex the condition, the more potential advantage for MCDC over branch coverage.

The present work also shows a proof-based approach to generating test suites satisfying MCDC, which is an extension of the previous approach for branch coverage. With this approach, although generating an MCDC test suite is generally more expensive (larger test suite and longer generation run) than generating a branch-compliant test suite, the performance overhead is still at an acceptable level if it is performed automatically. The benefit from the extra cost is that MCDC testing can detect more than 10% additional failures than branch coverage testing or automated random testing, which makes it significantly better.

As far as we know MCDC-SC is the first tool that makes such analyses possible since it generates, completely automatically, test suites satisfying MCDC based on code. We next plan to apply the approach to safety-critical programs from key industries.

References

1. Ammann, P., Offutt, J.: Introduction to Software Testing, 2nd edn. Cambridge University Press, Cambridge (2017)
2. Ammann, P., Offutt, J., Huang, H.: Coverage criteria for logical expressions. In: 2003 14th International Symposium on Software Reliability Engineering, ISSRE 2003, pp. 99–107. IEEE (2003)
3. AutoProof. http://autoproof.sit.org/
4. Awedikian, Z., Ayari, K., Antoniol, G.: MC/DC automatic test input data generation. In: Proceedings of the 11th Annual Conference on Genetic and Evolutionary Computation, pp. 1657–1664 (2009)
5. Barnett, M., Chang, B.Y.E., DeLine, R., Jacobs, B., Leino, K.R.M.: Boogie: a modular reusable verifier for object-oriented programs. In: de Boer, F.S., Bonsangue, M.M., Graf, S., de Roever, W.P. (eds.) Formal Methods for Components and Objects. Lecture Notes in Computer Science, vol. 4111, pp. 364–387. Springer, Heidelberg (2005). https://doi.org/10.1007/11804192_17
6. Bhansali, P.V.: The MCDC paradox. ACM SIGSOFT Softw. Eng. Notes **32**(3), 1–4 (2007)
7. Bormer, T., et al.: The COST IC0701 verification competition 2011. In: Beckert, B., Damiani, F., Gurov, D. (eds.) FoVeOOS 2011. LNCS, vol. 7421, pp. 3–21. Springer, Heidelberg (2012). https://doi.org/10.1007/978-3-642-31762-0_2
8. Carlier, M., Dubois, C., Gotlieb, A.: Constraint reasoning in FocalTest. In: ICSOFT (2010)
9. Chilenski, J., Miller, S.P.: Applicability of modified condition/decision coverage to software testing. Softw. Eng. J. **9**, 193–200 (1994). https://api.semanticscholar.org/CorpusID:27283960
10. Chilenski, J.J., Miller, S.P.: Applicability of modified condition/decision coverage to software testing. Softw. Eng. J. **9**(5), 193–200 (1994)

11. Ciupa, I., Leitner, A., Oriol, M., Meyer, B.: Experimental assessment of random testing for object-oriented software. In: Proceedings of the 2007 International Symposium on Software Testing and Analysis, pp. 84–94 (2007)
12. Ciupa, I., Leitner, A., Oriol, M., Meyer, B.: ARTOO: adaptive random testing for object-oriented software. In: International Conference on Software Engineering (ICSE), p. 71–80 (2008)
13. de Moura, L., Bjørner, N.: Z3: an efficient SMT solver. In: Ramakrishnan, C.R., Rehof, J. (eds.) TACAS 2008. LNCS, vol. 4963, pp. 337–340. Springer, Heidelberg (2008). https://doi.org/10.1007/978-3-540-78800-3_24
14. Dijkstra, E.W.: A Discipline of Programming. Prentice Hall (1976)
15. DO-178B: Software considerations in airborne systems and equipment certification (1992)
16. DO-178C: Software considerations in airborne systems and equipment certification (2011)
17. Dupuy, A., Leveson, N.: An empirical evaluation of the MC/DC coverage criterion on the HETE-2 satellite software. In: IEEE DASC: Digital Aviation Systems Conference, pp. 1B6/1–1B6/7 (2000)
18. Dutta, A., Kumar, S., Godboley, S.: Enhancing test cases generated by concolic testing. In: Proceedings of the 12th Innovations on Software Engineering Conference (formerly known as India Software Engineering Conference), pp. 1–11 (2019)
19. Huang, L., Meyer, B.: A failed proof can yield a useful test. arXiv:2208.09873 (2022)
20. Huang, L., Meyer, B., Oriol, M.: Improving counterexample quality from failed program verification. In: International Symposium on Software Reliability Engineering Workshops (ISSREW), pp. 268–273. IEEE (2022)
21. Huang, L., Meyer, B., Oriol, M.: Seeding contradiction: a fast method for generating full-coverage test suites. In: Bonfanti, S., Gargantini, A., Salvaneschi, P. (eds.) ICTSS 2023. LNCS, vol. 14131, pp. 52–70. Springer, Cham (2023). https://doi.org/10.1007/978-3-031-43240-8_4
22. International Electrotechnical Commission (IEC): IEC 61508-3:2010 - Functional safety of electrical/electronic/programmable electronic safety-related systems - Part 3: Software requirements (see Functional Safety and IEC 61508) (2010)
23. International Organization for Standardization (ISO): ISO 26262-3:2011 - Road vehicles — Functional safety (2011)
24. Just, R., Jalali, D., Inozemtseva, L., Ernst, M.D., Holmes, R., Fraser, G.: Are mutants a valid substitute for real faults in software testing? In: Proceedings of the 22nd ACM SIGSOFT International Symposium on Foundations of Software Engineering, pp. 654–665 (2014)
25. Kitamura, T., Maissonneuve, Q., Choi, E.-H., Artho, C., Gargantini, A.: Optimal test suite generation for modified condition decision coverage using SAT solving. In: Gallina, B., Skavhaug, A., Bitsch, F. (eds.) SAFECOMP 2018. LNCS, vol. 11093, pp. 123–138. Springer, Cham (2018). https://doi.org/10.1007/978-3-319-99130-6_9
26. Klebanov, V., et al.: The 1st verified software competition: experience report. In: Butler, M., Schulte, W. (eds.) FM 2011. LNCS, vol. 6664, pp. 154–168. Springer, Heidelberg (2011). https://doi.org/10.1007/978-3-642-21437-0_14
27. Leino, K.R.M.: Program Proofs. MIT Press (2023)
28. Leino, K.R.M., Rümmer, P.: The Boogie 2 type system: design and verification condition generation. https://citeseerx.ist.psu.edu/viewdoc/summary?doi=10.1.1.146.4277

29. Marcozzi, M., Bardin, S., Delahaye, M., Kosmatov, N., Prevosto, V.: Taming coverage criteria heterogeneity with LTest. In: 2017 IEEE International Conference on Software Testing, Verification and Validation (ICST), pp. 500–507. IEEE (2017)
30. Meyer, B.: Applying "design by contract." Computer **25**(10), 40–51 (1992)
31. Meyer, B.: Object-Oriented Software Construction, 2nd edn. Prentice Hall (1997)
32. Meyer, B.: Touch of Class: Learning to Program Well with Objects and Contracts. Springer, Heidelberg (2016). https://doi.org/10.1007/978-3-540-92145-5
33. Mustafin, I., Schena, A., Weber, R.: buggy-java-jml-eiffel (2024). https://github.com/CI-CSE/buggy-java-jml-eiffel
34. Nilizadeh, A., Leavens, G.T., Le, X.B.D., Păsăreanu, C.S., Cok, D.R.: Exploring true test overfitting in dynamic automated program repair using formal methods. In: 2021 14th IEEE Conference on Software Testing, Verification and Validation (ICST), pp. 229–240. IEEE (2021)
35. Paul, T.K., Lau, M.F.: A systematic literature review on modified condition and decision coverage. In: Proceedings of the 29th Annual ACM Symposium on Applied Computing, SAC 2014, pp. 1301–1308. Association for Computing Machinery, New York (2014). https://doi.org/10.1145/2554850.2555004
36. Radio Technical Commission for Aeronautics (RTCA): RTCA/DO-178B Software Considerations in Airborne Systems and Equipment Certification (1992)
37. Rani, G.M., Godboley, S.: Poster: a gCov based new profiler, gMCov, for MC/DC and SC-MCC. In: 2022 IEEE Conference on Software Testing, Verification and Validation (ICST), pp. 469–472 (2022https://doi.org/10.1109/ICST53961.2022.00058
38. Rayadurgam, S., Heimdahl, M.P.E.: Coverage based test-case generation using model checkers. In: Proceedings. Eighth Annual IEEE International Conference and Workshop On the Engineering of Computer-Based Systems-ECBS 2001, pp. 83–91. IEEE (2001)
39. Tillmann, N., de Halleux, J.: Pex–white box test generation for .NET. In: Beckert, B., Hähnle, R. (eds.) TAP 2008. LNCS, vol. 4966, pp. 134–153. Springer, Heidelberg (2008). https://doi.org/10.1007/978-3-540-79124-9_10
40. Tschannen, J., Furia, C.A., Nordio, M., Polikarpova, N.: AutoProof: auto-active functional verification of object-oriented programs. In: Baier, C., Tinelli, C. (eds.) TACAS 2015. LNCS, vol. 9035, pp. 566–580. Springer, Heidelberg (2015). https://doi.org/10.1007/978-3-662-46681-0_53
41. US Department of Transportation: An Investigation of Three Forms of the Modified Condition Decision Coverage (MCDC) Criterion, final report, DOT/FAA/AR-01/18 (2001)
42. Vilkomir, S.A., Bowen, J.P.: Reinforced condition/decision coverage (RC/DC): a new criterion for software testing. In: Bert, D., Bowen, J.P., Henson, M.C., Robinson, K. (eds.) ZB 2002. LNCS, vol. 2272, pp. 291–308. Springer, Heidelberg (2002). https://doi.org/10.1007/3-540-45648-1_15
43. Weide, B.W., et al.: Incremental benchmarks for software verification tools and techniques. In: Shankar, N., Woodcock, J. (eds.) VSTTE 2008. LNCS, vol. 5295, pp. 84–98. Springer, Heidelberg (2008). https://doi.org/10.1007/978-3-540-87873-5_10
44. Yang, L., Yan, J., Zhang, J.: Generating minimal test set satisfying MC/DC criterion via sat based approach. In: ACM Symposium on Applied Computing, pp. 1899–1906 (2018)

Refining CEGAR-Based Test-Case Generation with Feasibility Annotations

Max Barth and Marie-Christine Jakobs(✉)

LMU Munich, Munich, Germany
m.jakobs@lmu.de

Abstract. Often, testing is part of software quality assurance, in which testers may use automatic tools to generate test cases. To avoid redundant work, the tools may consider collateral coverage, i.e., use that a test case generated for a particular test goal, e.g., a branch, may cover further goals. We present a novel approach to use collateral coverage during test-case generation with software model checkers that apply counterexample-guided abstraction refinement. For every test goal, those model checkers perform a reachability analysis, which we plan to support with previous test inputs. More concretely, we use a feasibility annotation to map already covered goals to their test inputs. Whenever the reachability analysis detects a syntactical path to an uncovered test goal, we select a test input from the feasibility annotation that is likely a (partial) input for the path and use this input as a potential guide to check whether the path is semantically feasible. So far, we have integrated our approach into Ultimate TestGen and evaluated it on the Test-Comp tasks. Compared to the original Ultimate TestGen approach, our approach performs similar or better. In total, we increase the achieved branch coverage by 2%, but may achieve a significantly larger increase for some tasks.

1 Introduction

Testing is widely applied to examine software quality. However, manual test-case generation is laborious. Thus, plenty automatic test-case generators were developed. Since it is often not known in advance which part of the code is faulty, several of these generators [2,5,14,17,18,20–22,27,37] aim to generate test suites that optimize some adequacy criterion, e.g., branch coverage [5,17,18,37].

Often, such automatic test-case generation approaches face the phenomenon of collateral coverage, i.e., a test case generated to cover a test goal g (e.g., a particular branch) may cover other test goals $g' \neq g$ by accident. To deal with this phenomenon, EvoSuite [18] performs whole test suite optimization. Other approaches [3,5,9,37] ignore the phenomenon completely, perform test suite reduction [36] after they finished their test-case generation process [22,33], or discard test cases that do not increase the value of the adequacy criterion [28, 29]. Thus, they miss an opportunity to profit from collateral coverage. Further

This work was partially funded by the Deutsche Forschungsgemeinschaft (DFG, German Research Foundation) - 496852682.

© The Author(s), under exclusive license to Springer Nature Switzerland AG 2025
M. Huisman and F. Howar (Eds.): TAP 2024, LNCS 15153, pp. 45–64, 2025.
https://doi.org/10.1007/978-3-031-72044-4_3

approaches [2,7,10,21,22,27] determine the collaterally covered test goals of a generated test case by measuring the coverage while executing the test case. Typically, these approaches rely on external tools for coverage measurement [2, 7,10,21,27], which requires information exchange between the tools and typically introduces overhead. An exception may be approaches [14] that extend a test case after it reaches an uncovered test goal since they aim to construct test cases that provide enough inputs for the program execution to terminate, i.e., to reach the end of the program. However, this objective makes test-case generation more complex and may lead to failures, e.g., in case of infinite program paths. In contrast to the above approaches, test goal reduction techniques [1,15,24,31] aim to statically detect test goals that are subsumed by other test goals, i.e., they will always be automatically covered if the other test goals are covered. Test-case generation thereafter ignores subsumed test goals, but also does not profit from collateral coverage if only some but not all test cases that cover a test goal also accidentally cover a particular other test goal.

In this paper, we present a new concept to profit from collateral coverage. While generating a test case to cover a goal g, we aim to reuse inputs of an already existing test case. Thereby, we add additional inputs required to cover the test goal. Since reuse may not always be possible, we will generate test cases starting from scratch without reusing any inputs if the reuse fails. We believe that one can adopt our idea to any test-case generator built on top of a reachability analysis. However, we employ our idea for test-case generators like e.g., CoVeriTest [9] and Ultimate TestGen [5][1] that apply software model checking with counterexample-guided abstraction refinement (CEGAR) [16]. As shown in the international competition on software testing (Test-Comp) [6], these test-case generators achieve high coverage, but still deal well with large state spaces.

Like most test-case generators relying on model checkers, test-case generators that apply software model checking with counterexample-guided abstraction refinement encode reaching an uncovered test goal as property violation and generate test cases from counterexamples [7]. To this end, they maintain and iteratively refine an abstraction of the program, which describes an over-approximation of the feasible program executions. In each iteration, they select a counterexample, a path π of the abstraction that reaches an uncovered test goal g, and check its feasibility. If path π is feasible, a test case that covers g will be exported. Otherwise, the abstraction is refined to exclude path π.

Our approach hooks into the feasibility check of the above procedure. To this end, we publish previously generated test cases in a feasibility annotation, which maps covered test goals to their test inputs. During feasibility checking, we then use path π to look up the test inputs of a covered goal that has a high chance to provide a partial input for path π. Thereafter, we guide the feasibility check with those inputs, i.e., we check whether π is feasible with the selected inputs. If the guided check fails, we will fall back to the standard feasibility check. In case of a failure, we may however derive a test case for another test goal if the

[1] While the evaluation in this paper only considers the implementation in Ultimate TestGen, a master student currently integrates the approach in CoVeriTest.

```
0: r = 1;
1: while x > 0
2:     r = r*x;
3:     x = x - 1;
4: if x < 0
5:     r = 0;
```

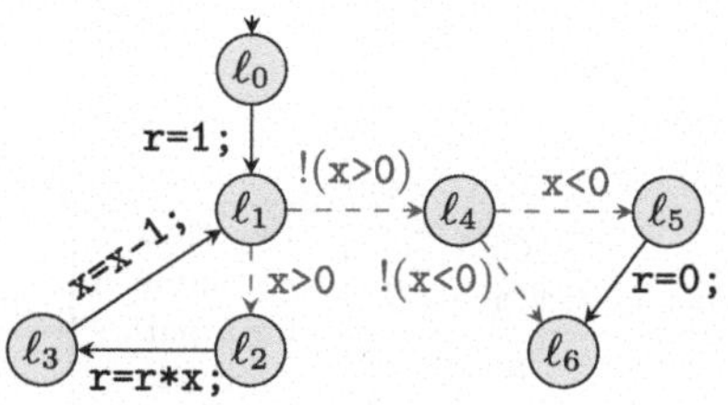

Fig. 1. Source code (left) and CFA (right) of our example program `fac`

inputs were generated for a prefix of π and after the prefix path π evaluates at most one condition of an if or while statement.

As a proof of concept, we integrate our approach into ULTIMATE TESTGEN [5] and compare its performance against the performance of ULTIMATE TESTGEN when it ignores collateral coverage. Our evaluation on the Test-Comp tasks shows that a smart use of previously generated test cases allows us to significantly improve the achieved coverage for some tasks. For the remaining tasks, we perform similar to ULTIMATE TESTGEN when it ignores collateral coverage.

2 Overview of CEGAR-Based Test-Case Generation

Programs and Their Test Goals. Our goal is to generate test cases to cover test goals, e.g., the branches of a program. For our presentation, we consider sequential programs that execute assignment $v := \mathit{aexpr}$ and assume statements bexpr over a set V of (integer) variables.[2] Given the set Σ of all possible program statements, we model a program by a *control-flow-automaton* (CFA) [8] $P = (L, \ell_0, G)$ consisting of (1) a set L of locations, which represent the program counter values, (2) an initial location $\ell_0 \in L$, and (3) a set $G \subseteq (L \times \Sigma \times L)$ of control-flow edges, which determine the statements executable at a given program location and where to proceed after a statement's execution. We assume that CFAs are generated from program code and, therefore, ensure that the control-flow is deterministic, i.e., for all $(\ell, \mathit{stmt}, \ell'), (\ell, \mathit{stmt}', \ell'') \in G$ either $\mathit{stmt} = \mathit{stmt}'$ and $\ell' = \ell''$ or stmt and stmt' are assume statements such that $\mathit{stmt} \equiv \neg \mathit{stmt}'$. To detect the neighboring assume statement with the negated assumption, we define the following function.

$$NBR((\ell, \mathit{stmt}, \ell')) := \begin{cases} (\ell, \mathit{stmt}', \ell'') & \text{if } \mathit{stmt} \text{ is an assume statement} \wedge \\ & \exists (\ell, \mathit{stmt}', \ell'') \in G : \mathit{stmt} \equiv \neg \mathit{stmt}' \\ \bot & \text{otherwise} \end{cases}$$

Figure 1 shows our example program `fac` and its CFA. The CFA contains one edge per assignment and two assume edges per condition of an if or while statement, namely one for each evaluation of the condition.

[2] Our implementation supports sequential C programs.

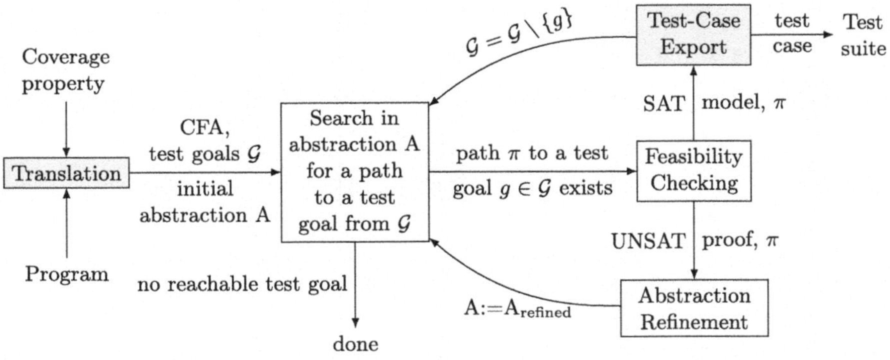

Fig. 2. Overview of a CEGAR-based model checker that generates test cases

In our example, the assume edges highlighted in dashed, blue are our test goals. In general, our approach supports *test goals* $\mathcal{G} \subseteq G$, which are a subset of the control-flow edges. This allows us to support different elementary coverage criteria [23] like statement or branch coverage as in our example. Note that in case of branch coverage, the set $\mathcal{G}$ of test goals will contain all assume edges.

To generate test cases that cover test goals, we need to analyze (syntactical) program paths that end in a test goal. Formally, a *program path* π of a program $P = (L, \ell_0, G)$ is a sequence of consecutive control-flow edges, i.e., $\pi = (g_0, \ldots, g_n) \in G^+$ with $g_0 = (\ell_0, \cdot, \cdot)$ and for all $1 \leq i \leq n$ there exists $\ell_i \in L$ such $g_{i-1} = (\cdot, \cdot, \ell_i)$ and $g_i = (\ell_i, \cdot, \cdot)$. We order two program paths π and π' based on their prefix relation and write $\pi' \preceq \pi$ if π' is a prefix of π, i.e., there exists $\pi'' \in G^*$ such that $\pi = \pi'\pi''$. Next, we extend the concept of neighboring assume edges to syntactic path and define the neighboring path of π as follows.

$$NBR(\pi) := \begin{cases} \pi' NBR(g) & \text{if } \pi' \in G^* \wedge \pi = \pi' g \ \wedge \ NBR(g) \neq \bot \\ \bot & \text{otherwise} \end{cases}$$

Generating Test Cases with CEGAR-Based Software Model Checking. As underlying procedure to generate test cases that cover our test goals, we employ a software model checker that applies counterexample-guided abstraction refinement (CEGAR) [16]. Examples of such model checkers are Blast [7], CPAchecker [9,33], and Ultimate Automizer [5]. Test-case generation utilizes that these model checkers already examine whether a property violation is reachable and that they produce a counterexample if a property violation is reached. To turn such model checkers into test-case generators, it is therefore sufficient to (1) encode the reachability of a test goal as a property violation, e.g., using monitors [9,33] or extending the program with appropriate assertions [5], and to (2) derive tests from counterexamples [7].

Figure 2 shows an overview of the test-case generation procedure with a CEGAR-based model checker. Extensions to the standard CEGAR approach are highlighted in gray. The procedure starts with the translation of the program and the desired coverage property into the CFA and the corresponding test goal representation. Thereafter, the standard CEGAR iteration starts. During the iteration procedure, the model checker maintains an abstraction over-approximating the program's execution paths. Initially, the abstraction contains all syntactical paths of the program and then, each iteration refines the abstraction by reducing the number of paths that reach a property violation (i.e., that reach an uncovered test goal). At the beginning of each iteration, the model checker searches for a (syntactic) program path π in the current abstraction that violates the property, i.e., that ends in an uncovered test goal. If no such path exists, our procedure stops because it either covered all test goals or the remaining test goals are proven to be unreachable. Otherwise, the model checker continues with the analysis of π's feasibility, i.e., π's executability. To this end, the model checker investigates whether the formula encoding φ_π of path π is satisfiable. If π is executable, the model checker exports a test case from the resulting counterexample. More concretely, it derives the test inputs from the model showing that π's formula encoding is satisfiable. Afterwards, the covered test goal is removed such that it can no longer cause a property violation.[3] If π is not executable, the model checker uses the proof of unsatisfiability to refine the abstraction, i.e., it removes π and paths that cannot be executed due to similar reasons as π from the abstraction. In both cases, the next iteration starts.

Partial Models of Satisfiability and Their Formula Encoding. Our approach builds on the following observation in the context of collateral coverage. A model m satisfying the formula encoding φ_π of a path π may also be useful to show the satisfiability of a path π' that extends π. In general, a model m for formula φ_π provides for any variable of φ_π a value of its domain. Since we assume an SSA-based encoding of π, the formula may use more than one variable for a specific program variable. Without loss of generality, we expect that variables are indexed. Thus, we can define a model as a partial function $m : V \times \mathbb{N} \rightharpoonup \mathbb{Z}$. In the following, we use $\mathcal{M}$ to denote the set of all such models. While we could reuse complete models, we want to avoid providing too many constraints to a later feasibility check. Thus, we utilize that we can derive values for those variables that do not define inputs. In contrast, input variables $I \subseteq V \times \mathbb{N}$ save input values like the initial values of input parameters or the values of external functions like e.g., `random`, `scanf`. We can easily extract input variables from φ_π using a not further specified function $\mathcal{I} : \Phi \to 2^{V\times\mathbb{N}}$, where Φ represents the set of formula encodings of paths π. Based on function $\mathcal{I}$, we can now define a function $\downarrow: \mathcal{M}\times\Phi \to \mathcal{M}$ to restrict models to partial models that only consider values of input variables such that $m \downarrow \varphi_\pi = \{(v, val) \mid (v, val) \in m \ \wedge \ v \in \mathcal{I}(\varphi_\pi)\}$. To make use of these models m, we need to encode them into a constraint, a formula, that provides the values for the input variables. To this end, we compute a conjunction $\varphi_m = \bigwedge_{(v,val)\in m} v = val$ of atoms that assign each (input)

[3] While the generated test case covers all test goals occurring in π, the model checker typically detects a path π that only contains one uncovered goal, namely g.

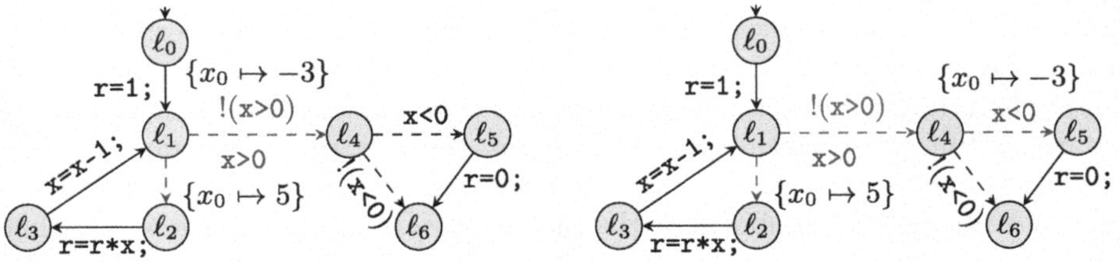

Fig. 3. Example CFA with a feasibility annotation (left) and an adaption of that feasibility annotation (right) performed after analyzing the feasibility of path $\pi = (\ell_0, r = 1;, \ell_1)(\ell_1, !(x > 0), \ell_4)(\ell_4, x < 0, \ell_5)$.

variable of the model to its value stored in the model. Next, we explain how to integrate these conjunctions into the test-case generation process from above.

3 Feasibility Checking with Feasibility Annotations

To simplify the generation of test cases, we want to use our observation that a test case for a test goal g may also cover further test goals g' that are reachable from test goal g or at least may provide a partial input to cover such further test goals g'. For example, consider path $\pi = (\ell_0, r = 1;, \ell_1)(\ell_1, !(x > 0), \ell_4)$ executable with e.g., test case $x \mapsto -3$. Test case $x \mapsto -3$ also covers test goal $(\ell_4, x < 0, \ell_5)$ along the path $\pi = (\ell_0, r = 1;, \ell_1)(\ell_1, !(x > 0), \ell_4)(\ell_4, x < 0, \ell_5)$. Our goal is to use this observation during the feasibility check of a path π. More concretely, we try to guide the satisfiability check of π's formula encoding with the test case of an already covered test goal that occurs earlier on path π.

Feasibility Annotation. To make the relation between covered test goals and their test cases accessible, we introduce the concept of a feasibility annotation. A *feasibility annotation* for a program $P = (L, \ell_0, G)$ is a partial function $\mathcal{F}_A : G \rightharpoonup \mathcal{M}$ that maps control-flow edges, in particular test goals, to partial models. Note that we use partial models instead of test cases because models are easier to integrate into the satisfiaiblity check of a formula encoding. A conjunction of model and formula is sufficient. Figure 3 shows one feasibility annotation for our example CFA that assigns test cases (in the form of partial models) to both branches of the loop. We continue to explain how we extend our test-case generation procedure (see Fig. 2) to use and assemble feasibility annotations.

3.1 Integrating Feasibility Annotations Into Satisfiability Checking

Our goal is to use feasibility annotations during the feasibility check. Figure 4 gives an overview on how we extend the feasibility checking for this purpose. In the following, we explain the basic extension without the dashed elements, which assumes that opt?(π) always returns false. First, we maintain a feasibility

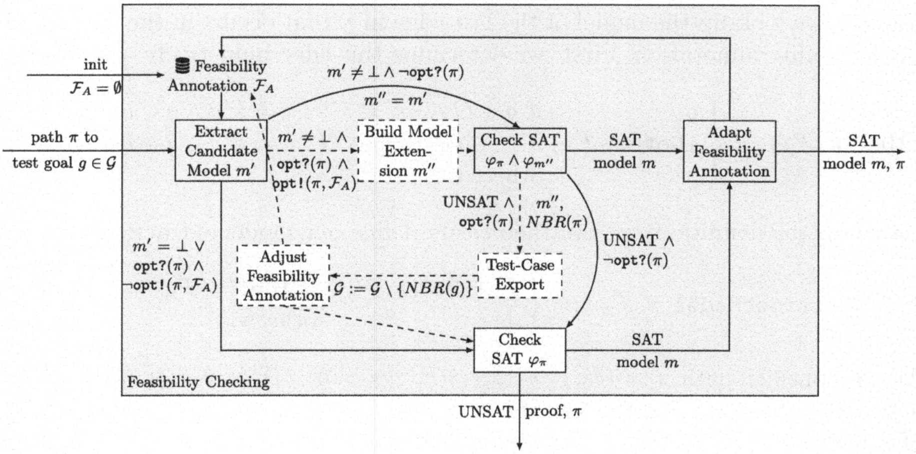

Fig. 4. Extended feasibility checking that uses feasibility annotation, basic extension does not use dashed elements

annotation that is adapted during test-case generation. Initially, the feasibility annotation is empty, i.e., no control-flow edge maps to a partial model. At the beginning of each feasibility check, we use the path π to extract a candidate model m' from the current feasibility annotation. The details of the extraction are described in the next paragraph. If a candidate model can be extracted ($m' \neq \bot$), we assume that it provides a partial input for π and use it ($m'' = m'$) to guide and hopefully speed up the satisfiability check with the (partial) input. More concretely, we check the satisfiability of π's formula encoding φ_π conjuncted with the encoding $\varphi_{m''}$ of the model. Note that this guided satisfiability check may return unsatisfiable because π is not executable at all or cannot be executed with the inputs provided by (partial) candidate model m'', i.e., our assumption was wrong. Hence, if the conjunction of π's formula encoding φ_π with model m'' is proven unsatisfiable or no candidate model can be extracted, we will simply perform the satisfiability check of φ_π like the original procedure. In case one of the satisfiability checks succeeds, i.e., returns formula satisfiable, we adapt the feasibility annotation, e.g., we integrate the new test case in form of a partial model. The details of the adaption are explained later.

Extracting a Candidate Model from a Feasibility Annotation. To profit from feasibility annotations, we need to extract a candidate model m' for a given path π that has a high chance to provide a (partial) input for π. The highest chances to provide a partial input have those models that witness the feasibility of a prefix of path π because they already partially execute π. Out of those models we expect the model whose associated path has the largest length to be most likely successful because its execution is closest to π. Since our experience is that prefix matching makes the look-up too expensive and, therefore, is not supported by our feasibility annotation, we decide to use a proxy for prefixes.

Namely, we look-up the model of the last edge in π that occurs in the domain of the feasibility annotation. First, we determine this edge inductively as follows.

$$\mathtt{lDef}(\pi, \mathcal{F}_A) := \begin{cases} g & \text{if } g \in G \wedge \exists \pi' \in G^* : \pi = \pi' g \wedge g \in dom(\mathcal{F}_A) \\ \mathtt{lDef}(\pi', \mathcal{F}_A) & \text{if } \pi' \in G^* \wedge \exists g \in G : \pi = \pi' g \wedge g \notin dom(\mathcal{F}_A) \\ \bot & \text{otherwise} \end{cases}$$

Based on the definition, we can then easily define our model extraction.

$$\mathtt{extractModel}(\pi, \mathcal{F}_A) := \begin{cases} \mathcal{F}_A(\mathtt{lDef}(\pi, \mathcal{F}_A)) & \text{if } \mathtt{lDef}(\pi, \mathcal{F}_A) \neq \bot \\ \bot & \text{otherwise} \end{cases}$$

Again, consider path $\pi = (\ell_0, r = 1;, \ell_1)(\ell_1, !(x > 0), \ell_4)(\ell_4, x < 0, \ell_5)$ and the feasibility annotation on the left of Fig. 3. Since $(\ell_1, !(x > 0), \ell_4)$ is the last edge of π for which the feasibility annotation is defined, we extract its corresponding model $\{x_0 \mapsto -3\}$. The input derivable from this model suffices to execute π.

Adapting the Feasibility Annotation. To make test cases for already covered test goals accessible, we need to add them to the feasibility annotation. Remember that our test-case generation procedure generates a test case when one of the two satisfiability checks in Fig. 4 returns satisfiable. In these cases, we should also adapt the feasibility annotation. We know that the model m provided by one of the checks proved the executability of path π, which ends in test goal g. Furthermore, we know that no explicit test case has been generated for g before, i.e., $g \notin dom(\mathcal{F}_A)$, and the test case is derived from m. Therefore, we may extend the feasibility annotation with an entry for test goal g. As explained before, we do not store the complete model m but like a test case only keep those model parts $m \downarrow \varphi_\pi$ that specify the inputs. Consequently, we add the following entry $g \mapsto m \downarrow \varphi_\pi$ to the feasibility annotation, i.e., $\mathcal{F}_A^{\text{new}} = \mathcal{F}_A \cup \{(g, m \downarrow \varphi_\pi)\}$. In case of our example path $\pi = (\ell_0, r = 1;, \ell_1)(\ell_1, !(x > 0), \ell_4)(\ell_4, x < 0, \ell_5)$ from above, which we proved feasible with model $\{x_0 \mapsto -3\}$, we extend the feasibility annotation from Fig. 3 with $((\ell_4, x < 0, \ell_5), \{x_0 \mapsto -3\})$.

So far, we only added new entries to the feasibility annotation. Since unsatisfiability proofs are costly, we want to reduce the number of times that we suggest an incorrect partial input, i.e., the satisfiability check of $\varphi_\pi \wedge \varphi_{m''}$ returns unsatisfiable. Our goal is to delete entries that have a low chance of being successfully reused again. The deletion is based on the following observations. After assigning a model m to the last edge g of π, for many extension π' of path π we will have $\mathtt{lDef}(\pi, \mathcal{F}_A) \neq \mathtt{lDef}(\pi', \mathcal{F}_A^{\text{new}})$. Exceptions may be caused by loops in the program, but even for those extensions model m might be a better candidate because it is an input for a longer prefix of the extension and according to our assumption preferable. Furthermore, consider that we assume programs are deterministic, i.e., control-flow only branches at assume edges and the branch direction is determined by the values of the program's variable. Unless we provide the program with further inputs, i.e., we need to extend model m' with further inputs, after a successful reuse of m' for π, model m' would likely not be usable for paths π'' that branch from π after the last occurrence of $\mathtt{lDef}(\pi, \mathcal{F}_A)$. Moreover, the exploration order typically guarantees that prefixes π' of π are explored before π. We conclude that after successfully using a model m' (i.e., $\varphi_\pi \wedge \varphi_{m''}$ is satisfiable), the likelihood of being useful in future decreases significantly. Therefore, we suggest that in case we check the satisfiability of $\varphi_\pi \wedge \varphi_{m''}$ and that check returns satisfiable, we perform the following extended update $\mathcal{F}_A^{\text{new}} = (\mathcal{F}_A \setminus \{(\mathtt{lDef}(\pi, \mathcal{F}_A), m')\}) \cup \{(g, m \downarrow \varphi_\pi)\}$ of the feasibility annotation, which also removes the successfully used model m'. In case of our example path $\pi = (\ell_0, r = 1;, \ell_1)(\ell_1, !(x > 0), \ell_4)(\ell_4, x < 0, \ell_5)$ from above, which we proved feasible while reusing model $\{x_0 \mapsto -3\}$, we adapt the feasibility annotation on the left of Fig. 3 by deleting $((\ell_1, !(x > 0), \ell_4), \{x_0 \mapsto -3\})$ and adding $((\ell_4, x < 0, \ell_5), \{x_0 \mapsto -3\})$ (result shown on the right of Fig. 3).

3.2 Learning from Unsatisfiability Proofs of Model-Guided Checks

While deletion of entries in the feasibility annotation tries to reduce the number of unsatisfiability proofs, we now consider an optimization that aims to derive a test case despite $\varphi_\pi \wedge \varphi_{m''}$ being unsatisfiable. Our observation is that under certain conditions that include a prefix relation between the path for which the extracted model was generated and the current path π, we can conclude from the unsatisfiability result that the (extension of the) extracted model is a valid test case for covering the neighboring edge $NBR(g)$ of goal g. Note that this optimization is only applicable if a neighboring edge exists as e.g., for any test goal in branch coverage. In the next two paragraphs, we discuss the precondition condition for the optimization in more detail.

Precondition for Learning. From now on, we assume that the neighboring edge exists, i.e., $\bot \neq NBR(g)$. First, we discuss the conditions under which the extracted model m' is already a valid test case for covering the neighboring edge $NBR(g)$ of goal g, i.e., we can use $m'' = m'$ to cover $NBR(g)$. Remember we only want to use m' if $\varphi_\pi \wedge \varphi_{m''}$ is unsatisfiable. Hence, we consider m' valid if it can execute neighboring path $NBR(\pi)$ (and thus, covers $NBR(g)$) whenever it cannot execute π. Syntactically, m' must provide values for all inputs in $\varphi_{NBR(\pi)}$. Semantically, the unsatisfiability of $\varphi_\pi \wedge \varphi_{m''}$ must imply the satisfiability of $\varphi_{NBR(\pi)} \wedge \varphi_{m''}$, i.e., if $m'' = m'$ cannot execute π, it will execute $NBR(\pi)$. By definition and $NBR(g) \neq \bot$, we know that g and $NBR(g)$ are assume edges, both executing the negated assumption of the other. Hence, $\varphi_g \vee \varphi_{NBR(g)} \equiv true$. To ensure the semantic constraint, we thus require that the largest common prefix $\pi_\prec$ of π and $NBR(\pi)$, which is by definition π without its last edge, is executable with m', i.e., $\varphi_{\pi_\prec} \wedge \varphi_{m'}$ is satisfiable. Assuming that only assume edges can restrict a path's executability, which is fulfilled for deterministic programs, $\pi_\prec$ is executable if the path $\pi_{m'}$ used to generate the test case for $\mathtt{lDef}(\pi, \mathcal{F}_A)$[4] can be extended to $\pi_\prec$ without using any assume edges. We expect this condition often to be true when considering branch coverage because

[4] $\mathtt{lDef}(\pi, \mathcal{F}_A)$ is the test goal used to extract model m' from the feasibility annotation.

our approach typically covers previous assume edges first and then stores their test case in the feasibility annotation until it is used. Following the structure of the requirement for $\pi_{\prec}$, we split its evaluation into two parts. More concretely, we mentally split path $\pi_{\prec}$ at the last occurrence of $\mathtt{lDef}(\pi, \mathcal{F}_A)$ into two parts and provide one check for each part. The check on the first half, i.e., the path starting at the beginning of $\pi_{\prec}$ and ending at the last occurrence of $\mathtt{lDef}(\pi, \mathcal{F}_A)$, tests whether the first half is identical to $\pi_{m'}$, i.e., $\pi_{m'}$ can be extended to $\pi_{\prec}$. To this end, we use the following recursive definition to determine the first half.

$$\mathtt{pre}(\pi, \mathcal{F}_A) := \begin{cases} \pi & \text{if } \exists \pi' \in G^*, g \in G : \pi = \pi' g \wedge g \in dom(\mathcal{F}_A) \\ \mathtt{pre}(\pi', \mathcal{F}_A) & \text{if } \pi' \in G^* \wedge \exists g \in G : \pi = \pi' g \wedge g \notin dom(\mathcal{F}_A) \\ \bot & \text{otherwise} \end{cases}$$

The check $\mathtt{nA}$ inspects the edges of the second half backwards, i.e., it inspects $\pi_{\prec}$ from its end until the first occurrence (in the reverse order) of $\mathtt{lDef}(\pi, \mathcal{F}_A)$. During inspection, it checks recursively that no assume statements occur.

$$\mathtt{nA}(\pi, \mathcal{F}_A) := \begin{cases} true & \text{if } \exists \pi' \in G^*, g \in G : \pi = \pi' g \wedge g \in dom(\mathcal{F}_A) \\ \mathtt{nA}(\pi', \mathcal{F}_A) & \text{if } \pi' \in G^* \wedge \exists (\ell, stmt, \ell') \in G : \pi = \pi'(\ell, stmt, \ell') \wedge \\ & \quad (\ell, stmt, \ell') \notin dom(\mathcal{F}_A) \wedge \ stmt \text{ is no assume statement} \\ false & \text{otherwise} \end{cases}$$

Weakening Precondition via Model Extension. Next, we want to weaken the assumption that m' must define all test inputs. First, we observe that if predicate $\mathtt{pre}$ evalutes to true, the values for exactly all inputs on the prefix $\mathtt{pre}(\pi, \mathcal{F}_A)$ will be provided by m' because $\pi_{m'} = \mathtt{pre}(\pi, \mathcal{F}_A)$ and m' provides all inputs for $\pi_{m'}$ by construction. Second, we observe that if $\mathtt{nA}$ evaluates to true, the only assume edge occuring in π after the prefix may be g. Hence, providing arbitrary values for inputs after that prefix cannot restrict the condition that either π or $NBR(\pi)$ is executable when $\pi_{m'} = \mathtt{pre}(\pi, \mathcal{F}_A)$. Practically, we can easily determine those input variables from the formula encoding. Although we could use arbitrary values, as an example we define an extension m'' that always adds zero values: $m'' = m' \cup \{(v, 0) \mid v \in \mathcal{I}(\varphi_\pi) \setminus \mathcal{I}(\varphi_{\mathtt{pre}(\pi, \mathcal{F}_A)})\}$.[5]

Integrating Learning Into the Extended Feasibility Check. Given the precondition for the optimization, we now explain how we integrate the optimization into feasibility checking (the dashed path in Fig. 4). After extracting a candidate model $m' \neq \bot$, we need to check whether the optimization should be applied. To this end, we first check that the optimization is enabled and appropriate, i.e., a neighboring edge exists that has not been covered yet.

$$\mathtt{opt?}(\pi) := \mathtt{enabled} \ \wedge \exists \pi' \in G^*, g \in G : \pi = \pi' g \wedge NBR(g) \neq \bot \wedge NBR(g) \in \mathcal{G}$$

[5] Note that we only extend models while learning because adding arbitrary input values, e.g., always zeroes, can have a significant chance to make the formula $\varphi_\pi \wedge \varphi_{m''}$ unsatisfiable. However, only while learning we can profit from unsatisfiability results.

Afterwards, we examine whether the optimization is applicable. Remember we need to check two aspects. On the one hand, check $\texttt{nA}$ ensures that there are no assume edges between the last occurrence of $\texttt{lDef}(\pi, \mathcal{F}_A)$ and g. In principle, we can perform this check together with the computation of $\texttt{lDef}(\pi, \mathcal{F}_A)$. On the other hand, we check that the prefix of path π ending at the last occurrence of $\texttt{lDef}(\pi, \mathcal{F}_A)$ is equivalent to $\pi_{m'}$, the path considered when generating test case $m' = \texttt{extractModel}(\pi, \mathcal{F}_A)$. While model m' would be sufficient for this check and we, therefore, do not include π'_m into our definition of a feasibility annotation, in practice we store $\pi_{m'}$ as part of the feasibility annotation to be more efficient. Hence, for the optimization we must introduce a prefix check that we wanted to avoid. However, the check is limited to at most one check in each CEGAR iteration. In our implementation, we combine it with the construction of φ_π, which needs to process the complete trace anyways. Combining these two checks, we get the following predicate $\texttt{opt!}$ that determines whether we are allowed to learn from the unsatisfiability result of $\varphi_\pi \wedge \varphi_{m''}$ if learning is enabled and appropriate (i.e., predicate $\texttt{opt?}$ is true).

$$\texttt{opt!}(\pi, \mathcal{F}_A) := \begin{array}{l} \pi_{\texttt{extractModel}(\pi, \mathcal{F}_A)} = \texttt{pre}(\pi, \mathcal{F}_A) \wedge \\ \exists \pi' \in G^*, g \in G : \pi = \pi' g \wedge \texttt{nA}(\pi', \mathcal{F}_A) \end{array}$$

After deciding that the optimization will be applied, we perform the first step. Namely if required, we add further inputs to candidate model m' as explained above. Like our basic extension, we then perform a satisfiability check to determine the feasibility of path π using the conjunction of π's formula encoding with the encoding of the extended candidate model instead of the candidate model. If the feasibility is shown (i.e., the result is SAT), the feasibility checking continues like the basic extension. In case of result UNSAT, we know that predicates $\texttt{opt?}(\pi)$ and $\texttt{opt!}(\pi, \mathcal{F}_A)$ are true, i.e. their checks ensure that the extended candidate model m'' covers the neighboring edge $NBR(g)$ along the neighboring path $NBR(\pi)$. Hence, we use the test-case export component of the original test-case generation procedure to export a test case for edge $NBR(g)$. Although not shown in Fig. 4[6], the test case is added to the test suite. Thereafter, the covered edge $NBR(g)$ is removed from the set of uncovered test goals $\mathcal{G}$ and we adjust the feasibility annotation. Adjustment is similar to the extended adaption. After reusing candidate model m', we remove it from the feasibility annotation and add the model m'' used to cover the neighboring edge to the feasibility annotation, i.e., $\mathcal{F}_A^{\text{new'}} = (\mathcal{F}_A \setminus \{(\texttt{lDef}(\pi, \mathcal{F}_A), m')\}) \cup \{(NBR(g), m'')\}$. Note that we do not need to restrict m'' to input variables because by construction it only defines values for those. Finally, we get back to the basic workflow and check feasibility of path π. The only difference is that if we adapt the feasibility annotation, we will adapt $\mathcal{F}_A^{\text{new'}}$. Further note that if predicate $\texttt{opt?}(\pi)$ is true but predicate $\texttt{opt!}(\pi, \mathcal{F}_A)$ is false, we do not reuse model m' and continue with the standard feasibility check because in our experience model m' has a low likelihood to be a candidate input.

[6] We excluded this part in favor of clarity of the figure.

3.3 Implementation

As a proof of concept, we integrated the described extensions of the feasibility check in the test-case generation procedure [5] of Ultimate Automizer. Next to the original procedure, which we call NoReuse, we provide two alternative modes for the feasibility check. The first mode Reuse realizes the basic extension described in Sect. 3.1. The second mode ReuseUNSAT applies all extensions described in the previous section. To make the second mode work with C programs, in particular those that use function calls and therefore do not fulfill our deterministic requirement, we need to ensure that all program paths π that are explored adhere to the callstack semantics. Ultimate Automizer ensures this. Furthermore, to examine whether the optimization of ReuseUNSAT is applicable we do not match the whole prefix of a program path but only the branching conditions along the path. To make feasibility checking more efficient in case reusing the candidate model fails, we utilize the assertion stack of the underlying SMT solver. Hence when checking the feasibility of $\varphi_\pi \wedge \varphi_{m''}$, we first push the formula φ_π that represents the program path and then we push the candidate model $\varphi_{m''}$. If the SMT solver returns unsatisfiable, we pop the candidate model $\varphi_{m''}$ and check satisfiability again. Finally, note that Ultimate Automizer encodes the reachability of a test goal into the reachability of an error location modeled as an accepting state. Therefore, our implementation annotates locations and not edges. For readers familiar with the details of Ultimate Automizer's test-case generation procedure, we add the annotation to locations ℓ_g^n instead of edges g.

4 Experiments

The goal of our evaluation is to investigate the performance difference of Ultimate TestGen with respect to the three modes NoReuse, Reuse, and ReuseUNSAT. Thereby, our focus is on achieved coverage and required CPU time.

4.1 Experimental Setup

Tasks. For our evaluation, we consider the Test-Comp tasks from 2024[7]. Since most tasks in the cover-error category only have one test goal, we restrict our evaluation to the 9 825 tasks of the cover-branches category, for which a test suite should be constructed that optimizes branch coverage.

Tools and Environment. We run our experiments on machines with 33 GB of memory, an Intel Xeon E3-1230 v5 CPU with 8 processing units and a frequency of 3.40 GHz. The machines' operating system is a Ubuntu 22.04 (Linux kernel 5.15.0). For our evaluation, we use Ultimate Automizer (TestGeneration

[7] https://gitlab.com/sosy-lab/benchmarking/sv-benchmarks/-/tree/testcomp24-final.

branch[8] version cf97a5e2), which supports all three modes of ULTIMATE TESTGEN. Furthermore, we use TESTCOV (version 3.7) [11] to measure the achieved coverage. Following the Test-Comp rules, we allow ULTIMATE TESTGEN to use 4 cores, 15 min of CPU time, and 15 GB of memory per task. and restrict TESTCOV to use 2 cores, 10 min of CPU time, and 7 GB of memory to measure the coverage of a test-suite. All limits are enforced by BENCHEXEC 3.18 [12].

4.2 Experimental Results

In the following, we compare the performance ULTIMATE TESTGEN achieved in each of the three modes. Therefore, we exclude tasks in which none of the three ULTIMATE TESTGEN configurations achieved any coverage. These are tasks that ULTIMATE TESTGEN or TESTCOV cannot handle properly and are of no value. In total, we examine the performance on 9 399 tasks.

Comparing Achieved Coverage. First, let us compare the achieved coverage, the criterion that our approaches aim to optimize. We start with the comparison of REUSE and REUSEUNSAT, which use the two new modes suggested in this paper. Since REUSEUNSAT is an optimization of REUSE, we expect REUSEUNSAT to achieve a higher coverage. When summing up the coverage achieved per task overall 9 399 tasks, we observe that for REUSEUNSAT the achieved coverage sums up to 424 517.25 and for REUSE it sums up to 413 082.11. In sum, the coverage achieved by REUSEUNSAT is about 3% larger. A closer look at the individual tasks shows that for about 85% of the tasks (7 977 of 9 399 tasks), both approaches achieve the same coverage. For the remaining 1 422 tasks with different coverage, REUSEUNSAT achieves a higher coverage value for 70% (1 023 of 1 422 tasks) of the tasks. Also, we observe that if REUSEUNSAT gains additional coverage, i.e., if it achieves a higher coverage than REUSE, it gains about 13.1 additional coverage points in the mean with a median of 2.5. In contrast, if REUSEUNSAT loses coverage, it looses only about 5.3 in the mean and 1.7 in the a median. In summary, REUSEUNSAT improves but does not outperform REUSE.

Next, let us compare our approaches with NOREUSE, the original ULTIMATE TESTGEN mode, which ignores collateral coverage. First, we compare NOREUSE with REUSE, the worse of our two approaches. When summing up the coverage achieved per task overall 9 399 tasks, we observe that in sum REUSE achieves a coverage of 413 082.11 and NOREUSE of 414 773.9. Hence, REUSE shows no improvement. A detailed analysis of our results confirms that REUSE is hardly ever advantageous. For most tasks (8 364 of 9 399 tasks), the achieved coverage is the same. Examining the 1 035 tasks for which the achieved coverage differs, we observe that REUSE only improves the coverage for 25% of those tasks (263 of 1 035 tasks). We think that the time saved when REUSE successfully uses a previous input may be eaten up when a previous input is not helpful, i.e., the first feasibility check returns unsatisfiable. Thus, REUSE likely does not get additional time that it could spend on covering additional goals.

[8] https://github.com/ultimate-pa/ultimate/tree/TestGeneration.

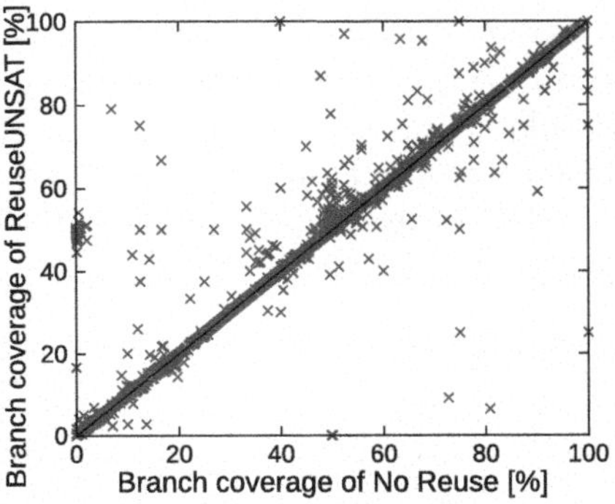

Fig. 5. Comparison of achieved coverage of NoReuse (x-axis) with achieved coverage of ReuseUNSAT (y-axis)

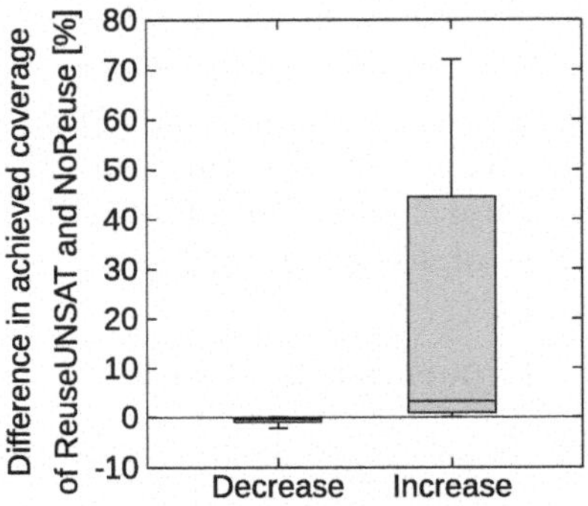

Fig. 6. Distribution of difference in achieved coverage of ReuseUNSAT and NoReuse when ReuseUNSAT performs worse (Decrease) and better (Increase)

Finally, let us compare NoReuse and ReuseUNSAT. When comparing the sum of the achieved coverage overall tasks, we observe that the overall coverage ReuseUNSAT achieves is about 2% larger (424 517.25 vs. 414 773.9). Next, let us compare the achieved coverage per task. The scatter plot in Fig. 5 shows for each task one point (x, y), where x denotes the coverage NoReuse achieves for the task and y the coverage achieved by ReuseUNSAT. Several points in the scatter plot are on the diagonal, i.e., both approaches achieve the same coverage. A detailed analysis reveals that both achieve the same coverage for about 85% of the tasks (8 088 of 9 399 tasks). Nevertheless, several points are in the upper left half, i.e., ReuseUNSAT achieves a higher coverage. Out of the 1 311 tasks, for which the coverage differs, we analyzed that ReuseUNSAT achieves a higher coverage value for about 58% of them (762 of 1 311 tasks).

Next, let us study how much more or less coverage ReuseUNSAT achieves. To this end, we study the distribution of the difference between the coverage achieved by ReuseUNSAT and NoReuse. The left box plot in Fig. 6 shows the difference distribution for those 629 tasks for which the difference is negative, i.e., ReuseUNSAT achieves less coverage. In contrast, the right box plot in Fig. 6 shows the difference distribution for those 762 tasks, for which ReuseUNSAT achieves higher coverage. The box in each box plot contains all data points (i.e., differences) from the second and third quartile, i.e., 25% of the difference values are larger than the top of the box and 25% of the difference values are smaller than the bottom of the box. The line through the box shows the median, which indicates in our case that the difference values are not uniformly distributed. The whiskers of each box shows the largest (smallest) data point that has a distance from the median of at most 1.5-times the height of the box. Looking at the left box plot, we observe that the decrease in coverage is mostly negligible. The median decrease is 0.3 coverage points and the mean decrease is 3.2 coverage points. However, the right box plot reveals that we may gain significant cover-

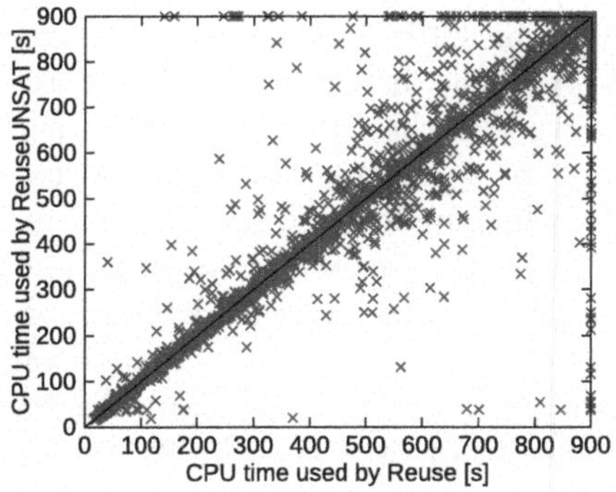

Fig. 7. Comparison of CPU time of NoReuse (x-axis) and ReuseUNSAT (y-axis)

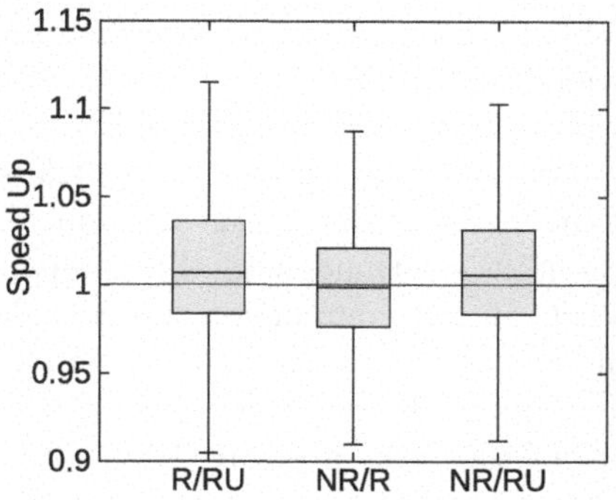

Fig. 8. Distribution of relation of CPU times of Reuse and ReuseUNSAT (R/RU), NoReuse and Reuse (NR/R), and NoReuse andReuseUNSAT (NR/RU)

age when using ReuseUNSAT, namely 15.6 coverage points in the mean with a median of 3.2. We think that further restricting the use of previous inputs to prefixes increases the chance of the inputs becoming useful, i.e., avoiding unsatisfiability results pays off. Also, spending time on proving path infeasibility under the guidance of a partial input is no longer a waste of effort because we gain a test case for the neighboring edge and, thus, save at least one CEGAR iteration. To sum up, ReuseUNSAT is a valuable extension because it may significantly increase coverage, but hardly has any penalties.

Comparing Efficiency (CPU Time). In our previous analysis, we observed that the analyses often achieved the same coverage. Still, it is beneficial to achieve the same coverage more efficiently, particularly using less CPU time. We cannot observe from the outside whether one approach is more efficient than another if both timeout. One of them might achieve the measured coverage faster, but then spends more time on proving additional goals. Also, comparing CPU times when different coverage is achieved is not very meaningful because it is acceptable to spend more time to cover more goals. Hence, when comparing the CPU time of two approaches, we restrict the comparison to tasks on which both approaches achieved the same coverage and at least one did not timeout.

Again, we start with the comparison of Reuse and ReuseUNSAT. Out of 7 977 tasks for which the two approaches achieved equal coverage, only 4 111 tasks fulfill our timeout requirement. The scatter plot in Fig. 7 compares the CPU time taken by Reuse (x-axis) with the CPU time taken by ReuseUNSAT (y-axis). While there exist points (tasks) on the top or right border, i.e., one of the approaches times out, for most considered tasks (95%) both approaches finish before the time out. Also, there exist points in both halves, i.e., Reuse is sometimes faster than ReuseUNSAT and vice versa. Taking a closer look at the raw data, we observe that ReuseUNSAT is faster for 58% of the tasks (2 399 of 4 111 tasks). Next, we consider the ratio of the CPU time taken by REUSE divided by the CPU time taken by REUSEUNSAT. The distribution of that ratio is shown in the left box plot of Fig. 8. We observe that the CPU times are rather similar, sometimes providing a little slow-down or speed-up. This is supported by the median value of one and a mean of 1.11, which indicates a small speed-up.

Let us continue with the comparison of the CPU times of NOREUSE and REUSE. In our comparison, we consider the 4 237 of 8 364 tasks for which both approaches achieve the same coverage. Since the scatter plot for the comparison looks similar to Fig. 7, we leave it out and directly look at the raw data. Again, 95% of the tasks are solved by both approaches before the time limit. Taking a closer look at the raw data, we observe that nearly half of the tasks (52%) are solved faster by NOREUSE and vice versa. When considering the ratio of the CPU time taken by NOREUSE divided by the CPU time taken by REUSE, which is shown in the middle box plot of Fig. 8, we again observe that CPU times are similar, which is backed up by a median of one and a mean of 1.02.

Finally, we compare the CPU times of NOREUSE and REUSEUNSAT. We compare 4 177 of the 8 088 tasks for which both approaches achieved the same coverage. Again, the scatter plot for the comparison looks similar to Fig. 7. Hence, we do not show the scatter plot and continue with our analysis of the raw data. Like before, 95% of the compared tasks are solved by both analyses before the time limit exceeds. A closer inspection of our data reveals that REUSEUNSAT is faster for 56% of the considered tasks (2 358 of 4 177 tasks). However, when examining the ratio of the CPU times taken by NOREUSE and REUSEUNSAT, which is shown in the right box plot of Fig. 8, we observe that CPU times are rather similar. This observation is confirmed by the median speed-up of 1.01 and a mean speed-up of 1.12.

To sum up, the performance with respect to CPU time is similar for our approaches and the original approach, i.e., our approaches do not introduce a computational overhead. In addition, REUSEUNSAT guarantees to achieve at least a similar coverage than NOREUSE and has the potential to increase the achieved coverage (significantly). We conclude that one should prefer REUSEUNSAT over NOREUSE.

4.3 Threats to Validity

Several reasons exist why our results may not generalize. While our evaluation uses an established benchmark set, the set may not properly reflect all real-world applications. Also, our measurements may not generalize. On the one hand, we use specific resource limits and the results may differ when changing the limits. On the other hand, the measurements of TESTCOV may be imprecise, e.g., due to bugs as well its memory and time limit per test case. Also, TESTCOV measurements include collateral coverage. Since we use TESTCOV to measure the coverage for all three modes, the modes are likewise affected. Moreover, test-case generation may be affected by implementation bugs. Since we use the same tool infrastructure for all three variants of ULTIMATE TESTGEN, we expect that implementation bugs in the feasibility check would have the largest effect. All other components are shared and bugs in those should affect all three variants similarly. However, bugs in the added components of the feasibility check more likely decrease the coverage of the resulting test-suite because the likelihood to mistakenly produce an input (candidate) for a particular goal is low. It is more likely that a bug leads to missed coverage of a branch. All in all, we think that bugs in Ultimate TestGen have hardly any affect.

5 Related Work

Our approach builds on the observation that a test case generated for a particular test goal may cover further test goals. While our approach may select a specific previous test case as a (partial) candidate input, many test-case generators [2, 7, 10, 21, 22, 27] execute a generated test case to determine additionally covered goals. Some test-case generators [2, 5, 17] even aim to cover deeper goals first to increase the likelihood of additionally covered goals. Nevertheless, test-case generation approaches still may (partially) use previous test cases. For example, DART [19] and SAGE [20] reuse previous values for those inputs that do not occur in the path constraint used to generate the new test case. In contrast, EvoSuite [18], Fizzer [27], or mutation-based fuzzers [30], may mutate parts of a previous input or combine different previous inputs.

We annotate the CFA edge to structure the generated test cases and make them available for reuse. Also, other approaches annotate control-flow like structures during test-case generation. Most closely to us, Fizzer [27] selects the previous input to consider based on an annotation of an atomic boolean execution tree. Memoization techniques for symbolic execution [13, 35] may store solver results with the symbolic execution tree to allow to repeat, to continue the analysis, etc. Instead of annotating programs with test cases or inputs, other approaches annotate programs with reasons for infeasibility, e.g., [32], or subsumption, e.g., [25]. Furthermore, some approaches [26, 34] allow to store and reuse the results of feasibility checks. In contrast to us, they do not associate the results directly with the program and may only provide the result but not the test input.

6 Conclusion

Testing is standard in software quality assurance and may employ test-case generation tools. Due to their goal-orientation, CEGAR-based test-case generators are well-suited to automatically generate test cases for complex branching conditions. To avoid that these test-case generators do redundant work in case of collateral coverage, we suggest to guide their feasibility check with previous test inputs. To this end, we store previous inputs in a feasibility annotation until they have been used. In our basic approach (Reuse), we only use a candidate input when checking the feasibility of a syntactical path to a test goal. Our extension of the basic approach (ReuseUNSAT), also outputs a test case for the neighboring test goal if it learns that the candidate input is not appropriate for the current test goal. Our evaluation of the basic approach and its extension on the Test-Comp tasks shows that only reusing test inputs is not enough to improve the performance of our CEGAR-based test-case generator Ultimate TestGen. However, extending the basic approach with learning improves the achieved coverage overall with significant improvements for some tasks.

Data-Availability Statement. All experimental data, all used software as well as the test tasks are publicly available in our supplementary artifact [4].

References

1. Agrawal, H.: Dominators, super blocks, and program coverage. In: POPL, pp. 25–34. ACM (1994). https://doi.org/10.1145/174675.175935
2. Alshmrany, K., Aldughaim, M., Bhayat, A., Cordeiro, L.: FuSeBMC v4: Improving code coverage with smart seeds via BMC, fuzzing and static analysis. FAC (2024). https://doi.org/10.1145/3665337
3. Alshmrany, K.M., Aldughaim, M., Bhayat, A., Cordeiro, L.C.: *FuSeBMC*: An energy-efficient test generator for finding security vulnerabilities in C programs. In: Loulergue, F., Wotawa, F. (eds.) TAP 2021. LNCS, vol. 12740, pp. 85–105. Springer, Cham (2021). https://doi.org/10.1007/978-3-030-79379-1_6
4. Barth, M., Jakobs, M.: Replication package for paper "Refining CEGAR-based test-case generation with feasibility annotations" (2024). https://doi.org/10.5281/zenodo.11641893
5. Barth, M., Jakobs, M.C.: Test-case generation with automata-based software model checking. In: Neele, T., Wijs A. (eds.) SPIN 2024. LNCS, vol. 14624, pp. 1–20. Spinger, Cham (2024). https://doi.org/10.1007/978-3-031-66149-5_14
6. Beyer, D.: Software testing: 5th comparative evaluation: Test-Comp 2023. In: Lambers, L., Uchitel, S. (eds.) FASE 2023. LNCS, vol. 13991, pp. 309–323. Springer, Cham (2023). https://doi.org/10.1007/978-3-031-30826-0_17
7. Beyer, D., Chlipala, A., Henzinger, T.A., Jhala, R., Majumdar, R.: Generating tests from counterexamples. In: ICSE, pp. 326–335. IEEE (2004). https://doi.org/10.1109/ICSE.2004.1317455
8. Beyer, D., Gulwani, S., Schmidt, D.A.: Combining model checking and data-flow analysis. In: Clarke, E., Henzinger, T., Veith, H., Bloem, R. (eds.) Handbook of Model Checking, pp. 493–540. Springer, Cham (2018). https://doi.org/10.1007/978-3-319-10575-8_16
9. Beyer, D., Jakobs, M.-C.: CoVeriTest: Cooperative verifier-based testing. In: Hähnle, R., van der Aalst, W. (eds.) FASE 2019. LNCS, vol. 11424, pp. 389–408. Springer, Cham (2019). https://doi.org/10.1007/978-3-030-16722-6_23
10. Beyer, D., Lemberger, T.: Conditional testing - off-the-shelf combination of test-case generators. In: Chen, Y.-F., Cheng, C.-H., Esparza, J. (eds.) ATVA 2019. LNCS, vol. 11781, pp. 189–208. Springer, Cham (2019). https://doi.org/10.1007/978-3-030-31784-3_11
11. Beyer, D., Lemberger, T.: TestCov: Robust test-suite execution and coverage measurement. In: ASE, pp. 1074–1077. IEEE (2019).https://doi.org/10.1109/ASE.2019.00105
12. Beyer, D., Löwe, S., Wendler, P.: Reliable benchmarking: Requirements and solutions. STTT **21**(1), 1–29 (2019). https://doi.org/10.1007/s10009-017-0469-y

13. Busse, F., Nowack, M., Cadar, C.: Running symbolic execution forever. In: ISSTA, pp. 63–74. ACM (2020) https://doi.org/10.1145/3395363.3397360
14. Cadar, C., Dunbar, D., Engler, D.R.: KLEE: Unassisted and automatic generation of high-coverage tests for complex systems programs. In: OSDI, pp. 209–224. USENIX Association (2008). http://www.usenix.org/events/osdi08/tech/full_papers/cadar/cadar.pdf
15. Chusho, T.: Test data selection and quality estimation based on the concept of esssential branches for path testing. IEEE TSE **13**(5), 509–517 (1987). https://doi.org/10.1109/TSE.1987.233196
16. Clarke, E., Grumberg, O., Jha, S., Lu, Y., Veith, H.: Counterexample-guided abstraction refinement. In: Emerson, E.A., Sistla, A.P. (eds.) CAV 2000. LNCS, vol. 1855, pp. 154–169. Springer, Heidelberg (2000). https://doi.org/10.1007/10722167_15
17. Fedchin, A., et al.: A toolkit for automated testing of Dafny. In: Rozier, K.Y., Chaudhuri, S. (eds.) NFM 2023. LNCS, vol. 13903, pp. 397–413. Springer, Cham (2023). https://doi.org/10.1007/978-3-031-33170-1_24
18. Fraser, G., Arcuri, A.: Evolutionary generation of whole test suites. In: QSIC, pp. 31–40. IEEE (2011). https://doi.org/10.1109/QSIC.2011.19
19. Godefroid, P., Klarlund, N., Sen, K.: DART: Directed automated random testing. In: PLDI, pp. 213–223. ACM (2005). https://doi.org/10.1145/1065010.1065036
20. Godefroid, P., Levin, M.Y., Molnar, D.A.: Automated whitebox fuzz testing. In: NDSS. The Internet Society (2008). https://www.ndss-symposium.org/ndss2008/automated-whitebox-fuzz-testing/
21. Güdemann, M., Schrammel, P.: BlueCov: Integrating test coverage and model checking with JBMC. In: SAC, pp. 1695–1697. ACM (2023). https://doi.org/10.1145/3555776.3577829
22. Holzer, A., Schallhart, C., Tautschnig, M., Veith, H.: Query-driven program testing. In: Jones, N.D., Müller-Olm, M. (eds.) VMCAI 2009. LNCS, vol. 5403, pp. 151–166. Springer, Heidelberg (2008). https://doi.org/10.1007/978-3-540-93900-9_15
23. Holzer, A., Schallhart, C., Tautschnig, M., Veith, H.: How did you specify your test suite. In: ASE, pp. 407–416. ACM (2010).https://doi.org/10.1145/1858996.1859084
24. Hong, H.S., Ural, H.: Using model checking for reducing the cost of test generation. In: Grabowski, J., Nielsen, B. (eds.) FATES 2004. LNCS, vol. 3395, pp. 110–124. Springer, Heidelberg (2005). https://doi.org/10.1007/978-3-540-31848-4_8
25. Jaffar, J., Murali, V., Navas, J.A., Santosa, A.E.: TRACER: A symbolic execution tool for verification. In: Madhusudan, P., Seshia, S.A. (eds.) CAV 2012. LNCS, vol. 7358, pp. 758–766. Springer, Heidelberg (2012). https://doi.org/10.1007/978-3-642-31424-7_61
26. Jia, X., Ghezzi, C., Ying, S.: Enhancing reuse of constraint solutions to improve symbolic execution. In: ISSTA, pp. 177–187. ACM (2015). https://doi.org/10.1145/2771783.2771806
27. Jonás, M., Strejcek, J., Trtík, M., Urban, L.: Gray-box fuzzing via gradient descent and Boolean expression coverage. In: Finkbeiner, B., Kovács, L. (eds.) TACAS 2024. LNCS, vol. 14572, pp. 90–109. Springer, Cham (2024). https://doi.org/10.1007/978-3-031-57256-2_5
28. Lemberger, T.: Plain random test generation with PRTest. STTT **23**(6), 871–873 (2021). https://doi.org/10.1007/s10009-020-00568-x
29. Lemieux, C., Sen, K.: FairFuzz: A targeted mutation strategy for increasing greybox fuzz testing coverage. In: ASE, pp. 475–485. ACM (2018).https://doi.org/10.1145/3238147.3238176

30. Manès, V.J.M., et al.: The art, science, and engineering of fuzzing: A survey. IEEE TSE **47**(11), 2312–2331 (2021). https://doi.org/10.1109/TSE.2019.2946563
31. Marré, M., Bertolino, A.: Using spanning sets for coverage testing. IEEE TSE **29**(11), 974–984 (2003). https://doi.org/10.1109/TSE.2003.1245299
32. McMillan, K.L.: Lazy annotation for program testing and verification. In: Touili, T., Cook, B., Jackson, P. (eds.) CAV 2010. LNCS, vol. 6174, pp. 104–118. Springer, Heidelberg (2010). https://doi.org/10.1007/978-3-642-14295-6_10
33. Ruland, S., Lochau, M., Fehse, O., Schürr, A.: CPA/Tiger-MGP: Test-goal set partitioning for efficient multi-goal test-suite generation. STTT **23**(6), 853–856 (2021). https://doi.org/10.1007/s10009-020-00574-z
34. Visser, W., Geldenhuys, J., Dwyer, M.B.: Green: Reducing, reusing and recycling constraints in program analysis. In: FSE, p. 58. ACM (2012).https://doi.org/10.1145/2393596.2393665
35. Yang, G., Pasareanu, C.S., Khurshid, S.: Memoized symbolic execution. In: ISSTA, pp. 144–154. ACM (2012)https://doi.org/10.1145/2338965.2336771
36. Yoo, S., Harman, M.: Regression testing minimization, selection and prioritization: A survey. STVR **22**(2), 67–120 (2012). https://doi.org/10.1002/STV.430
37. Zlatkin, I., Fedyukovich, G.: Maximizing branch coverage with constrained horn clauses. In: Fisman, D., Rosu, G. (eds.) TACAS 2022. LNCS, vol. 13244, pp. 254–272. Springer, Cham (2022). https://doi.org/10.1007/978-3-030-99527-0_14

No Smoke Without Fire: Detecting Specification Inconsistencies with Frama-C/WP

Allan Blanchard[1], Loïc Correnson[1], Adel Djoudi[2], and Nikolai Kosmatov[3](✉)

[1] Université Paris-Saclay, CEA, List, Palaiseau, France
{allan.blanchard,loic.correnson}@cea.fr
[2] Thales Digital Identity and Security, Meudon, France
adel.djoudi@thalesgroup.com
[3] Thales Research and Technology, Palaiseau, France
nikolai.kosmatov@thalesgroup.com

Abstract. Deductive verification provides a proof that, under the provided pre-conditions, each terminating execution of a given function satisfies the stated post-conditions. In general, pre- and post-conditions are expressed in a logical specification language and typically rely on theories including abstract definitions, axioms and lemmas. As they are written by humans, errors may be introduced into specifications. Some errors can be detected when the proof fails, but sometimes, they remain unnoticed due to misleading proofs: most of the program may become dead code under the provided pre-conditions, or the proof may succeed because of inconsistencies in hypotheses and axioms. In this tool paper, we explore how to detect such unwanted situations by using deductive verification techniques and describe the smoke test mechanism in Frama-C/WP, a popular deductive verifier for C code. We show that, while the intuitive idea is simple, making it practical requires optimizations to scale up, and report on experiments with critical industrial code. Although our method is based on proof techniques, it is not complete and is similar to testing. In the end, can we ever be sure that our programs are proved well enough?

1 Introduction

Deductive verification [14] is aimed at proving that a given program respects its formal specification. The specification is an essential ingredient of the process: if the specification is wrong, the whole verification is of no interest. Similarly, too strong specification requirements might silently eliminate large portions of the code, dramatically reducing the effective scope of the verification claim.

The purpose of this paper is to describe a mechanism for tracking inconsistent specifications and unwanted dead code that we implemented in Frama-C/WP [6], a mature and popular deductive verification tool for C programs annotated in ACSL specification language [7]. It is based on so-called *smoke tests*, which are

© The Author(s), under exclusive license to Springer Nature Switzerland AG 2025
M. Huisman and F. Howar (Eds.): TAP 2024, LNCS 15153, pp. 65–83, 2025.
https://doi.org/10.1007/978-3-031-72044-4_4

specific annotations generated by WP such that their proof would demonstrate the presence of such unwanted situations.[1] Such annotations typically assert `false` at specific program points. Then, an unwanted situation can be revealed if the corresponding assertion of `false` is proved. Such an assertion of `false` is provable only if the corresponding program point is not reachable by a *valid execution path*[2], i.e. an execution path leading to this program point such that all annotations met on this path are satisfied. In this way, detecting inconsistencies can be reduced to the detection of program points that are unreachable (or dead) *from the point of view* of a deductive verification tool. Notice that this unreachability property is larger than the usual notion of dead code—when a program point is not reachable by *any* execution path. In the following sections, when talking from the point of view of WP, unreachable (dead) code will be understood in this broader sense.

This mechanism is potentially capable to detect various kinds of inconsistencies and dead code—but only those explicitly tracked, and only if the prover manages to prove the corresponding annotation. By essence, this approach amounts to testing whether the tracked unwanted situations occur or not, without any guarantee to detect them, nor any guarantee that there is no *other* sources of inconsistency in user specifications.

This tool paper describes the design and implementation of the smoke tests feature of Frama-C/WP, optimizations to make this mechanism more scalable and more practical, and presents some evaluation results on industrial code.

2 Tracked Inconsistencies

Specifications can contain various kinds of errors. They are often related to inconsistencies among the hypotheses that form the context of the proof. The context typically includes pre-conditions of the entry point function, global variables and global properties such as axioms. Sometimes, the user configuration of the deductive verification engine can also introduce additional hypotheses in the proof context, for instance, global assumptions regarding the memory model or the absence of specific kinds of runtime errors. These hypotheses might also interfere with the specification or with the code in a misleading way.

In this section, we explore different situations where inconsistencies in specifications might remain unnoticed during modular deductive verification. Most examples presented in the article are simple enough to be fully and trivially verified by Frama-C/WP [6,17] with a simple command `frama-c myfile.c -wp`. However, all the presented examples are actually *doomed* by specification errors. We also show that all these situations are trivially revealed by WP thanks to smoke tests by simply adding the option `-wp-smoke-tests` to the command.[3]

[1] some of which can be justified in some specific cases (e.g. by a partial verification scope, architecture assumptions), but should not remain unnoticed (cf. Sect. 2.7).

[2] See Sect. 3.3 for a formal definition of a valid execution path.

[3] All examples were run with Frama-C 29 (Copper) and Alt-Ergo 2.5.3 public releases. Terminal outputs are shortened or omitted, and only focus on relevant parts.

2.1 Pre-condition Errors

Inconsistent pre-conditions can be revealed as they can never be proved at their call sites. Indeed, WP checks that pre-conditions are valid at every call site. But for root functions in the call graph, there is no way to check this property. For instance, consider the following program (say, in file `requires.c`):

```
/*@ requires x < 0 ;
    requires x > 0 ;
    ensures \result == 42 ; */
int f(int x){ return x ; }
```

The post-condition is obviously wrong: there is no reason for the result of function `f` to be equal to 42. However, this program is fully verified by WP:

```
> frama-c requires.c -wp
[wp] Proved goals:    3 / 3
```

Indeed, the two pre-conditions of `f` are mutually exclusive: it is not possible to call it with valid pre-conditions. Hence, the program is valid because there is *no* valid call context for it. Fortunately, WP with smoke tests trivially detects this misleading specification:

```
> frama-c requires.c -wp -wp-smoke-tests
[wp] [Failed] (Doomed) typed_f_wp_smoke_default_requires (Qed)
[wp] requires.c:4: Warning: Failed smoke-test
[wp] Proved goals:    3 / 4
[wp] Smoke Tests:     0 / 1
```

When a function's contract is split into different ACSL behaviors, inconsistencies may also occur among a behavior's assumptions, or between the default behavior pre-conditions and the assumptions of a specific behavior. For instance, consider the following program (file `assumes.c`):

```
/*@ requires x < 0 ;
    behavior Positive:
      assumes x > 0 ;
      ensures \result == 42 ; */
int f(int x){ return x ; }
```

Here also, the program is fully verified by WP, although its `Positive` behavior is doomed since its assumption is inconsistent with the function pre-condition, a situation trivially detected by WP smoke tests:

```
> frama-c assumes.c -wp
[wp] Proved goals:    3 / 3

> frama-c assumes.c -wp -wp-smoke-tests
[wp] [Failed] (Doomed) typed_f_wp_smoke_Positive_assumes (Qed)
[wp] assumes.c:5: Warning: Failed smoke-test
[wp] Proved goals:    4 / 5
[wp] Smoke Tests:     1 / 2
```

Detecting errors at the level of pre-conditions naturally extends to inconsistencies with respect to the global context. Consider the example (file `axioms.c`):

```
/*@ axiomatic Ax {
      logic integer A reads \nothing ;
      axiom Positive: A >= 0 ;
    } */
```

```
/*@ requires A < 0 ;
    ensures \result == 42 ; */
int f(void){ return 0 ; }
```

The ACSL axiomatic block introduces logical variable A assumed to be positive. This function is also proven valid by WP, while, contrary to its post-condition, it never returns 42. Indeed, its pre-condition is doomed: it is inconsistent with the global assumption on logic parameter A, as revealed by WP smoke tests:

```
> frama-c axioms.c -wp -wp-smoke-tests
[wp] [Failed] (Doomed) typed_f_wp_smoke_default_requires (Alt-Ergo 14ms)
[wp] axioms.c:8: Warning: Failed smoke-test
[wp] Proved goals:    3 / 4
[wp] Smoke Tests:     0 / 1
```

2.2 Post-condition Errors

Post-conditions of a function are verified by WP with respect to the function body and its pre-conditions. Now consider external functions that only have a specification but no code. Their post-conditions cannot be verified, hence, they might silently introduce inconsistencies with respect to their calling context.

Consider for instance the following program (file `ensures.c`), where function `main` is indeed wrong, since it always returns 1 according to the post-condition of `incr` function, and hence cannot return 42 as claimed by its specification:

```
//@ ensures \result == 42;
int main(void){
  int x = 0 ;
  incr(&x) ;
  return x ;
}

/*@ assigns \nothing ;
    ensures *p == \old(*p) + 1 ; */
void incr(int* p);
```

However, this program is fully proved by WP. Here, the problem comes from external function `incr` whose post-condition is doomed by an inconsistency with its assigns clause: `*p` and `\old(*p)` shall be indeed equal since `incr` is assumed to have no side-effects. Its correct assigns clause would be `assigns *p`. Such an inconsistency is trivially detected by WP smoke tests:

```
> frama-c ensures.c -wp -wp-smoke-tests
[wp] [Failed] (Doomed) typed_incr_wp_smoke_dead_call_s2 (Qed)
[wp] ensures.c:4: Warning: Failed smoke-test
[wp] [Failed] (Doomed) typed_main_wp_smoke_dead_code_s4 (Qed)
[wp] ensures.c:5: Warning: Failed smoke-test
[wp] Proved goals:    3 / 5
[wp] Smoke Tests:     0 / 2
```

In this case, the doomed post-condition leads to detecting two issues. First, because the post-condition of function `incr` is inconsistent with its assigns clause. Second, because the code in `main` *after* calling `incr(&x)` becomes unreachable (or dead) code (from the point of view of WP, cf. Sect. 1). Recall that for a function call, its pre-conditions are verified while its post-conditions are assumed. Hence, inconsistent post-conditions introduce a `false` hypothesis into the proof context for any property after the call.

2.3 Dead Code Errors

Dead code generally stays outside the eyes of deductive verification: any properties for infeasible execution paths are silently proved valid because their associated branching conditions are always false. However, as illustrated with doomed post-conditions in the previous section, some execution paths might be silently discarded by doomed specifications. Consider the following code (file `dead.c`):

```
/*@ requires \valid(x);
    ensures \result == *x; */
int read(int *x) {
  if (!x) return 42;
  return *x;
}
```

The program is proven valid by WP. The if statement makes the function return 42 when it receives a `NULL` pointer in argument. Although it might be the expected function behavior, this is *not* reflected by the specification, which assumes a valid (hence, non-null) pointer, that makes unreachable the statement `return 42`. Such an unwanted doomed code is detected by WP smoke tests:

```
> frama-c dead.c -wp -wp-smoke-tests
[wp] [Failed] (Doomed) typed_read_wp_smoke_dead_code_s2 (Qed)
[wp] dead.c:4: Warning: Failed smoke-test
[wp] Proved goals:    5 / 6
[wp] Smoke Tests:     2 / 3
```

Dead code is generally unwanted for software quality, so even if the function above is correct according to ACSL, it is still important to track dead code.

2.4 Non-terminating Loops and Other Loop Errors

Non-terminating loops can be left undetected by deductive verification, unless explicit termination proofs are required by the user through `loop variant` and `terminates` clauses. By lack of such specifications, which are optional in ACSL and Frama-C, buggy non-terminating code might be silently verified.[4]

Consider for instance the following program (file `loop.c`):

```
/*@ requires x >= 0;
    ensures \result == 0;
*/
int f(int x) {
  /*@
    loop invariant x >= 0;
    loop assigns x;
  */
  while (x > 0) ;
  return 42;
}
```

This program seems to incorrectly return 42, contrary to its specification. However, the program is fully verified by WP. Actually, there are two bugs in the code: the loop is non-terminating (making the code after it unreachable), and the

[4] Since the Frama-C 29 (Copper) release, terminating annotations are generated by default. In this example, it has been turned off by `-generated-spec-custom terminates:skip` command line option.

return statement is incorrect. Both problems are silently ignored by deductive verification. Fortunately, WP smoke tests detect them:

```
> frama-c loop.c -wp -wp-smoke-tests
[wp] [Failed] (Doomed) typed_f_wp_smoke_dead_code_s6 (Qed)
[wp] loop.c:10: Warning: Failed smoke-test
[wp] Proved goals:     7 / 8
[wp] Smoke Tests:      2 / 3
```

A possible corrected version of the code, where the loop terminates and the returned value is correct, is the following:

```
/*@ requires x >= 0;
    ensures \result == 0;
*/
int f(int x) {
  /*@
    loop invariant x >= 0;
    loop assigns x;
  */
  while (x > 0)
    { x--; }
  return x;
}
```

Another common issue with loops occurs when there is an inconsistency in loop invariants, or between them and the current proof context: this makes the entire loop provably dead code. Moreover, it is often the case where a buggy, non-proved loop specification introduces such an inconsistency. Hence, detecting inconsistent loop invariants early might help to fix buggy loop specifications. WP smoke tests are also able to detect inconsistencies in loop invariants.

2.5 Exiting Errors

Functions that might exit (by calling `exit` function) typically have explicit `false` post-conditions, that are indeed good candidates for introducing unwanted inconsistencies in proof contexts.

Consider for instance the following program (file `exit.c`):

```
/*@ ensures \false ;
    exits \true ; */
void exit(void);

/*@ ensures \result == 0; */
int main()
{
  exit();
  return 42;
}
```

This program is verified by WP[5], although it contains a buggy statement returning 42, which is silently ignored after the `exit()` call. As expected, WP smoke tests detect such a dead code:

```
> frama-c exit.c -wp -wp-smoke-tests
[wp] [Failed] (Doomed) typed_main_wp_smoke_dead_code_s2 (Qed)
[wp] exit.c:8: Warning: Failed smoke-test
[wp] Proved goals:     2 / 3
```

[5] To reproduce this example with Frama-C 29 (Copper), clause generation shall be customized with `-generated-spec-custom terminates:skip,exits:skip`.

The main function and its specification are actually completely wrong: it never returns a value, always exits and its `return` statement is never executed.

2.6 Avoiding Redundant Alarms

As illustrated above, inconsistencies are closely related to unreachable code. However, unreachability of a program point extends to a sequence of the following instructions, provided there is no goto leading into the middle of the sequence.

From a user perspective, we should avoid reporting as unreachable all instructions along an entire *sequence* of instructions. Similarly, for performance reasons, when WP has put some effort in deciding whether a given program point is reachable or not, it is not useful to spend the effort again on subsequent instructions, unless they might become reachable through another execution path. Hence, it is important to focus on *necessary* program points for generating smoke tests.

2.7 Avoiding Spurious Alarms

In the case of dead code, alarms might be raised by WP smoke tests whereas the developer knows that the code is dead for *good* reasons (such as verification scope or architecture restrictions, countermeasures against fault injection attacks, etc.). In this case, the developer may provide an `assert \false` annotation[6] to tell WP that a given branch is intentionally dead and that it should not warn about it.

Consider for instance the following program (file `div.c`):

```
/*@ requires b > 0;
    ensures \result == a/b;
    assigns \nothing; */
int div(int a, int b) {
  if (b==0) {
    /*@ assert \false; */
    return 0;
  }
  return a/b;
}
```

The defensive code to avoid the division by zero is actually not needed thanks to the pre-condition. Normally, WP smoke tests would detect dead code. However, in this example, the user provides `assert \false` annotation indicating that this dead code is expected.[7] The program is fully verified by WP, including the assert annotation indicating the dead code, annotations generated to prove the absence of runtime errors and remaining smoke tests:

```
> frama-c div.c -wp -wp-rte -wp-smoke-tests
[wp] Proved goals:    10 / 10
[wp] Smoke Tests:      2 / 2
```

[6] ACSL has two assertion clauses, `assert p;` and `check p;`, whose only difference is that with the former, property `p` is verified and preserved in the proof context, while with the latter, `p` is just verified.

[7] We do not debate here whether this is a good practice or not.

3 Design and Implementation

As illustrated in Sect. 2, misleading or inconsistent specifications can be revealed by the fact that specific program points are unreachable. In the context of deductive verification, this can be implemented by checking that `false` is provable at the considered program point. Hence, tracking inconsistencies can be implemented by inserting `false` annotations at the right places. Those annotations will play the role of *Smoke* detectors that would reveal misleading specifications, if any. We discuss later the incompleteness of the method, but for now, it suffices to state that a smoke test expresses the unreachability of some program point.

Let us also recall that, from the ACSL point of view, any code annotation attached to unreachable program points is *de facto* valid because there will be no execution path to invalidate it. However, it is important for the end users to have a feedback regarding the *source* of a program point's unreachability. For instance, as pointed out in Sect. 2.7, we shall take into account user-defined intended dead code. We shall also take into account that the property of being dead code may propagate through the program control flow (cf. Sect. 2.6).

Hence, reachability, explicit dead code, unreachable annotations and smoke tests are closely related with each other and need specific feedback to users.

In this section, we provide a method to determine an optimized collection of program points that shall be equipped with a smoke test. First, we introduce a reachability analysis dedicated to smoke tests (Sect. 3.1). For an efficient generation of smoke tests, we also introduce the concept of nodes protected by smoke tests and how this concept propagates through the control flow graph (Sect. 3.2). Then, we illustrate how we can derive the generation of smoke tests from standard Weakest-Precondition Calculus of the WP plug-in (Sect. 3.3). We finally discuss the completeness of the method (Sect. 3.4) and how to provide users with accurate feedback (Sect. 3.5) for smoke test results.

3.1 Reachability Analysis

Although reachability is a standard problem in static analysis and compilation techniques, we need some adaptations to take redundancy and spurious alarms into account.

We use a Control Flow Graph (CFG) of functions. As illustrated in Fig. 1, the CFG is made of program points (statements, Stmt) and edges labeled with instructions (Instr). We assume here that the CFG is *normalized*, that is, the large variety of C instructions and statements, such as loops, switches, and conditional operators are decomposed into branching statements and elementary instructions. Moreover, expressions with side effects are assumed to be decomposed into assignments $l = e$ of a side-effect-free expression $e \in \mathsf{Expr}$ to an l-value $l \in \mathsf{Lval}$ and function calls $l = e(\overline{e})$. Expressions and l-values are not detailed here since this is mostly irrelevant for generating smoke tests. Jumping C instructions such as `goto`, `break` and `continue` are represented by transitions labeled with the `skip` instruction, which has no effect at all.

Program points:	$a, b \in \mathsf{Stmt}$
Instructions:	$k \in \mathsf{Instr} ::= l = e \mid l = e(\overline{e}) \mid \texttt{if}(e) \mid \texttt{skip} \mid \texttt{return}(e)$
Control Flow Graph:	$\{a \xrightarrow{k} b, \ldots\} \in \mathsf{Cfg}$
Entry point:	$\mathsf{entry} \in \mathsf{Stmt}$
Predecessors:	$\mathsf{pred}(b) \triangleq \{\, a \mid a \xrightarrow{k} b \in \mathsf{Cfg} \,\}$

Fig. 1. Normalized Control Flow Graph (CFG) definition

We consider sequential C programs (without threads), hence the CFG is deterministic, which means that a branching node a has a complete and disjoint collection of transitions of the form $a \xrightarrow{\texttt{if}(e)} b$. A non-branching node a has exactly *one* outcoming transition $a \xrightarrow{k} b$, where k is an assignment $l = e$, a function call $l = e(\overline{e})$, a `skip` or a `return`(e) instruction. Moreover, since we need to distinguish the program point right after each call, we further decompose a call $l = e(\overline{e})$ into the sequence $\{\texttt{r} = e(\overline{e}); l = \texttt{r}\}$ with an intermediate temporary variable `r` to store the result. We can thus define the following classification of node categories—with the first category for a branching node and the others for non-branching ones—that will be very handy when defining smoke tests:

- $\mathsf{branch}(a)$ when a has multiple outcoming instructions $\texttt{if}(e)$;
- $\mathsf{skip}(a)$ when a has a unique outcoming instruction `skip`;
- $\mathsf{call}(a)$ when a has a unique outcoming instruction $\texttt{r} = e(\overline{e})$;
- $\mathsf{write}(a)$ when a has a unique outcoming instruction $l = e$;
- $\mathsf{return}(a)$ when a has a unique outcoming instruction $\texttt{return}(e)$.

Nodes after a $\texttt{return}(e)$ transition have no outcoming transition, and for a given function, there is a unique entry point denoted by $\mathsf{entry} \in \mathsf{Stmt}$.

Standard reachability analysis can be formally defined as the smallest set $R \subset \mathsf{Stmt}$ of program points satisfying the following equation:

$$\mathsf{entry} \in R \quad \wedge \quad \forall (a \xrightarrow{k} b) \in \mathsf{Cfg},\ a \in R \implies b \in R.$$

In practice, a well-known efficient algorithm to compute reachable program points uses a memoization table and the following lazy definition[8]:

$$R(n) \triangleq \quad n = \mathsf{entry} \ \vee\ \exists p \in \mathsf{pred}(n),\ R(p),$$

where $\mathsf{pred}(n)$ is the set of predecessors p of n in the CFG defined in Fig. 1. For WP smoke tests, we also need to account for user-defined dead code annotations, as stated in Sect. 2.7. To this end, let us introduce predicate $\mathsf{dead}(a)$ that checks if a program point a has been annotated with an explicit `assert \false`

[8] The memoization table is initialized to `false` before recursive calls to cut off cycles in the CFG. All recursive definitions presented use this technique. This is completely standard and not represented here for simplicity.

annotation[9]. Hence, we introduce the following lazy definition for reachability:

$$\mathsf{reachable}(n) \triangleq \neg\,\mathsf{dead}(n) \wedge (\, n = \mathsf{entry} \vee \exists p \in \mathsf{pred}(n),\, \mathsf{reachable}(p)\,).$$

Indeed, $\mathsf{dead}(a)$ corresponds to a program point that is explicitly marked to be unreachable by the user. The associated annotation `assert \false` is expected to be eventually proved as part of the user specification. In this case, such program points will be provably unreachable.

3.2 Protected and Protecting Nodes

In theory, it suffices to equip all reachable nodes (according to the above definition) with a smoke test to detect any specification inconsistency. However, doing so will generate far too many smoke tests. As a simple example, consider a block consisting of a sequence of write instructions, without any call or jump from/into the block: then all instructions in the block have the same reachability status, and a smoke test is necessary only for the first instruction. All the following instructions of the sequence will be *protected*: the smoke test for the first instruction will be sufficient to detect a potential unreachability (from the point of view of WP, cf. Sect. 1) for any of the following instructions of the sequence, hence they do not need to be equipped with smoke tests. Of course, the situation becomes more complex in the general case.

We give here an overview of different heuristics that we have implemented in order to efficiently remove most redundant smoke tests. This section is relatively technical and might be skipped by readers who are not interested in the underlying implementation details.

Strictly speaking, computing the optimal set of protected nodes is hard and would require to compute the *dominators* of nodes throughout the CFG, which is complex and costly. Instead, we consider a lightweight heuristic based on local transitions and a weak definition of protecting nodes. Although non-optimal, our approach appears to be sufficient in practice and avoids most redundancies.

Let us start with the actual implementation, which is based on three mutually inductive predicates, formally defined in Fig. 2, that we can briefly summarize as follows:

- $\mathsf{smoking}(a)$ indicates that program point a shall be finally equipped with a smoke test;
- $\mathsf{protected}(a)$ indicates that program point a *does not require* additional protection (by a smoke test) because its predecessor nodes in the CFG are already sufficiently (directly or indirectly) protected by smoke tests, or because a is provably unreachable according to the user-provided specification.
- $\mathsf{protecting}(a)$ is the dual notion and indicates that program point a is already protected by smoke tests so that its immediate successors are *also* protected by a.

[9] Actually, any code annotation or loop invariant syntactically equivalent to `false` is accepted by WP as well.

$$\begin{aligned}
\mathsf{smoking}(a) &\triangleq \mathsf{entry}(a) \lor (\ \mathsf{reachable}(a) \land \neg\,\mathsf{protected}(a)\ ),\\
\mathsf{protected}(a) &\triangleq \mathsf{entry}(a) \lor \mathsf{dead}(a) \lor (\ \forall p \in \mathsf{pred}(a),\ \mathsf{protecting}(p)\ ),\\
\mathsf{protecting}(a) &\triangleq \mathsf{entry}(a) \lor \mathsf{dead}(a) \lor \mathsf{return}(a)\\
&\quad \lor (\ \mathsf{write}(a) \land \mathsf{protected}(a)\ )\\
&\quad \lor (\ \mathsf{skip}(a) \land \mathsf{protected}(a)\ )\\
&\quad \lor (\ \mathsf{branch}(a) \land \neg\,\mathsf{reachable}(a)\ ).
\end{aligned}$$

Fig. 2. Characterization of smoking nodes

Typically, consider a single write instruction $l = e$ from node a to node b. Assume that node a is already equipped with a smoke test and that b has no other predecessor than a. Then a is protecting b and, dually, b is protected by a. Indeed, they have the same reachability status, hence it is not necessary to equip b with a smoke test.

Not all nodes are *protecting*. Typically, consider now that a is a branching node, already equipped with a smoke test, having two conditional outcomes: $\mathsf{if}(e)$ to node b and $\mathsf{if}(\neg e)$ to node c. In this case, nodes b and c are *not* protected by a, since condition e or condition $\neg e$ might be inconsistent with previous conditions or user specifications from the above context. Node b does not necessarily have the same reachability status as node a, and neither does node c. Dually, we shall consider that node a is *not* protecting its successors. Both nodes b and c will then need to be equipped with a smoke test, even if a is already protected.

Let us now comment on our definitions of predicates smoking, protected and protecting given in Fig. 2.

Smoking Nodes. Predicate $\mathsf{smoking}(a)$ characterizes all nodes a that require a smoke test. The function entry point and loop entry points, characterized by predicate $\mathsf{entry}(a)$, must always be equipped with smoke tests in order to detect inconsistencies in function pre-conditions and loop contracts. Then, only *reachable* nodes a that are *not* already protected by other means shall be equipped with a new smoke test. This explains the definition.

Protected Nodes. Predicate $\mathsf{protected}(a)$ notably includes nodes that are *de facto* equipped by a smoke test or that are provably unreachable by user specifications. Moreover, if all predecessors of node a are protecting nodes, then a will be sufficiently protected and no additional smoke test will be needed. This explains the definition.

Protecting Nodes. Predicate $\mathsf{protecing}(a)$ designates nodes a that propagate their protection to their successors. All nodes that are *de facto* equipped by smoke tests or user-indicated as unreachable will be protecting. Non-branching nodes (write and skip instructions) will be protecting as soon as they are already protected. Branching nodes are protecting only when they are unreachable.

This heuristic appears to be pretty efficient in practice: we have observed quite few redundant smoke tests, and only for very complex control flow graphs with weird inter-block gotos.

3.3 Weakest-Precondition Calculus for Smoke Tests

We are now ready to (semi-formally) define the generation of WP smoke tests to address all potential unwanted situations described in Sect. 2. This section is more technical: it assumes that the reader is familiar with the weakest precondition calculus and can be skipped by the readers who are not interested in implementation details.

As introduced above, a smoke test at program point $a \in \mathsf{Stmt}$ shall detect an inconsistency in the proof context that makes a to be unreachable through valid execution paths. Hence, such a smoke test amounts to checking the satisfiability or unsatisfiability of the so-called *path predicate* over a path towards the corresponding node.

Indeed, the Frama-C/WP deductive verification engine is based on an efficient *Weakest Precondition Calculus* that relies on unsatisfiability of formulas that also involve path predicates. Hence, we want to adapt our WP calculus in order to efficiently generate smoke tests on-the-fly.

First, recall the main objective of WP. Given an ACSL assertion P attached to program point $a \in \mathsf{Stmt}$, we want to prove that predicate P holds for every memory state m reached by a valid execution path going through node a.

More generally, every ACSL annotation [5] can be decomposed into a collection of predicates attached to the relevant program points in the CFG. Hence, we denote by $\mathsf{asserts}(a)$ the set of ACSL predicates P to be proved at node a, and $\mathsf{assumes}(a)$ the set of ACSL predicates P assumed at node a.

More formally, let us consider an execution path $\sigma = (a_i, m_i)_{i<n}$ where $a_i \in \mathsf{Stmt}$ are program points and $m_i \in \mathsf{Mem}$ are memory states $(0 \leq i < n)$. Execution paths shall be consistent with the semantics of C programs and the CFG of executed functions, as defined in Fig. 3. Moreover, *valid* execution paths shall also satisfy ACSL annotations of the program, that is, $[\![P]\!](m_i)$ holds for every $P \in \mathsf{asserts}(a_i)$ at every step i (with $0 \leq i < n$), provided that $[\![H]\!](m_j)$ holds for every $H \in \mathsf{assumes}(a_j)$ at every preceding step j (with $0 \leq j < i$). We write $\mathsf{valid}(\sigma)$ for an execution path σ that satisfies both the program semantics and ACSL annotations. Notice that we consider below execution paths from arbitrary nodes, not only those originating from the function entry point.

The Frama-C/WP engine actually computes a collection of proof obligations for each ACSL annotation. The intuitive meaning is that, provided all the proof obligations are valid, then all execution paths are valid. We now expose the classical definition of WP and extend it to generating proof obligations.

A proof obligation $A : \phi \in \Omega$ is a logical formula ϕ labelled with its originating ACSL annotation A. For the sake of simplicity, we consider collections of proof obligations represented by sets, although their efficient implementation in WP is completely different.

$$
\begin{array}{rl}
\text{Memory states:} & m \in \mathsf{Mem} \\
\text{Logical formula:} & \varphi,\ \phi,\ (\varphi \Rightarrow \phi), \ldots \in \mathsf{Prop} \\
\text{C instruction semantics:} & [\![k]\!](m, m') \in \mathsf{Prop} \\
\text{ACSL predicate semantics:} & [\![P]\!](m) \in \mathsf{Prop} \\
\text{ACSL predicate collection:} & [\![P_1, \ldots, P_n]\!](m) \ \equiv\ \forall i,\ [\![P_i]\!](m) \\
\text{Execution paths} & \sigma = (a_i, m_i)_{i<n} \\
\text{Program semantics:} & \forall i,\ \exists k,\ a_i \xrightarrow{k} a_{i+1} \in \mathsf{Cfg}\ \wedge\ [\![k]\!](m_i, m_{i+1}) \\
\text{Valid execution paths :} & \forall i,\ (\forall j < i, [\![\mathsf{assumes}(a_j)]\!](m_j)) \implies [\![\mathsf{asserts}(a_i)]\!](m_i)
\end{array}
$$

Fig. 3. Semantics of C programs annotated in ACSL

$$
\begin{array}{rl}
\mathsf{wp}(a) \triangleq & \mathsf{wpGoals}(a) \cup \mathsf{wpCfg}(a) \\
\mathsf{wpGoals}(a) \triangleq & \bigcup \{\, A : [\![P]\!](m_a) \mid A : P \in \mathsf{asserts}(a) \,\} \\
\mathsf{wpCfg}(a) \triangleq & \bigcup \{\, A : \mathsf{wpPath}(a, k, b, \varphi) \mid a \xrightarrow{k} b \in \mathsf{Cfg},\ A : \varphi \in \mathsf{wp}(b) \,\} \\
\mathsf{wpPath}(a, k, b, \varphi) \triangleq & [\![\mathsf{assumes}(a)]\!](m_a) \Rightarrow [\![k]\!](m_a, m_b) \Rightarrow \varphi
\end{array}
$$

Fig. 4. Weakest pre-condition calculus

We introduce a collection of free memory state variables $(m_a)_{a \in \mathsf{Stmt}}$ indexed by program points. WP generates for each node a a collection of partial proof obligations formally defined in Fig. 4. Informally, from the bottom-up:

- $\mathsf{wpGoals}(a)$ ensures that all asserted ACSL predicates at node a are valid in memory state m_a;
- $\mathsf{wpPath}(a, k, b, \varphi)$ ensures that, if property φ holds for execution paths originating from b, then $\mathsf{wpPath}(a, k, b, \varphi)$ holds for execution paths going through transition $a \xrightarrow{k} b$. To achieve that, the assumed assertions at point a on memory state m_a are added to the proof context, together with the instruction semantics $[\![k]\!](m_a, m_b)$. Then, $\mathsf{wpCfg}(a)$ aggregates $\mathsf{wpPath}(a, k, b, \varphi)$ for every transition $a \xrightarrow{k} b$ of the CFG and partial proof obligations $\varphi \in \mathsf{wp}(b)$ computed for node b;
- Finally, $\mathsf{wp}(a)$ collects both $\mathsf{wpGoals}(a)$ and $\mathsf{wpCfg}(a)$.

Inductively, one can then easily prove that, provided all proof obligations computed by $\mathsf{wp}(\mathsf{entry})$ are valid formulas, all execution paths in the CFG are actually *valid.*

Now to generate a WP smoke test for node a, it suffices to augment the definition of $\mathsf{wp}(a)$ with a new proof obligation for detecting that valid execution paths cannot reach node a. For this purpose, we simply generate a proof obligation $\varphi = \mathsf{false}$ for smoking nodes. A smoke test proof obligation at node a is labelled with a special ACSL annotations denoted by Smoke_a, and we finally update the definition of proof obligations at node a as follows:

$$
\mathsf{wp}(a) \triangleq \quad \ldots \cup \{\ \mathsf{Smoke}_a : \mathsf{false} \mid \mathsf{smoking}(a)\ \}
$$

Moreover, since we now have the unreachable(a) analysis at hand, we can further optimize the generation of proof obligations for explicit dead code. We omit here those details for lack of place, but this is actually implemented in WP.

The interpretation of wp(a) shall now be interpreted in a slightly different way: actually, each proof obligation $A : \varphi$ labelled with non-smoking ACSL annotation A still means that the annotation is valid on all execution paths. But proof obligation $\mathsf{Smoke}_a : \varphi$ labelled with a smoke test annotation at node a actually entails that node a is provably unreachable for valid execution paths. This is indeed equivalent to verifying the ACSL annotation `check \false` at node a. Notice that this would *not* be same to verify the ACSL annotation `assert \false` , since such an annotation would be also inserted as an assumption into the proof context of other proof obligations, which would be completely incorrect.

Hence, the global objective of WP for smoke tests has now changed: we still want to succeed in proving all proof obligations $A : \varphi$ labeled by non-smoking ACSL annotations A, but we want to *invalidate* the proof obligations $\mathsf{Smoke}_a : \varphi$ labeled by smoke tests. We debate further on how to fulfill those proof objectives when using SMT solvers in Sect. 3.4. We will then discuss how to provide users with informative feedback on smoke test results in Sect. 3.5.

3.4 Proof Method

In this section, we discuss the smoke test verification method itself. As explained previously, smoke tests are similar to standard proof obligations for a `check \false` annotation, although we expect this annotation to be *unprovable*.

Since we use SMT solvers to discharge proof obligations, let us reformulate smoke test verification in terms of satisfiability. A logical formula is submitted to an SMT solver, and it outputs one of the following possible answers:

- UNSAT: the formula is *not* satisfiable.
- SAT: the formula is satisfiable, and sometimes, the SMT solver can output a model validating the formula.
- UNKNOWN: the solver has failed to decide the satisfiability of the formula, or it has exhausted the allocated resources (time or memory).

The proof obligation $A : \phi$ shall be understood as universally quantified over its free variables. WP submits its negation, $\exists \neg \phi$, to SMT solvers. Hence, an UNSAT result means that $\forall \phi$ is true, which is actually the expected result. SAT results are currently not exploited by WP, although they can be used to generate counter-examples for debugging[10].

For a smoke test, WP submits the negated formula as usual, but the expected result is now SAT, in order to prove that the associated program point is *actually* reachable. If the SMT solver replies with UNSAT—which is not the expected result—we actually have detected some dead code or a *proven* inconsistency in

[10] Counter-examples have been integrated into WP in the latest release Frama-C 29 (Copper).

the program specifications, and we can report the doomed program point to the user. However, when the SMT solver replies UNKNOWN, we have *no* guarantee that the formula is satisfiable or not.

Hence, smoke test verification is an incomplete process. This is the fundamental reason to refer to such a verification artifact as a *test* rather than a proof.

3.5 Providing Feedback to Users

The various results obtained from the generated proof obligations, especially smoke tests, deserve various kinds of feedback to users. Let us first consider the (set of possibly several, e.g. for loop invariants) proof obligations $A : \phi$ associated to some non-smoking ACSL annotation A. When *all* proof obligations labelled with A are discharged, we obviously report that the ACSL annotation A is valid[11].

For smoke test results, there are several situations to consider. Consider first a successful smoke test, that is, proof obligation $\mathsf{Smoke}_a : \phi$ is unproven. Indeed, no inconsistency at node a has been detected, and no further feedback is provided to the user: sanity checks are all right in this situation.

Consider now a failed smoke test, that is, proof obligation $\mathsf{Smoke}_a : \phi$ is proved. Here, the program point a is proved to be unreachable although *not* explicitly specified by the user to be intentional dead code. As illustrated by examples of Sect. 2, we report a failed smoke test. Further, in order to communicate this result to other plug-ins, WP also generates a new ACSL annotation `assert \false` at program point a, with a *valid* status, hence promoting the implicit `check \false` —actually proved by the smoke test—to a newly proven dead-code program point.

Moreover, all other ACSL annotations attached to the same program point become also *de facto* valid because of unreachability. More generally, all annotations that are associated to node a such that $\neg\mathsf{reachable}(a)$ are also valid because of unreachability. To inform the user, WP assigns a special validity status "Valid but Unreachable" to all those properties.

4 Industrial Experiments

The smoke test generation has been experimented on large industrial case studies, in particular, on real code bases under certification processes. Generating smoke tests during normal WP processing does not produce any visible overhead. However, as mentioned earlier, *verifying* smoke tests implies an additional cost, which can become significant for large projects, since we need to wait for SMT solvers to *fail* at proving satisfiability. Most of the time, on complex industrial studies, we must wait for external provers to timeout for each generated

[11] More precisely, other proof obligations used as hypotheses for A are also taken into account by WP. We omit those details here for simplicity.

	dead-requires	dead-assumes	dead-call	dead-code	dead-loop	total
Total generated	363	150	732	1089	16	2350
Proved by CFG	0	0	0	7	0	7
Proved by Qed	0	0	0	24	0	24
Proved by SMT	0	0	0	6	0	6

Fig. 5. Generated and failing smoke tests per category and proving analyzer (with a default timeout of 2 s per smoke test) for the JCVM project

smoke test. This delay is alleviated by using prover caches, however, users generally turn smoke test verification off during specification and proof debugging, and only turn smoke tests on for nightly builds and final proof replay.

Despite its operational cost, smoke tests generation proves to be very useful for early detection of specification bugs, that can sometimes be difficult and time-prone to find. We also found internal soundness bugs of WP thanks to smoke tests, especially inside its standard logic library which contains many axioms. To avoid those kinds of inconsistencies, we have decided to turn most of our axioms into proper lemmas or Coq realizations.

Industrial Application on the JavaCard Virtual Machine (JCVM). WP has been applied on a large industrial code (a JavaCard Virtual Machine with over 7,000 lines of C code) to prove functional and global security properties [12] at Thales. This project was conducted according to a stringent common criteria certification process [19] and succeeded to reach the highest assurance level (EAL7, certificate available at [1]). Besides the effort to specify target properties with more than 30,000 lines of ACSL, the most important challenge was to ensure the full consistency of the formal specification.

Smoke tests have been systematically applied throughout the project to monitor the consistency of formal specification. They effectively guided the initial steps of verification especially when introducing hypotheses to define the perimeter of analyzed code. Given the already high cost of proof computation (over 4 h on a PC with 3.10 GHz 12-core CPU and 64 GB RAM for more than 80,000 verification conditions generated by WP), smoke tests provided a convenient way for sanity checks with a reasonable overhead. The generation of smoke tests is very efficient and fully automatic. The verification of smoke tests has a reasonable cost thanks to proof parallelization and prover cache. Overall, only a 20min (i.e., $\approx$8%) overhead is observed for the full proof time of the JCVM due to smoke tests.

Figure 5 shows the number of various kinds of generated smoke tests: precondition errors (dead-requires, dead-assumes), non-terminating calls (dead-call), dead-code and post-condition errors (dead-code), and inconsistent loop invariants (dead-loop). In total, 2,350 smoke tests were generated and 37 of them were proved to be failing. The last three lines of the table show the number of smoke tests proved as failing by different analyzers with the default timeout of 2 s per smoke test. The lines for the three analyzers are shown in the order in which they are applied, so that an SMT solver is used only for goals not proved with CFG and Qed. In this project, we used only one SMT solver, Alt-Ergo [18]. All failing smoke tests belong to the dead-code category and are justified by the assumptions for the considered version. They are spurious alarms and may be avoided with explicit `assert \false` annotations at the corresponding code locations. Most smoke tests were simple enough to be either detected as unreachable by the CFG (control flow graph) analysis of Frama-C (7), or discharged by Qed (24). The default timeout of 2 s per smoke test seems to be sufficient in practice to detect failing smoke tests for the JCVM. Proof sessions with a bigger timeout (3 s, 5 s and even 10 s) did not detect more failing smoke tests. However, with a smaller timeout of 1 s, 5 of them were not detected: the SMT solver identified only one failing smoke test instead of 6 (so for this timeout, in the last line of Fig. 5, 6 should be replaced by 1). As expected (for theoretical reasons of proof incompleteness), this illustrates that the absence of proof of the proof obligation for a smoke test *increases confidence* but *cannot guarantee* that the smoke test does not fail. Thus, a suitable timeout duration should be chosen. Our experiments and observations give confidence that the default timeout of 2 s is suitable for the JCVM project. Indeed, rigorous code and specification review did not allow us to suspect other failing smoke tests in the project.

5 Related Work

Hoenicke et al. [15] define the notion of doomed statement we use in this work and relies on weakest pre-condition calculus with Boogie [4]. Bertoloni et al. [8] follow the same path. The main difference is that our work was originally meant to find inconsistencies in *specifications*, yet we have extended the analysis to error detection, in particular, the presence of dead code and, in a limited way, memory access errors. Other efforts, instead of deductive verification, use pattern-based and dataflow-based approaches [2] or constrain solving through Horn clauses [16].

The authors of [8,11,15,22] focus mainly on undefined behavior detection. For this, they make some assumptions about pointers that we do not currently make with WP. While useful to detect true errors, these assumptions might create false alarms (for example when a pointer is supposed not to be in the beginning of a memory block in the input of a function). We plan to extend WP with such kinds of assumptions but in a more controlled way, in order to optimize detection of runtime errors.

Most of these efforts were meant to tackle the problem of having too many false alarms, like [13], or for example WP without smoke tests, where we have proof failures on verification of absence of runtime errors but no way to know whether the alarm is a false alarm. Another approach for this is using model checking to find traces that bring to problems like in [10], or at least to find an explanation about the failure [21], or to produce a counter-example to the correct behavior through a specialized mechanism [20]. While we plan to add this last capability to WP, we prefer to rely on the ability of SMT solvers like CVC5 [3] or Z3 [9] to produce counter-examples.

6 Conclusion

This tool paper presented the design and implementation of smoke tests in Frama-C/WP. Introduced to address potential inconsistencies in specifications, they provide to verification engineers a practical and pragmatic solution for detecting inconsistencies and dead code, even if it is incomplete and cannot guarantee their absence. Along with the extensions we mentioned in Sect. 5, future work directions include a larger evaluation, as well as proof of correct generation of smoke tests, as part of a long-term effort on formalization of WP. Suggesting a suitable timeout for a smoke test in a given project (e.g. based on statistics or machine-learning) is another work perspective.

Acknowledgment. Part of this work was supported by ANR grants ANR-22-CE39-0014 and ANR-22-CE25-0018.

References

1. ANSSI: The EAL7 certificate ANSSI-CC-2023/45. https://cyber.gouv.fr/sites/default/files/document_type/Certificat-CC-2023_45fr_0.pdf
2. Ayewah, N., Pugh, W.W., Morgenthaler, J.D., Penix, J., Zhou, Y.: Evaluating static analysis defect warnings on production software. In: Das, M., Grossman, D. (eds.) Proceedings of the 7th ACM SIGPLAN-SIGSOFT Workshop on Program Analysis for Software Tools and Engineering, PASTE 2007, San Diego, California, USA, 13–14 June 2007, pp. 1–8. ACM (2007). https://doi.org/10.1145/1251535.1251536
3. Barbosa, H., et al.: cvc5: a versatile and industrial-strength SMT solver. In: Fisman, D., Rosu, G. (eds.) TACAS 2022, Part I. LNCS, vol. 13243, pp. 415–442. Springer, Cham (2022). https://doi.org/10.1007/978-3-030-99524-9_24
4. Barnett, M., Chang, B.-Y.E., DeLine, R., Jacobs, B., Leino, K.R.M.: Boogie: a modular reusable verifier for object-oriented programs. In: de Boer, F.S., Bonsangue, M.M., Graf, S., de Roever, W.-P. (eds.) FMCO 2005. LNCS, vol. 4111, pp. 364–387. Springer, Heidelberg (2006). https://doi.org/10.1007/11804192_17
5. Barnett, M., Leino, K.R.M.: Weakest-precondition of unstructured programs. SIGSOFT Softw. Eng. Notes **31**(1), 82–87 (2005)
6. Baudin, P., et al.: The dogged pursuit of bug-free C programs: the Frama-C software analysis platform. Commun. ACM **64**(8), 56–68 (2021). https://doi.org/10.1145/3470569
7. Baudin, P., et al.: ACSL: ANSI/ISO C specification language. http://frama-c.com/acsl.html
8. Bertolini, C., Schäf, M., Schweitzer, P.: Infeasible code detection. In: Joshi, R., Müller, P., Podelski, A. (eds.) VSTTE 2012. LNCS, vol. 7152, pp. 310–325. Springer, Heidelberg (2012). https://doi.org/10.1007/978-3-642-27705-4_24
9. Bjørner, N.S., Eisenhofer, C., Kovács, L.: Satisfiability modulo custom theories in Z3. In: Dragoi, C., Emmi, M., Wang, J. (eds.) VMCAI 2023. LNCS, vol. 13881, pp. 91–105. Springer, Cham (2023). https://doi.org/10.1007/978-3-031-24950-1_5
10. David, C., Kesseli, P., Kroening, D., Lewis, M.: Danger invariants. In: Fitzgerald, J., Heitmeyer, C., Gnesi, S., Philippou, A. (eds.) FM 2016. LNCS, vol. 9995, pp. 182–198. Springer, Cham (2016). https://doi.org/10.1007/978-3-319-48989-6_12

11. Dillig, I., Dillig, T., Aiken, A.: Static error detection using semantic inconsistency inference. In: Ferrante, J., McKinley, K.S. (eds.) Proceedings of the ACM SIGPLAN 2007 Conference on Programming Language Design and Implementation, San Diego, California, USA, 10–13 June 2007, pp. 435–445. ACM (2007). https://doi.org/10.1145/1250734.1250784
12. Djoudi, A., Hána, M., Kosmatov, N.: Formal verification of a JavaCard virtual machine with Frama-C. In: Huisman, M., Păsăreanu, C., Zhan, N. (eds.) FM 2021. LNCS, vol. 13047, pp. 427–444. Springer, Cham (2021). https://doi.org/10.1007/978-3-030-90870-6_23
13. Flanagan, C., Leino, K.R.M., Lillibridge, M., Nelson, G., Saxe, J.B., Stata, R.: PLDI 2002: extended static checking for java. ACM SIGPLAN Not. **48**(4S), 22–33 (2013). https://doi.org/10.1145/2502508.2502520
14. Hähnle, R., Huisman, M.: Deductive software verification: from pen-and-paper proofs to industrial tools. In: Steffen, B., Woeginger, G. (eds.) Computing and Software Science. LNCS, vol. 10000, pp. 345–373. Springer, Cham (2019). https://doi.org/10.1007/978-3-319-91908-9_18
15. Hoenicke, J., Leino, K.R.M., Podelski, A., Schäf, M., Wies, T.: It's doomed; we can prove it. In: Cavalcanti, A., Dams, D.R. (eds.) FM 2009. LNCS, vol. 5850, pp. 338–353. Springer, Heidelberg (2009). https://doi.org/10.1007/978-3-642-05089-3_22
16. Kahsai, T., Navas, J.A., Jovanović, D., Schäf, M.: Finding inconsistencies in programs with loops. In: Davis, M., Fehnker, A., McIver, A., Voronkov, A. (eds.) LPAR 2015. LNCS, vol. 9450, pp. 499–514. Springer, Heidelberg (2015). https://doi.org/10.1007/978-3-662-48899-7_35
17. Kirchner, F., Kosmatov, N., Prevosto, V., Signoles, J., Yakobowski, B.: Frama-C: a software analysis perspective. Formal Asp. Comput. **27**(3), 573–609 (2015). https://doi.org/10.1007/s00165-014-0326-7
18. OCamlPro: The Alt-Ergo solver. https://alt-ergo.ocamlpro.com/
19. Portal, T.C.C.: Common criteria for information technology security evaluation. https://www.commoncriteriaportal.org/
20. Rümmer, P., Shah, M.A.: Proving programs incorrect using a sequent calculus for java dynamic logic. In: Gurevich, Y., Meyer, B. (eds.) TAP 2007. LNCS, vol. 4454, pp. 41–60. Springer, Heidelberg (2007). https://doi.org/10.1007/978-3-540-73770-4_3
21. Schäf, M., Schwartz-Narbonne, D., Wies, T.: Explaining inconsistent code. In: Meyer, B., Baresi, L., Mezini, M. (eds.) Joint Meeting of the European Software Engineering Conference and the ACM SIGSOFT Symposium on the Foundations of Software Engineering, ESEC/FSE 2013, Saint Petersburg, Russian Federation, 18–26 August 2013, pp. 521–531. ACM (2013). https://doi.org/10.1145/2491411.2491448
22. Wang, X., Zeldovich, N., Kaashoek, M.F., Solar-Lezama, A.: A differential approach to undefined behavior detection. Commun. ACM **59**(3), 99–106 (2016). https://doi.org/10.1145/2885256

Testing and Proving Advanced Properties

Runtime Verification for High-Level Security Properties: Case Study on the TPM Software Stack

Yani Ziani[1,2], Nikolai Kosmatov[1(✉)], Frédéric Loulergue[2], and Daniel Gracia Pérez[1]

[1] Thales Research and Technology, Palaiseau, France
{yani.ziani,nikolai.kosmatov, daniel.gracia-perez}@thalesgroup.com
[2] Univ. Orléans, INSA Centre Val de Loire, LIFO EA 4022, Orléans, France
frederic.loulergue@univ-orleans.fr

Abstract. The Trusted Platform Module (TPM) is a cryptoprocessor designed to provide hardware-based secure storage and protect integrity of modern computers. Communications with the TPM go through the TPM Software Stack (TSS), a popular implementation of which is the open-source library *tpm2-tss*. It is thus crucial to ensure that no leak of sensitive data may occur in the TSS during communications between the host platform and the TPM. Recent work on deductive verification of functional and safety properties for this library faced several challenges. The purpose of this case study paper is to focus on high-level security properties, and to propose an alternative validation approach for such properties on the library by using runtime verification. We describe the proposed approach, apply it to specify and verify at runtime some key security properties using the Frama-C verification platform and report on our first evaluation results.

1 Introduction

The *Trusted Platform Module* (TPM) [21] has become a key security component in modern computers. The TPM defines a standard for a cryptoprocessor designed to ensure security properties such as the integrity of the platform it is a component of, or the secure storage of encryption keys inside it.

Operating systems and applications can communicate with the TPM through a standard API provided by a software specification known as the *TPM Software Stack* (TSS). A widely-used implementation of the TSS is the open-source library *tpm2-tss*. Safety and security of operations involving the TPM thus rely on both the component itself and its access API, and are highly critical in modern computers. Therefore, ensuring the security of the library is crucial, making it a key target for verification and validation.

Verification of security properties was the purpose of several recent case studies. A large-scale formal verification of global security properties on the C code

© The Author(s), under exclusive license to Springer Nature Switzerland AG 2025
M. Huisman and F. Howar (Eds.): TAP 2024, LNCS 15153, pp. 87–106, 2025.
https://doi.org/10.1007/978-3-031-72044-4_5

of the JavaCard Virtual Machine for Common Criteria certification was successfully conducted in [8]. Our recent work [24] used the FRAMA-C verification platform [11] and its deductive verification plug-in WP in order to verify safety and functional properties on a subset of high-level functions of the tpm2-tss library involved in the secure storage of an encryption key on the TPM. This target was highly complex, based on complex data structures, low-level code, dynamic memory allocation and recursive data structures. It highlighted several current tool limitations, which required workarounds and minor yet necessary code rewriting, and make the verification of larger subsets of code—and in particular lower-level functions—very challenging.

The main motivations of this work are to extend previous verification efforts to high-level security properties, and to offer an alternative validation approach for such properties on the library by using runtime verification, complementary—but of course less rigorous—with respect to deductive verification.

In this paper we extend the previous case study [24] on formal verification of tpm2-tss using the FRAMA-C verification platform. We use the METACSL plug-in [17,18] of FRAMA-C, which provides an extension of the ACSL specification language [3] to define high-level security properties, and translates them into regular ACSL specifications. The runtime verification plug-in E-ACSL [12] then allows us to translate such ACSL specifications into instrumented C code, to be compiled and executed in order to verify annotations at runtime. However, much like the WP plug-in, E-ACSL faces its fair share of limitations, for example, its capacity to handle logic definitions such as those used for linked list specification [4], direct comparisons between complex structures and unions, and various other features of the C language. On the other hand, runtime verification presents opportunities to handle more easily dynamic allocations, byte-level assignments, and varying representations of complex data structures, which presented important challenges for deductive verification [24].

We focus here on the subset of functions necessary to store an encryption key on the TPM, from which we exclude calls to cryptographic operations from external libraries, as well as linked list manipulations. We use such simplifications to fit with runtime verification. We also modify a few of the lowest-level functions, some to intentionally induce TSS errors, and some to avoid the necessity to directly use a TPM. The code is available online as a companion artifact[1].

Contributions. The contributions of this paper include:

- a modeling approach relying on specific data structures, usable for the specification and verification of high-level security properties;
- specification and runtime verification in FRAMA-C of high-level security properties on a representative simplified subset of functions of tpm2-tss;
- presentation of the main issues we faced;
- evaluation results including detection of simulated errors.

[1] Available (with all necessary annotations) on https://doi.org/10.5281/zenodo.12773113.

Outline. The rest of the paper is organized as follows. Section 2 presents FRAMA-C and the plug-ins used. Section 3 briefly introduces the TPM, and the tpm2-tss library, an implementation of its software stack. Sections 4 and 5 present our approach to model sensitive data and to define high-level security properties on it. Section 6 describes our evaluation and verification results. Finally, Sects. 7 and 8 present related work and a conclusion with necessary tool improvements.

2 The Frama-C Verification Platform and Its Wp, E-ACSL and MetAcsl Plug-ins

FRAMA-C [2,11] is a framework for the analysis and verification of ANSI/ISO C programs organized as a set of plug-ins around a common kernel. The mean of communication between the various plug-ins is the specification language ACSL [3,6] (ANSI/ISO C Specification Language). ACSL is basically a typed first-order logic embedding C types and pure expressions as well as logic types and built-in predicates.

There are four main plug-ins used for annotating and verifying programs:

- RTE [10] generates ACSL annotations that, if proved, ensure that there are no runtime errors in the analyzed program.
- EVA [5] is an automatic abstract interpretation based value analysis. It performs a whole program analysis.
- WP [2] offers deductive verification. In this case, the verification is modular: the contract and annotations of each function are verified independently from the other functions, using only the contracts of the callees. WP generates verification conditions that can be proved by external automatic or interactive provers via WHY3 [9].
- E-ACSL [12] provides a way to dynamically verify ACSL annotations. A subset of ACSL, named E-ACSL, is translated into C code which allows the annotations to be verified at runtime. This is *runtime assertion checking* (RAC) [7,20]. Of course, unlike EVA and WP, E-ACSL cannot, in general, guarantee the absence of errors for all possible executions but detects and precisely locates errors for a concrete input, thus helping to find their reason.

There are other plug-ins in the FRAMA-C distribution for understanding the code (for example by code metrics) and for simplifying the analyzed source code (for example by slicing), as well as external plug-ins. In particular, METACSL [16] is not part of the FRAMA-C distribution but is an actively maintained plug-in. METACSL considers high-level properties expressed at the global level. These properties are especially suited to state security properties. High-level properties can be proved using other high-level properties by a specific prover, but most of the time they are translated into additional local annotations in function contracts and bodies.

Annotation generators (like RTE and METACSL) are naturally combined with verification plug-ins. But analyzers can be combined too, which makes FRAMA-C even more powerful. For example, EVA was used [14] to detect pieces of code for which there may exist a vulnerability and E-ACSL to generate a monitor to check at runtime that these potential vulnerabilities are not exploited.

3 Overview of the TPM and its Software Stack

The TPM[2] is a standard conceived by the Trusted Computing Group (TCG)[3] for a passive secure cryptoprocessor designed to protect hardware from software-based threats. It is usually implemented as a discrete chip and designed to perform cryptographic operations, but it can however also be implemented as part of the firmware of a regular processor, or as a software component.

Nowadays, the TPM is well known for its usage in consumer computers to ensure integrity and the secure storage of the keys used by *Bitlocker* or *dm-crypt* to encrypt the disk, but it may also be used to provide other cryptographic services to the Operating System (OS) and applications. The TCG defines the TPM Software Stack (TSS), a set of specifications providing standard APIs to access the functionalities and commands of the TPM, regardless of the environment.

The TSS provides different levels of complexity for its APIs, from the Feature API (FAPI) (for simple and common cryptographic services), to the System API (SAPI) (for a one-to-one mapping to the TPM commands) and the TPM Command Transmission Interface (TCTI) (for connection with the TPM). Data on the SAPI and the TCTI is stored in the form of buffers of bytes. Between the FAPI and SAPI lies the Enhanced System API (ESAPI), which provides functionalities similar to that of SAPI, with a higher level of abstraction but slightly limited flexibility. Other APIs such as the Marshaling/Serialization API complete the previous ones for common operations like data formatting.

The TSS, as any software component or the TPM itself, can have vulnerabilities[4] that attackers can exploit to recover sensitive data communicated with the TPM or to take control of the system. We center our study on the verification of the tpm2-tss library, an open-source and popular implementation of the TSS.

More precisely, we focus on the import of a sensitive information (for example, an encryption key) onto the TPM, without parameter encryption, from the ESAPI layer. This can be done using the `Esys_Create` function of the ESAPI, corresponding to the `Tss2_Sys_Create` function of the SAPI and the `TPM2_Create` TPM command. For each involved layer (including the TCTI), the TSS relies on a notion of context containing all the data the layers need to store between calls, and to transfer data from one layer to the next (and vice-versa). This is done by design, so that the TSS does not need to maintain a global state or global variables. The imported sensitive data is transferred from one layer to the next through these contexts, written in high-level structures in the ESAPI context, and low-level buffers in the SAPI and TCTI contexts.

We focus here on the security of sensitive data, when going through the TSS, as it is transformed between layers to be sent to the TPM for import.

[2] See the TPM specification [21] and reference books as [1] for more detail.
[3] https://trustedcomputinggroup.org/.
[4] Like CVE-2023-22745 and CVE-2020-24455, documented on www.cve.org.

4 Companion Memory Modeling for Sensitive Data

Function Subset. To construct our target subset of functions, we simplified an integration test of the library for the `Esys_Create` function, to import an object onto the TPM without using parameter encryption.

To do so, we remove from the TSS dependencies to other function calls to TPM commands for authorizations, parameter encryption (and thus dependencies to an external library such as OpenSSL), and we replace the command transmission interface with a dummy that receives the command buffer sent to the TPM, but replies to higher layers of the TSS with an empty response buffer. We do not change anything else, and keep each dynamic memory allocation, freeing, and memory manipulation operation as is.

Thus, we consider the import of a single object acting as sensitive data, that is statically allocated in the test function. In this scenario, the call to `Esys_Create` will succeed in sending the TPM command to the TCTI, and will fail at the very end when receiving the invalid TPM response buffer. Regardless of the failure or success of the ESAPI call to the `TPM2_Create` command, it is expected that the TSS should not retain any sensitive data at the end of the integration test.

Examples Overview. To illustrate our verification approach, we provide our modeling of the memory for sensitive data with Figs. 1 and 2. We isolate with Figs. 3, 4, 5 and 6 a few small examples of code and structure definitions from our subset representative of the manipulation of the imported sensitive information. Figure 7 provides the security properties we verify in this work. Figures 1 and 2 will be described step-by-step in this section, and Figs. 3, 4, 5, 6 and 7 will be explained in Sect. 5. As it is often done, some ACSL notation (e.g. `\forall`, `integer`, `==>`, `<=`, `!=`) is pretty-printed (resp., as $\forall$, $\mathbb{Z}$, $\Rightarrow$, $\leq$, $\neq$).

Memory Representation. Lines 1–4 of Fig. 1 show our companion memory representation for sensitive data defined as global variables. All sensitive data shall be uniquely represented by its memory location and its size. Thus, we define `_all_sens` on line 3 as an array of `char *` pointers to be used to store the addresses of all the possible representations and copies of the imported object and other pieces of sensitive data throughout the layers of the TSS. With the `_len_sens` array of `int` on line 2, we couple each of these addresses with the size (in bytes) of the associated sensitive data. For convenience, the macro on line 1 defines `MAX_SENS`, a maximum number of sensitive data to be modeled. The `_nb_sens` variable on line 4 serves to determine whether it is possible to add another piece of sensitive data to our representation: it stores the number of stored pointers (which gives also the index of the next available one). Lines 7–10 define indices we use to record where each type of sensitive information is located in our model. We define `_sens_A_B_idx` as the index of `A` or information `A` in location `B`, where `A` is the name of the original variable referred to by `_all_sens[_sens_A_B_idx]`, and `B` describes whether the original is a local variable in a specific layer, or stored in the ESAPI context, or in a command buffer.

```
1 #define MAX_SENS 100
2 int _len_sens[MAX_SENS];
3 char * _all_sens[MAX_SENS];
4 int _nb_sens;
5
6 // define _sens_##vartype##_##usage##_idx here
7 int _sens_inSensitive_esys_Create_idx = -1;
8 int _sens_inSensitiveData_esys_Create_ctx_idx = -1;
9 int _sens_outPrivate_esys_Create_idx = -1;
10 int _sens_inSens_sys_Create_cmdbuff_idx = -1;
11
12 bool is_sens(void *ptr, int size, int idx)
13 {
14   if (0 > idx ∨ idx ≥ MAX_SENS){return false;}
15   else if (0 ≤ idx ∧ idx < MAX_SENS){
16     return(_all_sens[idx] == ptr ∧ _len_sens[idx] == size);
17   }
18 }
19
20 void remove_sens(int idx){_len_sens[idx] = 0;}
21
22 int add_as_sens(void *ptr, int size)
23 {
24   int idx;
25   if(_nb_sens ≥ MAX_SENS ∨ _nb_sens < 0){idx =-1;}
26   else {
27     _all_sens[_nb_sens] = (char*) (ptr);
28     _len_sens[_nb_sens] = size;
29     idx = _nb_sens++;
30   }
31   return idx;
32 }
```

Fig. 1. Companion memory representation for sensitive data

Consequently, we consider that `_sens_A_B_idx` refers to sensitive data if we have `0≤_sens_A_B_idx<MAX_SIZE` and `0<_len_sens[_sens_A_B_idx]`. The fact that the corresponding memory block can be safely read and written, that is, `\valid(_all_sens[_sens_A_B_idx] + (0.._len_sens[_sens_A_B_idx]-1))`, is supposed to be true in this case (it will be verified in the global invariant given in Fig. 2, discussed below).

In particular, we define `is_sens` in lines 12–18, `remove_sens` in line 20, and `add_as_sens` in lines 22–32. Given a pointer `ptr`, a size `size` and an index `idx`, `is_sens` is used to determine whether the memory block of size `size` at address `ptr` corresponds to the sensitive data at index `idx` of the representation, returns `true` in this case, and `false` otherwise. The `remove_sens` function in line 20 sets the size `_len_sens[idx]` of the sensitive data at index `idx` of our model to `0`, to express that `idx` is not considered to refer to sensitive data anymore.[5] `remove_sens` is typically used, for instance, when dynamically allocated sensitive data is freed, overwritten with non-sensitive data, or when we exit the scope of automatically allocated variables (such as local variables) with sensitive data.

[5] For simplicity, when an element is removed, we do not shift the following array elements to the left. This feature can be easily added and particularly useful for long-running programs, where pieces of sensitive data are frequently added and removed.

```
1 /*@ meta \prop, \name(valid_sensitive),
2   \targets(\ALL),
3   \context(\strong_invariant),
4   ∀ int i; 0 ≤ i < _nb_sens ⇒ 0 < _nb_sens ≤ MAX_SENS ⇒
5     0 < _len_sens[i] ⇒
6     \valid(_all_sens[i] + (0 .. _len_sens[i] - 1)); */
```

Fig. 2. Global invariant for the validity of memory accesses of modeled sensitive data

We use the `add_as_sens` function defined in lines 22–32 to add a new piece of sensitive data to the representation, given a pointer `ptr` and a size `size`. `add_as_sens` first checks with line 25 if `_nb_sens` is between 0 and `MAX_SENS`, that is to say if it is possible to add new data to the representation. If it is, `ptr` (resp. `size`) is added to the `_all_sens` array (resp. `_len_sens` array) at index `_nb_sens` (our tracking index), which is then incremented by 1. The new value of `_nb_sens` is then returned, to be used to set the indices defined in lines 7–10.

We use `is_sens` as a way to determine whether a piece of sensitive data exists in the representation before removing it with `remove_sens`, thus to determine whether `remove_sens` is safe to call.

Validity Invariant. In order to ensure that all sensitive data added to our representation is always safe for the TSS to read and write, we define as a MetAcsl meta-property a global validity invariant `valid_sensive` in Fig. 2. Line 2 defines the set of target functions in which this property should be satisfied, which in this case comprises all the defined functions of our representative subset. The `\context(\strong_invariant)` clause in line 3 indicates that the property must hold at every point of each target function. Subsequently, with lines 4–6, we express that for any index `i` for which sensitive data is defined (that is to say, for all indices within `[0, MAX_SIZE - 1]` such that `_len_sens[i]`>`0`) we must have `\valid(_all_sens[i] + (0.._len_sens[i] - 1))` (that is to say, the memory block at address `_all_sens[i]` of size `_len_sens[i]` bytes must be safe to read and write).

This property is expected to always be verified. Any violation of this invariant would imply that sensitive data was deleted or freed from the program before it was removed from our representation, which can only happen in one of two situations: either we neglected to remove sensitive data from the model when it should have been, or such data is freed too early.

5 Defining and Verifying High-Level Security Properties

This section presents how we use the definitions introduced in Sect. 4 to define and verify high-level security properties such as the integrity and the confidentiality of sensitive data (in our case, the object sent to the TPM). We also identify issues related to the limited support of ACSL clauses in E-ACSL related to logic labels, function pointers, and which currently prevent some of the possible extensions of the pool of verifiable security properties. In this section, we detail Figs. 3, 4, 5, 6 and 7.

```
1 /** Store sensitive data inside the ESYS_CONTEXT */
2 static void store_input_parameters (
3     ESYS_CONTEXT *esysContext,
4     const TPM2B_SENSITIVE_CREATE *inSensitive)
5 {
6   if (inSensitive == NULL) {esysContext->in.Create.inSensitive = NULL;}
7   else {
8     esysContext->in.Create.inSensitiveData = *inSensitive;
9     esysContext->in.Create.inSensitive =
10      &esysContext->in.Create.inSensitiveData;
11  /*For E-ACSL*/
12    /* We add the part of context containing the imported sensitive
13       object to our representation of sensitive data. */
14
15     _sens_inSensitiveData_esys_ctx_idx =
16      add_as_sens(esysContext->in.Create.inSensitive,
17             (int) sizeof(esysContext->in.Create.inSensitiveData));
18
19  /*end E-ACSL*/
20  }
21 }
```

Fig. 3. Adding sensitive data from ESAPI to the representation

Adding Sensitive Data on Higher-Level Layers. Figure 3 provides an example of addition of sensitive data from the ESAPI layer to our representation. More specifically, we focus on the `store_input_parameters` function in charge of storing the data from `inSensitive` inside the ESAPI context `esysContext`, before it can be sent to the lower layers. The ESAPI context as defined in tpm2-tss has specific fields to store the sensitive data to be imported, and its address.

The sensitive information passed as argument of `store_input_parameters` here is assumed to have already been added to the modeling in callers. The function checks with line 6 whether `inSensitive` is a `NULL` pointer, and sets the corresponding field in the context to `NULL` if such is the case. Otherwise, with lines 8–10, it adds a copy of the pointed memory—that is to say, the sensitive data itself—to the context (in the `in.Create.inSensitiveData` field), and sets its address within the context (in the `in.Create.inSensitive` field).

This new instance of the imported data is different from the one passed as argument of the function. As it refers to a memory location different from that of `inSensitive`, we need to add it to our representation as well. In lines 14–18, we add the new instance of the sensitive data, using its address given by the `in.Create.inSensitive` field, and its size defined as the `sizeof` of the `in.Create.inSensitiveData` field. The reason we can use `sizeof` is because the `TPM2B_SENSITIVE_CREATE` only contains fields of fixed size, as shown in Fig. 4. More specifically, this type is defined in lines 6–9 with two fields, an `int`-like field `size`, and a `sensitive` field of type `TPMS_SENSITIVE_CREATE` defined in lines 2–5 and comprised solely of two subfields `userAuth` and `data`, each defined with an `int`-like field and a fixed-size array, following the template in line 1.

While knowing the precise type definition is not paramount to handle sensitive data on high-level layers, knowing it is essential in understanding how such data is transferred to lower-level layers, and how to handle sensitive data on SAPI and TCTI. As the latter acts as a transmission layer to send the command

```
typedef struct {UINT16 size;BYTE buffer[TYPE_MAX_SIZE];} TPM2B_TYPE;
typedef struct  {
   TPM2B_AUTH userAuth;                //TPM2B_TYPE-like type
   TPM2B_SENSITIVE_DATA data;          //TPM2B_TYPE-like type
} TPMS_SENSITIVE_CREATE;
typedef struct  {
   UINT16 size;     // ignored by marshal according to the TCG specifications
   TPMS_SENSITIVE_CREATE sensitive;
} TPM2B_SENSITIVE_CREATE;
```

Fig. 4. Partial type definition used for `inSensitive`

buffer formed on the SAPI to the TPM (resp. to send the response buffer from the TPM to the SAPI), sensitive data is stored in the same way in both layers.

Adding Sensitive Data on Low-Level Layers. Figure 5 presents an example of addition of sensitive data, to our model, in a function of SAPI, a lower-level layer of the library. We focus here on the `Tss2_Sys_Create_Prepare` (line 1) library function which partially constructs the SAPI command for the Create command by copying and saving data passed as argument to the `cmdBuffer` of the `sysContext` context. It is typically used to transfer information such as `inSensitive` (used as argument in line 4) from higher layers to lower layers.

The snippet of code in lines 28–37 is in charge of such an operation. In particular, lines 29 checks whether the `inSensitive` pointer is `NULL` or not. If such is the case, the value `0` is copied byte per byte to the command buffer to indicate that the command will not have an imported object. Otherwise, it will copy the relevant content of `inSensitive` to the `ctx->cmdBuffer` buffer, starting at the `ctx->nextData`-th byte.

More specifically, the function call in lines 33–34 is used to read the subfields of `inSensitive`, and write byte per byte to position `ctx->nextData` of the command buffer, in this order (and as defined in Fig. 4), the size `userAuth.size`, the first `userAuth.size` bytes of the `userAuth.buffer` array, the size `data.size`, and the first `data.size` bytes of the `data.buffer` array. This function is a marshal/serialization function, which translates a data structure (in this case, objects of type `TPM2B_SENSITIVE_CREATE`) into a lower-level representation fit for data transmission (in this case, a buffer of bytes). This marshal function does not write `inSensitive->size` inside the command, but computes the size in bytes of the written area, and writes it. We define the total size in bytes of the written area in the command buffer with the `sys_sensitive_size` defined in lines 41–45. We base this definition on the behavior described in the official TSS SAPI Specification, rather than the behavior of this marshaling function as it is implemented in the tpm2-tss library. With line 28, we store in the `inSens_offset` variable the offset where the marshaling stores the transformed sensitive data in the command buffer. We then add to our model the SAPI command buffer instance of `inSensitive`, using its address `ctx->cmdBuffer + inSens_offset` and its size `sys_sensitive_size`, with lines 46–47.

```
TSS2_RC Tss2_Sys_Create_Prepare(
  TSS2_SYS_CONTEXT *sysContext,
  TPMI_DH_OBJECT parentHandle,
  const TPM2B_SENSITIVE_CREATE *inSensitive,
...
{
...
  size_t inSens_offset = ctx->nextData;
  if (!inSensitive) {
    rval = Tss2_MU_UINT16_Marshal(0, ctx->cmdBuffer,
                    ctx->maxCmdSize,&ctx->nextData);
  } else {
    rval = Tss2_MU_TPM2B_SENSITIVE_CREATE_Marshal(
      inSensitive, ctx->cmdBuffer, ctx->maxCmdSize, &ctx->nextData);
  }
  if (rval)
    return rval;
  /* We add the part of the command buffer containing the imported
    sensitive object to our representation of sensitive data. */

  int sys_sensitive_size = (int) sizeof(UINT16) +
              (int) sizeof(inSensitive->sensitive.userAuth.size) +
              (int) inSensitive->sensitive.userAuth.size +
              (int) sizeof(inSensitive->sensitive.data.size)+
              (int) inSensitive->sensitive.data.size;
  _sens_inSens_sys_Create_cmdbuff_idx =
      add_as_sens(ctx->cmdBuffer + inSens_offset, sys_sensitive_size);
...
}
```

Fig. 5. Adding sensitive data from SAPI to the representation

Removing Sensitive Data and Handling its Lifetime. In order to express high-level security properties on sensitive data in this subset, it is necessary to determine the lifetime of such data, so as to ascertain when such properties need to be verified. Thus, if we take for example the integrity of the imported key, for which we need to ensure it is only written or modified when it is supposed to be (as will be explained later on with Fig. 7), we need to precisely define for every instance of the key when they are freed or overwritten, and thus when their representation should be removed from the companion model.

We illustrate this with the two snippets of code in Fig. 6 (lines 387–395 and lines 494–502 refer to the same file in the considered subset of code, available in the companion artifact). Lines 389–392 allocate memory to be used to store sensitive data `outPrivate` returned by the TPM about the imported key, before the TSS receives the response buffer (which is empty in our example). Similarly to what we presented in Figs. 3 and 5, we add it to the companion model with lines 393–394. Lines 494–502 provide a typical usage, in the TSS, of dynamic deallocation of memory previously allocated for command or response parameters. The `if` statements in lines 494 and 495 correspond to checks to ensure the call to `free` line 499 is safe, before setting the corresponding pointer to `NULL` with line 500.

```
/* Allocate memory for response parameters */
if (outPrivate ≠ NULL) {
  *outPrivate = calloc(sizeof(TPM2B_PRIVATE), 1);
  if (*outPrivate == NULL) {
    return_error(TSS2_ESYS_RC_MEMORY, "Out␣of␣memory");
  }
  _sens_outPrivate_esys_Create_idx =
    add_as_sens(*outPrivate, (int) sizeof(TPM2B_PRIVATE));
}
...
if (outPrivate ≠ NULL){
  if((*outPrivate) ≠ NULL) {
    /*remove the sensitive data from the model before freeing*/
    if(is_sens(*outPrivate, size, (int) sizeof(TPM2B_PRIVATE)))
      remove_sens(_sens_outPrivate_esys_Create_idx);
    free((void*) (*outPrivate));
    (*outPrivate)=NULL;
  }
}
```

Fig. 6. Usage example for `remove_sens`

Defining Security Properties. To define high-level security properties over specific pieces of sensitive data (in our case, the key to be imported), we first need to add such data to the companion model as previously described in this section. Consequently, because our representation relies on both the address and the size in bytes to represent and describe sensitive data, we can verify high-level properties over all relevant memory locations by specifying and verifying the properties in question using their companion representation. Moreover, using this intermediary model is essential for two main reasons:

- Using a common global view of sensitive information leads to a smaller specification effort compared to using each instance of sensitive data separately, provided they all are added to the model when they are defined, and removed when they are freed or overwritten.
- The MetAcsl plug-in is mostly used to express properties over data that is visible at a global level. Therefore, it mostly relies on global variables to express properties, of which the library avoids the usage. Although it *is* possible to use the `\formal` operator to refer to arguments of target functions, it is limited in that it is not possible to use it to refer to existing memory locations unrelated to function arguments.

Figure 7 shows the meta-properties expressing the integrity and the confidentiality of sensitive data represented by the companion model. We define two additional arrays with lines 1–2, `_write_sens` and `_read_sens`, that we use in the properties defined in lines 4–32 to help determine whether a sensitive data should be read or written. Line 4 provides `all_sens_data_integrity` as a name for our property, and lines 6–9 provide the set of target functions for the property, that is to say the set of functions in which the property shall be verified. We define it as our full subset of functions, from which we exclude the set defined in lines 7–9. The functions in line 7 are excluded due to parsing issues with MetAcsl, and the functions lines 8–9 are removed from the target because they are called using function pointers, whose support is limited

```
1 int _write_sens[MAX_SENS];
2 int _read_sens[MAX_SENS];
3
4 /*@ meta \prop, \name(all_sens_data_integrity),
5   \targets(
6     \diff(\ALL,
7       \union({tcti_fake_init, doLog, doLogBlob, getLogFile, // F-C crash
8         tcti_proxy_transmit_fake_tpm, tcti_fake_receive,
9         tcti_proxy_receive_fake_tpm }))), //function pointers support
10  \context(\writing),
11  ∀ int i; 0 ≤ i < _nb_sens ⇒ 0 ≤ _nb_sens ≤ MAX_SENS ⇒ //idx within bounds
12    0 < _len_sens[i] ⇒ //sensitive data exists
13    _write_sens[i] ≠ 1 ⇒ //sensitive data should not be writable
14    \separated(\written, (char*)_all_sens[i]+(0..(size_t)(_len_sens[i]-1)));*/
15
16 /*@ meta \prop, \name(all_sens_data_confidentiality),
17  \targets(
18    \diff(\ALL,
19      \union({tcti_fake_init, doLog, doLogBlob, getLogFile, // F-C crash
...
27        tcti_proxy_receive_fake_tpm}))),
28  \context(\reading),
29  ∀ int i; 0 ≤ i < _nb_sens ⇒ 0 ≤ _nb_sens ≤ MAX_SENS ⇒
30    0 < _len_sens[i] ⇒
31    _read_sens[i] ≠ 1 ⇒ //sensitive data should not be readable
32    \separated(\read, (char*)_all_sens[i]+(0..(size_t)(_len_sens[i]-1)));*/
```

Fig. 7. Meta-property for the integrity and confidentiality of sensitive data

in E-ACSL. Line 10 establishes a writing context with `\context(\writing)` for `all_sens_data_integrity`, meaning that the predicate defined in lines 11–14 must hold whenever a variable or a memory location is written, where `\written` refers to the written location. The predicate lines 11–14 states that, provided the tracking index `_nb_sens` is within bounds, for any index `i` referring to existing sensitive data, *if* the data stored at index `i` is not supposed to be readable (line 13), then the written location must be separated from any sensitive data. While MetAcsl does provide a clause to locally relax strong invariants, it is currently not natively possible to locally relax other types of meta-properties without excluding entire functions. In order to do so, for specific data stored at index `idx` in the model, we manually set `_write_sens[idx]` to `1` in parts of code where the data should be written, before it is written, and we set it back to `0` afterwards. Similarly, we may define the confidentiality of sensitive data `all_sens_data_confidentiality` with lines 16–32, using the `\reading` context, and by stating any read location must be separated from existing sensitive data in the target set of functions defined with lines 19–27. We manually set `_read_sens[idx]` for data of index `idx`to `1` to locally relax confidentiality, for instance in functions like `store_input_parameters` of Fig. 3 and `Tss2_Sys_Create_Prepare` in Fig. 5, as they can read already existing sensitive data to create new instances and copy of it.

MetAcsl translates the meta-properties defined in Fig. 2 and Fig. 7 into local ACSL assertions at each relevant program point. For example, for the integrity, an assertion of the defined separation will be added to the code before each writing operation, where `\written` will be replaced by the written location. For the validity invariant, `valid_sensitive`, an assertion is generated at every program point of the target functions. Once generated, the resulting annotated

```
#include <string.h>
/*@ assigns ((char*)dest)[0..n - 1] \from ((char*)src)[0..n-1];*/
void *memcpy_e_acsl (void * dest, const void *src, size_t n)
{return memcpy(dest, src, n);}
```

Fig. 8. `memcpy` wrapper function

code can be given as input to E-ACSL to be instrumented, and to convert the logical ACSL assertions into executable assertions. E-ACSL can then use GCC to compile this version of the code. The meta-properties are verified if all the generated executable assertions are verified at runtime.

Handling Standard Memory Manipulation Functions. By default, FRAMA-C uses its own C standard library, providing a number of its functions with ACSL contracts to specify their behaviors. It is however possible for an analyzed program to use libc functions that have not been defined (yet) in the FRAMA-C libc, for some of the defined types to mismatch those of the system libc, or even for other plug-ins to generate code that may be unusable by or incompatible with E-ACSL. In order to instrument and compile a program with E-ACSL, it can in turn be necessary to force the usage of the standard library of the system. Our subset of functions (and tpm2-tss in general) represent a case of such obligation.

However, some of these contracts include information about which parts of the memory may be modified by the corresponding function, through the use of the `assigns` clauses. In particular, `assigns A, B \from C, D;` specifies that the memory locations referred by variables `A` and `B` *can* be modified by the corresponding function, which reads variables `C` and `D` to do so. While E-ACSL does not currently support this clause, METACSL can rely on such annotations to generate assertions for meta-properties using the `\writing` or the `\reading` contexts. More specifically, if we consider our integrity (resp. confidentiality) meta-property applied to a function `f` specified with a minimal `assigns A \from C` clause, whenever `f` is called, METACSL will generate an assertion so that the written (resp. read) memory location referred by `A` is separated from any defined sensitive data. Without these specifications, METACSL will not be able to cover all situations where some meta-properties should be checked.

Thus, for functions of the libc such as `memcpy` that may read or write (non-local) variables, and whose contracts are unavailable to be used by METACSL for compatibility reasons with E-ACSL, we define wrapper functions with minimal contracts to describe such memory manipulation as shown in Fig. 8.

6 Evaluation and Key Lessons

The evaluation of our approach addresses the following research questions:

- **RQ1 (Expressiveness):** To what extent does this verification approach allow for the expression and the verification of high-level security properties on real-life code?

- **RQ2 (Effectiveness):** To what extent is this verification approach *effective* for the verification of high-level security properties on real-life code?
- **RQ3 (Efficiency):** To what extent is this verification approach *efficient* for the verification of high-level security properties on real-life code?

Verification Target. To answer the proposed research questions, we use a subset of 86 functions of the tpm2-tss library, of which 50 consist in marshal functions for different data types. The remaining 36 functions correspond to unique TSS operations involved in the import operation (without parameter encryption) defined by the `Esys_Create` function/the `TPM2_Create` command. The entire subset consists of approximately 20k lines of code, about 12k of which corresponding to interfaces and the remaining 8k corresponding to actual function implementations, with marshal functions defined as non-unfolded macros.

We construct the target using one of the integration tests of the library, and we remove from the subset cryptographic operations and their dependencies, and dependencies to libraries other than the C standard library. We also implement a few different versions of the code where we introduce faults designed to locally break the integrity and the confidentiality as they are defined in Fig. 7.

Tools Used. We use Frama-C v28.1 (Nickel) with the corresponding version of E-ACSL, and MetAcsl v0.6. We use MetAcsl to parse the defined high-level security properties and generate corresponding low-level ACSL assertions on each version of the code (with and without introduced errors). We then instrument the generated annotated code with E-ACSL to translate the annotations into C code to allow their verification at runtime. The output code is compiled by GCC through E-ACSL.

Verification Environment. For conducting our evaluation, we parse, instrument, compile and run each version of the code. All evaluations are performed on a desktop computer running Ubuntu 20.04.6 LTS, with an Intel(R) Core(TM) i5-6600 CPU @ 3.30 GHz, featuring 4 cores and 4 threads, with 16 GB RAM.

RQ1: Expressiveness. The MetAcsl plug-in allows users to define and express properties over data that are visible at a global level, thus mostly relying on global variables as targets. However, software specifications such as the TSS—and therefore library API code such as that of the tpm2-tss library—may require to avoid the usage of global state variables. Our approach allows rendering such data visible at a global level, and thus usable as target variables for the definition of high-level properties with MetAcsl, to be verified with other Frama-C plug-ins such as Wp or E-ACSL. In this way, it *extends* the capacities of MetAcsl, whose usage to handle data not visible at a global level is very challenging.

In our work, we focus on two high-level security properties, integrity and confidentiality of sensitive data, verified at runtime with E-ACSL. We do not define properties such as invariants relying directly on the values stored in modeled data between two program points, as their verification can appear difficult due to the current limitations of E-ACSL, and since lightweight runtime verification of security properties is an important goal by itself. However, such properties should be provable with WP, but would require a bigger specification effort.

RQ2: Effectiveness. In our approach, we use the E-ACSL plug-in to verify at runtime the assertions generated by METACSL for each security property. Using this method requires a much smaller specification effort on such real-life code than that of deductive verification for properties defined in ACSL.

Indeed, we define the integrity and the confidentiality of sensitive data by using the `\separated` clause to express memory separations, which are typically hard to prove with FRAMA-C on C codes relying on more dynamic management of the memory, as the WP plug-in does not currently rely on any aspect of separation logic; proving assertions about memory separations can require a lot of intermediary specifications, as highlighted in [13] and [24].

To ensure the integrity of sensitive data as defined in Fig. 7, METACSL generates about 800 low-level assertions on our subset of functions, and approximately 4200 low-level assertions for the confidentiality.

We did not detect any breach of integrity or confidentiality of sensitive data in our subset "as is". To ensure our approach is effective, we applied it to a few variations of the code in which we introduced errors to detect. For instance, we modified a few marshal functions to wrongly report where sensitive data was written. We also imagined a scenario in which a command buffer sent to the TPM could have been temporarily stored in a global variable for reissuing. We detected the resulting breaches of integrity in the former, and of confidentiality in the latter. In addition, we tested and detected situations where errors in specifications lead to sensitive data being added several times to the model, and the RTE safeguard checks performed by E-ACSL for each separation clause allowed for the detection of situations when sensitive data was wrongly removed from the representation after it had been deleted in the code.

RQ3: Efficiency. Parsing, instrumentation, compilation and execution times were similar for the main subset and its variations. Generating low-level assertions from high-level properties with METACSL took only about 8 s. Instrumentation with E-ACSL and compilation with GCC took much longer, reaching up to 15 min for the instrumentation, and up to 5 min for the compilation. Running a produced executable takes less than a second. Hence, the execution time remains compatible with executing numerous test cases on the same version of the code, as it should be typically required for a rigorous dynamic verification.

On average, the processing and evaluation of a version of the code takes approximately 19 min. We believe that this is considerably shorter than what would probably be required for deductive verification with WP, and requires much less time and effort for specification (from our experience with deductive verification). This should be confirmed with a more rigorous study focusing on comparing directly the usage of WP and E-ACSL for verifying the proposed properties. Additionally, the complete processing of a single version of the code is single-threaded, and thus can be further accelerated by running in parallel (for various versions of the code, or for different test cases).

6.1 Threats to Validity

Internal Validity. To verify the low-level specifications generated by MetAcsl from the high-level properties, we used E-ACSL to check them at runtime. The plug-in has however its fair share of limitations, including but not limited to the support of labels and logic definitions (which are supported by Wp), or the limited support of function pointers. Moreover, although our verification approach should not modify the behavior of the original code as is, we can not guarantee it to be on the same level as if using ghost code. Indeed, we have identified (and reported to developers) errors in ghost code instrumentation with E-ACSL.

External Validity. The conclusions about the expressiveness, effectiveness and efficiency of our approach might not hold for a complete TSS call to a TPM command, other programs using linked data structures, or with dependencies to external libraries. However, it should still be possible to conduct at least a partial verification by excluding problematic parts of the code.

6.2 Key Lessons

Verification Methodology. Our approach has allowed us to suggest a methodology for the verification of high-level security properties (such as integrity and confidentiality) of sensitive data on real-life code. We believe it to be relatively easy to apply for a user who does not possess in-depth prior knowledge of the target code. The methodology can be broken down into the following steps:

1. Define the memory representation to be used for sensitive data, as shown in Fig. 1.
2. Identify at a high level of abstraction the pieces of sensitive data whose security has to be ensured, and add them into the model.
3. Define security properties over sensitive data. Defining the integrity and the confidentiality as shown in Fig. 7 makes for a good starting point, and should help refine the approach in the following steps.
4. Parse, instrument, compile and execute the target code with the defined properties:
   (a) If the code lacks an entry point, it is up to the user to define a `main` function and to ensure the code can be compiled.
   (b) Parse the code and the properties with MetAcsl, instrument the resulting annotated code and compile the output with E-ACSL, and execute.
5. If possible, use the output of the executed code to refine the previous definitions:

(a) A detected violation of confidentiality should indicate either an "illegal" read of sensitive data, or that a sensitive data should not be considered as sensitive at the reported program point, or a "legal" read of sensitive data not yet handled by the current definitions. In the latter case, the user should locally relax the property by setting the corresponding element of `_read_sens` to `1` before the read, and setting it back to `0` after data has been read.

(b) Similarly, a detected violation of integrity should indicate either an "illegal" write of sensitive data, or that a sensitive data should not be considered as sensitive at the reported program point, or a "legal" write of sensitive data not yet handled by the current definitions. In the latter case, the user should locally relax the property by setting the corresponding element of `_write_sens` to `1` before the write, and setting it back to `0` after data has been written.

6. Repeat steps 4 and 5 until either no violation of properties are detected, or all reported violations correspond to breaches of integrity or confidentiality.

7 Related Work

TPM Related Safety and Security. Various case studies centered around functionalities of the TPM itself have emerged over the last decade. A recent formal analysis of the key exchange primitive of TPM 2.0 [23] provides a security model to capture TPM protections on keys and protocols. Authors of [22] propose a security model for the cryptographic support commands in TPM 2.0, proved using the CryptoVerif tool. A model of TPM commands was used to formalize the session-based HMAC authorization and encryption mechanisms [19]. Authors of [15] conducted a survey and established a study environment for the usability and security of TPM library APIs, including but not limited to the tpm2-tools library (which relies on tpm2-tss). They "conducted the first qualitative study targeting TPM library APIs and found that they are not developer-friendly".

To the best of our knowledge, none of the previously published works aim at verifying any implementation of the TSS.

Formal Verification of High-Level Properties and Real-Life Code. In Djoudi et al. [8] the authors present a large scale case study where deductive verification is applied on real-life C code to prove security properties.

Authors of [17] used MetAcsl to define meta-properties on two illustrative case studies, that they verified firstly with deductive verification using Wp, then secondly with testing using E-ACSL. The runtime verification of such properties in this work differs from ours in that they targeted a smaller code size, which relied on a more static management of the memory and global state variables, with unified representations, making it much easier to define meta-properties "out-of-the-box". In contrast, our approach provides the means to handle objects that conceptually contain the same information, but have different levels of representation in the code. Moreover, it provides a high level of automation, requiring very little specification work for *the chosen properties.*

We also validate the authors' claims that their "study demonstrates that it is easy to check meta-properties at runtime without extra annotation effort thanks to the combination of MetAcsl and E-ACSL, *as long as the specified properties are supported by the tools*".

8 Conclusion and Future Work

We presented in this paper preliminary work on how to define and verify security properties over sensitive data in real-life code. We targeted the tpm2-tss library, a popular implementation of the TPM Software Stack. As the communication layer between the TPM and the host platform or applications, this library is highly critical: to ensure the security of sensitive data to be stored on the TPM, it is highly desired to guarantee that such data can never be recovered without authorization while it is passing through the software stack. The library code is very different from more industrial codes, very complex, and challenging for verification tools.

We presented our verification result for a subset of 86 functions, on which we have verified, at runtime, that the target sensitive data is never modified or read when it is not supposed to. We have described some limitations of the tool and temporary solutions we used to address them. The real-life code was slightly simplified to remove dependencies to external libraries, but the logical behavior of the code corresponding to the function subset was maintained.

Future Work. Currently, only two high-level security properties over (some, but not all) pieces of sensitive data were verified at runtime, on a relatively simplified subset of the tpm2-tss library. In the future, we plan to perform a more complete verification work by reintroducing cryptographic capabilities of the TSS, and running the annotated code paired with a real TPM. Extending the range of security properties and improving the automation of this approach is another point of improvement, as well as establishing a method to perform a more extensive evaluation of this approach, and to allow for a careful comparison with deductive verification. Another interesting perspective of future work is to combine the deductive verification of Wp with the E-ACSL runtime verification to perform a more thorough and complete verification of high-level security properties.

Acknowledgment. Part of this work was supported by ANR (grants ANR-22-CE39-0014, ANR-22-CE25-0018) and French Ministry of Defense (PhD grant of Yani Ziani). We thank the anonymous referees for many helpful comments.

References

1. Arthur, W., Challener, D.: A Practical Guide to TPM 2.0: Using the Trusted Platform Module in the New Age of Security, 1st edn. Apress, USA (2015)
2. Baudin, P., et al.: The dogged pursuit of bug-free C programs: the Frama-C software analysis platform. Commun. ACM **64**(8), 56–68 (2021). https://doi.org/10.1145/3470569
3. Baudin, P., et al.: ACSL: ANSI/ISO C specification language. http://frama-c.com/acsl.html
4. Blanchard, A., Kosmatov, N., Loulergue, F.: Logic against ghosts: comparison of two proof approaches for a list module. In: Proceedings of the 34th Annual ACM/SIGAPP Symposium on Applied Computing, Software Verification and Testing Track (SAC-SVT 2019), pp. 2186–2195. ACM (2019). https://doi.org/10.1145/3297280.3297495
5. Blazy, S., Bühler, D., Yakobowski, B.: Structuring abstract interpreters through state and value abstractions. In: Bouajjani, A., Monniaux, D. (eds.) VMCAI 2017. LNCS, vol. 10145, pp. 112–130. Springer, Cham (2017). https://doi.org/10.1007/978-3-319-52234-0_7
6. Burghardt, J., Gerlach, J., Lapawczyk, T.: ACSL by example (2016). http://www.fokus.fraunhofer.de/download/acsl_by_example
7. Clarke, L.A., Rosenblum, D.S.: A historical perspective on runtime assertion checking in software development. SIGSOFT Softw. Eng. Notes **31**(3), 25–37 (2006). https://doi.org/10.1145/1127878.1127900
8. Djoudi, A., Hána, M., Kosmatov, N.: Formal verification of a JavaCard virtual machine with Frama-C. In: Huisman, M., Păsăreanu, C., Zhan, N. (eds.) FM 2021. LNCS, vol. 13047, pp. 427–444. Springer, Cham (2021). https://doi.org/10.1007/978-3-030-90870-6_23
9. Filliâtre, J.-C., Paskevich, A.: Why3—where programs meet provers. In: Felleisen, M., Gardner, P. (eds.) ESOP 2013. LNCS, vol. 7792, pp. 125–128. Springer, Heidelberg (2013). https://doi.org/10.1007/978-3-642-37036-6_8
10. Herrmann, P., Signoles, J.: RTE: runtime error annotation generation (2024). https://frama-c.com/download/frama-c-rte-manual.pdf
11. Kirchner, F., Kosmatov, N., Prevosto, V., Signoles, J., Yakobowski, B.: Frama-C: a software analysis perspective. Formal Asp. Comput. **27**(3), 573–609 (2015). https://doi.org/10.1007/s00165-014-0326-7
12. Kosmatov, N., Signoles, J.: A lesson on runtime assertion checking with Frama-C. In: Legay, A., Bensalem, S. (eds.) RV 2013. LNCS, vol. 8174, pp. 386–399. Springer, Heidelberg (2013). https://doi.org/10.1007/978-3-642-40787-1_29
13. Loulergue, F., Blanchard, A., Kosmatov, N.: Ghosts for lists: from axiomatic to executable specifications. In: Dubois, C., Wolff, B. (eds.) TAP 2018. LNCS, vol. 10889, pp. 177–184. Springer, Cham (2018). https://doi.org/10.1007/978-3-319-92994-1_11
14. Pariente, D., Signoles, J.: Static analysis and runtime assertion checking: contribution to security counter-measures. In: Symposium sur la Sécurité des Technologies de l'Information et des Communications (SSTIC) (2017)
15. Rao, S.P., Limonta, G., Lindqvist, J.: Usability and security of trusted platform module (TPM) library APIs. In: Chiasson, S., Kapadia, A. (eds.) Eighteenth Symposium on Usable Privacy and Security, SOUPS 2022, Boston, MA, USA, 7–9 August 2022, pp. 213–232. USENIX Association (2022). https://www.usenix.org/conference/soups2022/presentation/rao

16. Robles, V., Kosmatov, N., Prevosto, V., Rilling, L., Le Gall, P.: MetAcsl: specification and verification of high-level properties. In: Vojnar, T., Zhang, L. (eds.) TACAS 2019. LNCS, vol. 11427, pp. 358–364. Springer, Cham (2019). https://doi.org/10.1007/978-3-030-17462-0_22
17. Robles, V., Kosmatov, N., Prevosto, V., Rilling, L., Le Gall, P.: Tame your annotations with MetAcsl: specifying, testing and proving high-level properties. In: Beyer, D., Keller, C. (eds.) TAP 2019. LNCS, vol. 11823, pp. 167–185. Springer, Cham (2019). https://doi.org/10.1007/978-3-030-31157-5_11
18. Robles, V., Kosmatov, N., Prevosto, V., Rilling, L., Le Gall, P.: Methodology for specification and verification of high-level properties with MetAcsl. In: 9th IEEE/ACM International Conference on Formal Methods in Software Engineering (FormaliSE 2021), pp. 54–67. IEEE (2021). https://doi.org/10.1109/FormaliSE52586.2021.00012
19. Shao, J., Qin, Y., Feng, D.: Formal analysis of HMAC authorisation in the TPM2.0 specification. IET Inf. Secur. **12**(2), 133–140 (2018). https://doi.org/10.1049/iet-ifs.2016.0005
20. Signoles, J.: The E-ACSL perspective on runtime assertion checking. In: ACM International Workshop on Verification and mOnitoring at Runtime EXecution (VORTEX), pp. 8–12. ACM, New York (2021). https://doi.org/10.1145/3464974.3468451
21. Trusted Computing Group: Trusted Platform Module Library Specification, Family "2.0", Level 00, Revision 01.59 (2019). https://trustedcomputinggroup.org/work-groups/trusted-platform-module/. Accessed May 2023
22. Wang, W., Qin, Yu., Yang, B., Zhang, Y., Feng, D.: Automated security proof of cryptographic support commands in TPM 2.0. In: Lam, K.-Y., Chi, C.-H., Qing, S. (eds.) ICICS 2016. LNCS, vol. 9977, pp. 431–441. Springer, Cham (2016). https://doi.org/10.1007/978-3-319-50011-9_33
23. Zhang, Q., Zhao, S.: A comprehensive formal security analysis and revision of the two-phase key exchange primitive of TPM 2.0. Comput. Netw. **179** (2020). https://doi.org/10.1016/j.comnet.2020.107369
24. Ziani, Y., Kosmatov, N., Loulergue, F., Pérez, D.G., Bernier, T.: Towards formal verification of a TPM software stack. In: Herber, P., Wijs, A. (eds.) iFM 2023. LNCS, vol. 14300, pp. 93–112. Springer, Cham (2023). https://doi.org/10.1007/978-3-031-47705-8_6

Cyclone: A New Tool for Verifying/Testing Graph-Based Structures
Tool Paper

Hao Wu[1(✉)], Thomas Flinkow[1(✉)], and Dominique Méry[2(✉)]

[1] Department of Computer Science,
Maynooth University, Maynooth, Ireland
haowu@cs.nuim.ie, thomas.flinkow@mu.ie
[2] LORIA and Telecom Nancy,
University of Lorraine, Nancy, France
dominique.mery@loria.fr

Abstract. We present a new tool called Cyclone that can be used for verifying and testing graph-based models. Different from other verification tools, Cyclone provides users with a unique way of building models and specifying their properties, by explicitly constructing and reasoning about graphs. As graphs can naturally capture both static and dynamic behaviours of a system, this allows users to represent many challenging problems. In this tool paper, we describe Cyclone's basic features through different examples. Our preliminary evaluation results show that Cyclone has a promising potential in handling verification tasks from various domains and good usability for those who are not familiar with using verification tools.

1 Introduction

Formal methods aim to use mathematically rigorous techniques to help developers build reliable and dependable software. In the past few decades, an enormous number of tools and techniques have been created for different types of verification tasks. Those tools range from model checkers to theorem provers. This empowers software engineers to design and build more reliable software for modern society. The driverless Paris Metro line 14 is one successful application of using B models for deriving the correct code [1]. Another notable example is Airbus France, which uses a series of formal verification tools to develop avionics software for its aircraft [2–4].

Recent work has aimed to simplify the usage of formal methods tools. This often provides an integrated development environment (IDE) that helps developers write mathematical proofs, or a toolbox that can perform automated reasoning for a system. For example, the Rodin platform is an IDE for engineers writing

H. Wu—is supported by France Excellence-NUI Research Residency grant.
T. Flinkow—is supported by Science Foundation Ireland grant 20/FFP-P/8853.
D. Méry—is supported by EBRP Plus ANR Project (ANR-19-CE25-0010) and ICSPA ANR Project (ANR-21-CE25-0015).

© The Author(s), under exclusive license to Springer Nature Switzerland AG 2025
M. Huisman and F. Howar (Eds.): TAP 2024, LNCS 15153, pp. 107–124, 2025.
https://doi.org/10.1007/978-3-031-72044-4_6

Event-B proofs [5] while the TLA+ toolbox enables automatic translation from an algorithm written in PlusCal to a TLA specification [6,7]. Other tools such as Alloy advocate light-weight formal methods by providing an integrated IDE for writing relational logic to describe properties of a system [8,9].

Though many tools have been developed [6,10–12] very little efforts have been made to make formal verification tools more accessible to users without significant mathematical backgrounds [6,11,13–16]. In this paper, we introduce a new tool, called Cyclone, that is designed to make verification more accessible to a wider community, through an easy-to-understand graphical modelling environment.

Cyclone uses a novel algorithm for *bounded checking*. This algorithm traverses the graph representation of a Cyclone specification and outputs a set of graph conditions that can be efficiently verified by an SMT solver. This makes Cyclone particularly good at verifying/testing systems that can be represented as graphs such as a transition system.

The design philosophy of Cyclone is representing a verification task using a graph. Many interesting problems from different domains, including verification and testing, can be captured by graphs—for example, we could use a state machine to represent different states of dynamics of a free-fall ball, while a control flow diagram may be used to describe a computer program. This allows users to shift their focus from understanding complex formalism to building a simple graph. The visual impact and clarity of a graph can significantly help others to understand what problems they are trying to model.

2 Architecture

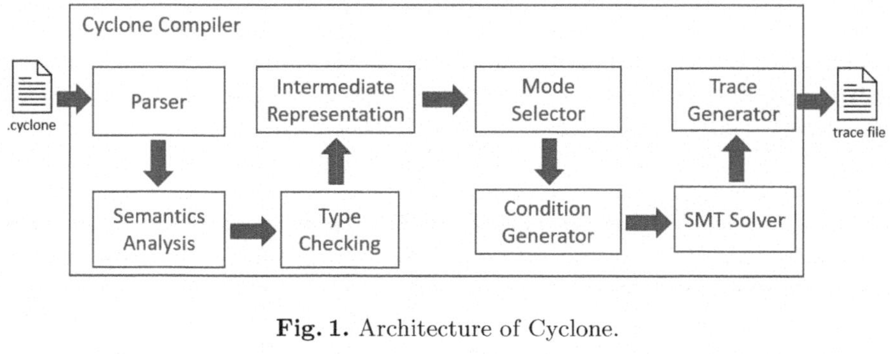

Fig. 1. Architecture of Cyclone.

The architecture of Cyclone is shown in Fig. 1. Cyclone is written in Java and consists of more than 100k lines of code including build scripts, test cases, configurations and other related projects. We designed about 180 grammar rules for the Cyclone specification language and use ANTLR for generating lexers and parsers. The type checker ensures the type safety of a specification, and produces relevant error messages if there are any semantic errors in a specification. We have designed a *state matrix* as an intermediate representation (IR) to capture all necessary information needed from the front-end of the Cyclone compiler. Once this IR is produced, we use a novel algorithm to generate a set of graph conditions with respect to the bounds chosen by users. These graph conditions can then efficiently be verified by an off-the-shelf SMT solver[1]. Finally, the trace generator produces a *trace* or *counter-example* for the specification (depending on the mode it is running as).

2.1 Usage

We provide the following 3 different ways of running Cyclone:

Command-line. Users can download the packages from https://classicwuhao.github.io/cyclone_tutorial/installation.html and launch Cyclone in a terminal window by typing the following command:

```
java -jar cyclone.jar <SampleSpec.cyclone>
```

where `<SampleSpec.cyclone>` is a Cyclone specification file (note the mandatory file ending `.cyclone`). The result of a successful check (verification) is written to standard output. If there is an example/counter-example, a trace file will be generated. The instructions can be found at: https://classicwuhao.github.io/cyclone_tutorial/instructions.html.

Visual Studio Code Extension. We provide a Visual Studio Code extension for users to run/check their cyclone specifications within Visual Studio code. This extension provides multiple features such as syntax highlighting, semantics checking, and viewing a trace in a graphical representation. To successfully use this Visual Studio Code extension, users are required to have Java preinstalled. This extension and detailed instructions can be downloaded from: https://github.com/classicwuhao/CycloneVSCodePlugin.

Web Interface. We also built a web interface for using Cyclone so that users do not need to install any packages locally. This web interface can be accessed from https://cyclone.cs.nuim.ie. It also links to a short Cyclone tutorial website that includes many interesting examples.

This tool paper describes the main features of Cyclone (Sects. 3 and 4) and finally the results from our preliminary evaluation (Sects. 5) show that Cyclone has the potential to verify models from various domains.

---

[1] Currently, Cyclone uses Z3 [17] as its default solver. Work is in progress to also support the CVC5 solver.

3 Building Graphs

In general, a Cyclone specification describes a *graph* structure and the kinds of properties to be checked/verified for that graph. Essentially, a valid Cyclone specification may contain the following 5 blocks in order:

1. A *variable* block: declares a set of variables that can be computed during the transition in a graph.
2. A *node* block: specifies a set of nodes in the graph.
3. An *edge* block: specifies a set of transitions in the graph.
4. An *invariant* block: specifies a set of properties to be hold after any transition.
5. A *goal* block: specifies properties of the graph and how Cyclone should find a set of particular paths.

All these blocks are optional—hence, the simplest complete specification is an *empty* graph: `graph G { }`. On the other hand, Listing 1.1 shows an example specification containing all 5 blocks.

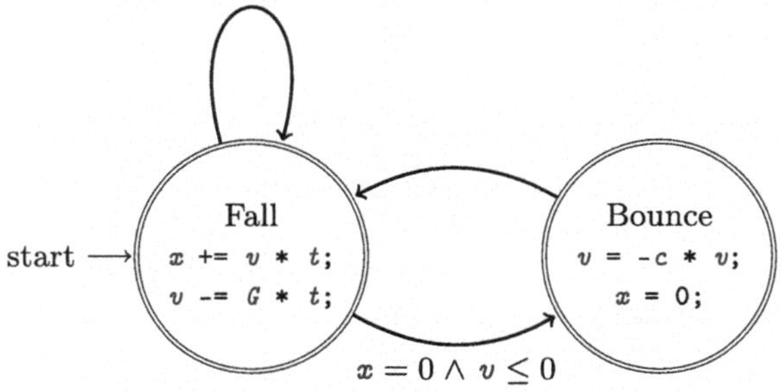

Fig. 2. A transition graph for a bouncing ball.

Listing 1.1. A Cyclone specification modelling a transition graph of a bouncing ball hybrid system depicted in Fig. 2. The variable block (Line 2–6) contains all necessary variables for computing the ball's position x, which can never be below 0 (Line 22). The node and edge blocks (Line 8–20) model different states of the ball. The goal block (Line 24–26) instructs Cyclone to explore a counter-example within a set of given bounds. Note that t is the discretisation unit for time.

```
1  graph Bouncing_Ball {
2      real x where x >= 0;                 // position
3      real v;                              // velocity
4      real t where t >= 0;                 // time
5      const real G = 9.81;                 // gravitational force
6      real c where c >= 0 && c <= 1;       // constant (energy loss)
7
8      normal start final node Fall {
9          x += v * t;
10         v -= G * t;
11     }
12
13     normal final node Bounce {
14         v = -c * v;
15         x = 0;
```

```
16         }
17
18         edge { Fall -> Fall }
19         edge { Fall -> Bounce where x == 0 && v <= 0; }
20         edge { Bounce -> Fall }
21
22         invariant inv { x >= 0; } // position of the ball is never < 0
23
24         goal { // defines different bounds for Cyclone to explore.
25             check for 2,3,4,5
26         }
27 }
```

3.1 Variables

Cyclone provides 6 different data types `int`, `bool`, `real`, `enum`, `record`, and `bv` (bitvector) to facilitate users building expressive models. The `enum` (enumeration) data type allows users to pre-define a list of constants while `record` data types can be used to build complex data structures. Further, sets and relations can be encoded using `bv`, operations over sets are captured by using bitwise operators for `bv`.

3.2 Conditional Variables

In Cyclone, users can create a special type of variable called *conditional variable*. This means that during any computation a variable must satisfy a boolean condition. To create a conditional variable, users create a normal variable followed by a `where` clause which specifies a condition. For example, Line 6 in Listing 1.1 uses a conditional (real data type) variable for representing energy loss, and (during any computation) this loss must stay between 0 and 1.

3.3 Nodes and Edges

Cyclone allows the use of modifiers to create different kinds of nodes in a graph. The modifiers that can be applied to construct different types of nodes are summarised in Table 1. The modifier `normal` can be used to create a computational node that contains code that is executed every time the node is visited, while a node that represents a pure node in a graph is declared using the modifier `abstract`.

Creating a set of edges one by one is a tedious task. To ease this, Cyclone provides a list of syntax to facilitate users to create multiple edges at a time. The syntax and its semantics are listed in Table 2.

Table 1. The list of modifiers for nodes in Cyclone.

Modifier	Type of Node
`abstract`	A pure node in a graph that does not contain any computational instructions
`start`	An entry node in a graph where a path (to be discovered) begins. Only exactly one starting node is allowed in a graph
`final`	A terminating node in a graph where a path (to be discovered) ends. Multiple terminating nodes can be defined
`normal`	A node that contains computational instructions

Table 2. Syntax for creating edges in Cyclone.

Syntax	Semantics
A -> *B*	Creates an *unidirectional* edge from *A* to *B*
A <-> *B*	Creates a *bidirectional* edge between *A* and *B*
A -> *B*, *C*, ..., *N*	Creates a set of *unidirectional* edges from *A* to each of *B*, *C*, ..., *N*, respectively
A <-> *B*, *C*, ..., *N*	Creates a set of *bidirectional* edges between *A* and each of *B*, *C*, ..., *N*
A -> *	Creates a set of *unidirectional* edges from node *A* to every other node in the graph, *including A itself*
A <-> *	Creates a set of *bidirectional* edges between node *A* to every other node in the graph, *including A itself*
A -> +	Creates a set of *unidirectional* edges from node *A* to every other node in the graph, *excluding A itself*
A <-> +	Creates a set of *bidirectional* edges between *A* to every other node in the graph, *excluding A itself*

The notation `[ ]` may be used to specify a list of nodes to be excluded from edge creation. This notation by default is optional but can be added to the syntax listed above to further facilitate edge creation. For example, `A -> * [B, C]` means that node *A* can go to every other node in the graph except for nodes *B* and *C*. Hence, `A -> * [A]` creates the same set of edges as `A -> +`.

3.4 Conditional Transitions

A conditional transition in Cyclone is an edge that is attached to a boolean condition. This means that a transition can happen only when its condition is satisfied. Otherwise, a transition can never be triggered. Similar to conditional variables, a `where` clause is used to specify conditions for a transition. For example, Line 19 in Listing 1.1 shows that to move from node *Fall* to *Bounce* the height of ball must be 0 and its velocity is equal or below 0.

Non-determinism. Non-determinism is introduced when multiple conditional transitions are satisfied. Typically, Cyclone will choose the *"first"* conditional transition. However, users can always use a path condition to instruct Cyclone to select a specific transition.

Listing 1.2. Multiple conditional transitions can occur when ***coin*** ≥ 4.

```
edge t1 { Select -> Coke where coin >= 2; }
edge t2 { Select -> Coffee where coin >= 3; }
edge t3 { Select -> Beer where coin >= 4; }
```

Given the example in Listing 1.2, we can select three different kinds of beverage here if we insert 4 coins. We can always force Cyclone to pick ***Coffee*** by specifying a single path condition: ***Select -> Coffee***, or use **enumerate** (see Sect. 4.3) like in Listing 1.4 to ensure that all satisfiable conditional transitions are selected.

3.5 Path Conditions

A path condition essentially is a constraint that allows Cyclone to discover the kind of paths users prefer, and can be built by using one or more predefined path operators (shown in Table 3). These predefined path operators can describe many interesting properties of a path. For example, Listing 1.3 asks Cyclone to find all possible Hamiltonian paths from any node—note that in order to define multiple starting nodes in Cyclone, we add a dummy starting node that connects to every other node in the graph.

Listing 1.3. Discovering all possible Hamiltonian paths from any node in the graph in Fig. 3. The `enumerate for 5` (Line 15) command instructs Cyclone to find all possible paths that have a length of 5 (since this graph has 6 nodes) with respect to the path condition describing that each node must be visited exactly once (Line 16–17).

```
1  graph G {
2      abstract start node S {}
3      abstract final node A {}
4      abstract final node B {}
5      abstract final node C {}
6      abstract final node D {}
7      abstract final node E {}
8      edge { S -> + } // from S to every other node but S
9      edge { A -> B,C,E }
10     edge { B -> D }
11     edge { C -> D }
12     edge { D -> E,C }
13     edge { E -> B,C }
14     goal {
15         enumerate for 5
16             condition (S^{1} && A^{1} && B^{1} &&
17                 C^{1} && D^{1} && E^{1})
18     }
19 }
```

Table 3. Path operators in Cyclone. p denotes a path to be discovered.

Operator	Meaning	Example	Explanation
n	a node named n	`A`	p must include node `A` at least once.
`_`	any valid node	`A -> _ -> A`	a cycle starting and ending at node `A` with path length 2.
`->`	a single transition	`A -> B`	p must include the transition `A -> B` at least once.
`^{`i`:`j`}`	a node or a transition must occur between i and j times (inclusive)	`(A -> B)^{2}`	p must include transition `A -> B` exactly twice.
`>>`i	place a node or transition in the i-th (starting from 0; default value is 0) position (from *left to right*) in a path	`>>2(A -> B)`	p must contain the transition `A -> B` which must appear in the third position of p.
`<<`i	place a node or transition in the i-th (starting from 0; default value is 0) position (from *right to left*) in a path	`<<(A -> B)`	p must contain the transition `A -> B` which must appear at the end of p.

4 Specifying Properties

4.1 Assertions

Different from path conditions, an assertion in Cyclone specifies a so-called *content condition*, which instructs Cyclone on how to explore a graph based on

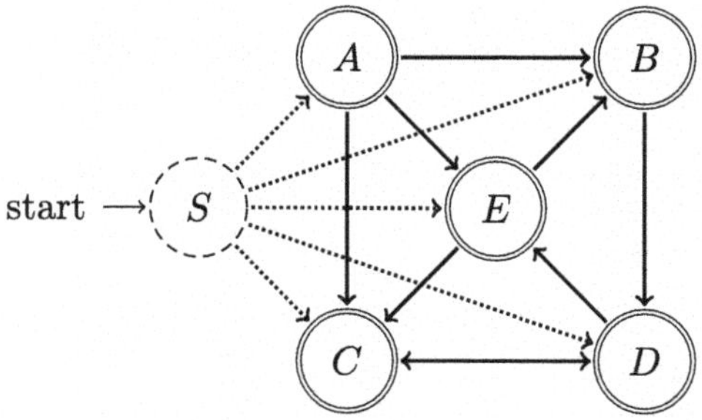

Fig. 3. A graph that is captured by the Cyclone specification in Listing 1.3. We add an additional node S so that the Hamiltonian path can start at any node A, B, C, D, or E.

specific computation instructions. Usually, both path and content conditions are required to specify the properties to be verified.

There are four different ways to write an assertion in Cyclone. In the following, let ϕ denote our property (or condition) to be checked within a graph.

`assert` ϕ; is the most common form of an assertion, requiring ϕ to be satisfied only in the last node of a path. This form of assertion is visualised in Fig. 4 and is useful for checking whether there exists a path that leads to the satisfaction of our property ϕ.

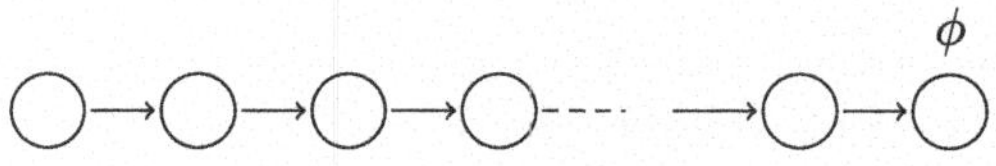

Fig. 4. ϕ is satisfied at the end of a path.

`assert` ϕ `in` $(S_1, S_2, \ldots, S_i)$; uses an `in` clause to specify a list of nodes. This means that ϕ only needs to be satisfied in one of the nodes specified in the `in` clause. A visualisation of `assert`ϕ`in` (S); is shown in Fig. 5, where ϕ must be satisfied whenever node S appears in the path. This is particularly useful for specifying a property for a subset of nodes.

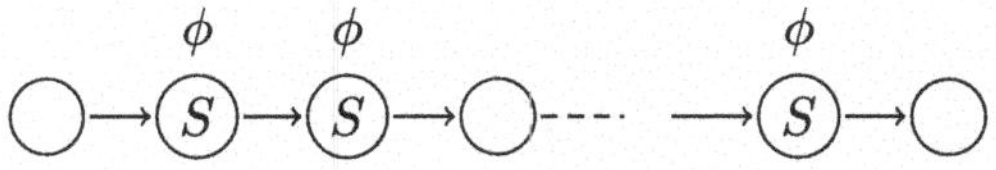

Fig. 5. ϕ is satisfied in node S.

`assert some` ϕ; means that ϕ needs to be satisfied in at least one of the nodes in a path. This is equivalent to the **EF** operator in Computation Tree Logic (CTL). This type of assertion is shown in Fig. 6.

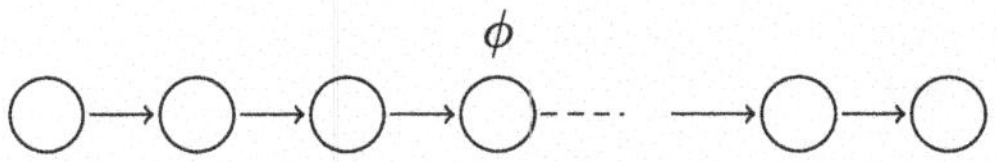

Fig. 6. ϕ must be satisfied in at least one of the nodes in the path to be discovered.

`assert always` ϕ; means that ϕ needs to be satisfied in every node in a path. This is equivalent to the **EG** operator in CTL. Thus, we can visualise this type of assertion as shown in Fig. 7.

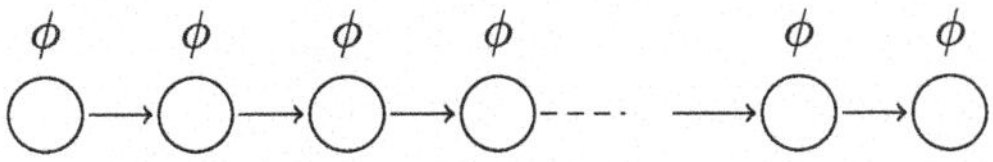

Fig. 7. ϕ is satisfied in every node in the path to be discovered.

Example. We now use a simple counting machine to illustrate how assertions can be used in Cyclone. This machine is depicted in Fig. 8. This counting machine uses an internal integer variable c as a counter and can use the following three different instructions:

1. Reset (R): reset counter c to 0.
2. Increment (I): increment counter c by 1.
3. Decrement (D): decrement counter c by 1.

To model all possible behaviours of this machine, we add transitions for each instruction resulting in a transition graph in Fig. 8. Assume that our initial instruction always begins with a reset (R). Then, an instruction sequence can now be formed by simply following the transitions in Fig. 8. For example, after executing the following instruction sequence our counter will be 0.

$$R \rightarrow I \rightarrow D \rightarrow D \rightarrow I$$

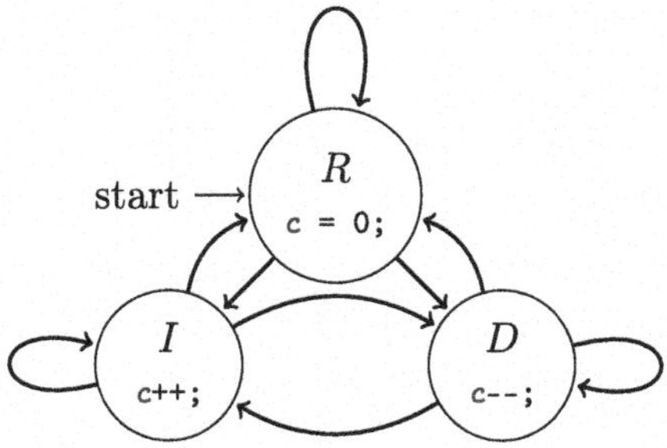

Fig. 8. A graph that models all possible transitions among three instructions: Reset, Increment and Decrement.

Now, suppose we would like to find all possible instruction sequences that have the following properties:

1. Each instruction sequence must use 6 instructions.
2. After evaluating each instruction sequence, our counter must be equal to 3.
3. The Decrement (D) instruction must appear in each instruction sequence.

To describe these properties, we can use an assertion together with our path condition described in Sect. 3. Listing 1.4 shows a complete Cyclone specification for this counting machine. After compiling and running this specification, Cyclone successfully finds a total of 6 different instruction sequences, shown in the following:

1. $R \rightarrow I \rightarrow I \rightarrow D \rightarrow I \rightarrow I$
2. $R \rightarrow I \rightarrow D \rightarrow I \rightarrow I \rightarrow I$
3. $R \rightarrow I \rightarrow I \rightarrow I \rightarrow I \rightarrow D$
4. $R \rightarrow I \rightarrow I \rightarrow I \rightarrow D \rightarrow I$
5. $R \rightarrow D \rightarrow I \rightarrow I \rightarrow I \rightarrow I$
6. $R \rightarrow D \rightarrow R \rightarrow I \rightarrow I \rightarrow I$

Listing 1.4. A Cyclone specification for the simple counting machine in Fig. 8. The `goal` section (Line 11–16) describes finding all possible instruction sequences satisfying the properties mentioned above. The `assert` statement (Line 12) indicates the content condition: our counter must be equal to 3 after executing an instruction sequence. The `condition` statement (Line 14) specifies a path condition: the Decrement (D) instruction must be used somewhere. The command `enumerate for 5` (Line 13) tells Cyclone to find all possible paths that have a length of 5 (6 instructions). The `reach` statement (Line 15) specifies that it can reach any one of the instructions at the end of an instruction sequence.

```
1  graph Counter {
2      int c;
3      normal start node R { c = 0; }
4      normal node I { c++; }
5      normal node D { c--; }
6
7      edge { R -> * }
8      edge { I -> * }
9      edge { D -> * }
10
11     goal {
12         assert c == 3;
13         enumerate for 5
14             condition (D)
15             reach (R, I, D)
16     }
17 }
```

4.2 Invariants

An invariant in Cyclone specifies a property or condition must always hold, no matter which transition takes place in a graph[2]. If a Cyclone specification contains at least one invariant, then Cyclone will switch to counter-example finding mode. This means Cyclone will try to discover a counter-example that violates the defined invariants. Semantically, an invariant in Cyclone must hold in each transition, i.e. after leaving a node—in other words, an invariant is allowed to be violated inside a node during computation. For example, the invariant at Line 22 in Listing 1.1 states that the height of a ball is never below 0.

By default, an invariant must hold after each transition in a graph (or, if the node is a final node, after computation in that node has finished). We refer to this type of invariant as a *global invariant* for a model. However, sometimes users may express an invariant for a subset of nodes, a so-called *local invariant*. In this case, an `in` clause is used for specifying a subset of nodes. The code in Listing 1.5 expresses that the invariant $y \geq 0$ must hold when transitioning away from the nodes *S1*, *S2*, and *S5* (or, if the nodes are final, when computation in these nodes has finished).

Listing 1.5. An invariant *A* with an `in` clause specifying a subset of nodes.

```
invariant A { y >= 0; } in (S1, S2, S5);
```

4.3 Checking Modes

Cyclone performs bounded checking for a specification. Users must specify one or more path lengths when checking a specification. If there exists a path that satisfies the conditions in a specification, Cyclone will generate a *trace*. A trace in Cyclone contains concrete values for each variable at each node in a path found.

Cyclone supports 5 checking modes. A summary of available checking modes is listed in Table 4. If *Combo Mode* is enabled, Cyclone will combine all specified path lengths into a single condition and perform *one* check. This is particularly useful for scenarios that users would like to quickly determine whether there exists a solution for multiple bounds. Operating in *Separation Mode* can help users determine whether each individual path length has a solution or not. Thus, when *Separation Mode* is enabled, Cyclone performs multiple checks.

[2] An **AG** operator can be directly mapped to an invariant in Cyclone.

Table 4. A summary of checking modes in Cyclone.

Mode	Command	Meaning	Example
Standard	`check for` k	Checks all paths that have exact length k. Returns a single solution if the specification is satisfied.	`check for 5`
Combo	`check for` $k_1, \ldots, k_i$	Performs a single check for all paths that have length $k_1, \ldots, k_i$. Returns a single solution if the specification can be satisfied by at least one of the path lengths.	`check for 3,6,7`
Separation	`check each` $k_1, \ldots, k_i$	Checks all paths that have length $k_1, \ldots, k_i$ individually. Returns multiple solutions if the specification can be satisfied by multiple path lengths.	`check each 2,9,10`
Range	`check upto` k	Checks all paths that have length from 1 upto k. Returns a single solution if the specification can be satisfied by at least one of the path lengths.	`check upto 10`
Enumeration	`enumerate for` k	Enumerates all possible solutions that have path length k.	`enumerate for 3`

5 Preliminary Evaluation

To extensively and effectively evaluate the robustness of Cyclone, we have collected and designed more than 200+ sample problems for testing Cyclone. We have found and fixed more than 120 issues in the past year. We have successfully used Cyclone to verify Event-B hybrid models [18]. All evaluation data including regression tests is available on our workflow. Each test workflow run produces a pack of trace files that can be downloaded to further validate the verification results from Cyclone. Due to the page limitation, we present some of our preliminary evaluation results in Table 5.

In Table 5, we use four categories (Graph, Program Verification, Hybrid Systems and Model Checking) to show that Cyclone is able to handle problems from different domains. In fact, all of our sample Cyclone specification files, including those shown in Table 5, can be run locally or online (using GitHub workflow). The results showed in Table 5 are from GitHub-hosted runners. The hardware specification for runners is 2-core CPU (x86_64) with 7 GB of RAM. The underlying solver Cyclone uses for evaluation is Z3-v4.12.4. The results can also be replicated locally on any machine that has java installed.

Table 5. Highlight of different category from our problem set. **Size(loc)**=line of code in a Cyclone specification (counted using sloc on GitHub, the size may vary if other tool is used.). **Mode**=checking mode. **Condition**= number of verification conditions generated. **Time (sec)**=the amount of time spending on verification. The unit here is second.

	Name	Size (loc)	Mode	Condition	Time (sec)
Graph	Dfa [19]	30	Enumeration	76	0.169
	Euler Path	37	Standard	506	0.037
	Hamilton Path	54	Standard	212	0.033
	Hamilton Cycle	50	Standard	252	0.031
	Package Installation	63	Enumeration	519	2.283
Program	Swap	34	Standard	87	0.038
	If-else [20]	27	Standard	224	0.021
	Loop [20]	28	Seperation	352	0.042
	Dijkstra's ring token [21]	50	Standard	22546	0.049
	McCarthy91	38	Standard	1452985	9.847
Hybrid	Bouncing Ball (v1)	27	Combo	7457	0.033
	Bouncing Ball (v2)	31	Combo	12377	0.045
	Car Position (v1)	76	Standard	560	0.108
	Car Position (v2) [22]	76	Standard	568	0.641
	Water Tank [23]	101	Standard	2549	17.985
h i i+ hModel Checking	Circuit (Sequential) [24]	56	Combo	443	0.036
	2 bit Counter	33	Combo	445	0.022
	Modulo 4 Counter[24]	29	Seperation	370	0.081
	Gate	26	Combo	1291	0.026
	Vending Machine (v1) [24]	31	Combo	780	0.021
	Vending Machine (v2) [24]	52	Combo	3839	0.071
	Defuse Bomb	94	Combo	21211	0.383

Performance. Overall, Cyclone is able to verify most of the problems within seconds. Depending on the checking mode specified, the verification time may vary. For example, Cyclone spends more time if combo mode is enabled since it can specify multiple path lengths. The larger the path length (bound) given, the more time is needed for verification. For example, we specified a 200 path length for McCarthy91 function and Cyclone generates more than 1.4 million conditions and took 9.87 s to verify. In general, Cyclone generates more conditions when verifying a hybrid system (Hybrid category in Table 5). This sometimes imposes a great challenge on the underlying solver. Modelling a hybrid system requires users to program the dynamics of a system using Cyclone. The code usually requires some complex computation over real numbers. For example, the *Bouncing Ball* ($v2$) example in Table 5 models the dynamics of a bouncing ball. Cyclone generates more than 12000 conditions and verifies it within a second using Combo mode. However, Cyclone generates 2549 conditions for the *Water Tank* example and it took nearly 18 s to verify. This indicates that the size of conditions does not always have an impact on verification. In fact, the verification performance is mainly affected by the computational complexity of each condition. The conditional transitions in the *Water Tank* example have many more complex calculations over the set of real numbers than the transitions in *Bouncing Ball* example. These conditions take Z3 much more time to solve compared to simpler conditions.

6 Related Work

In this section, we briefly discuss how Cyclone compares to some of the well-known tools to show its uniqueness in the area of formal verification. We choose the following tools mainly because their specifications are close to Cyclone's graph notations or can be explicitly represented as graphs.

Alloy. Alloy is a *model finder* that allows users to describe structural constraints and analyse them [25]. Its specification language is based on first-order logic. The initial design of Alloy is based on relational logic [8], later is extended to support higher-order relational constraint solver [9]. Alloy has been used in modelling software widely since. Cyclone is fundamentally different Alloy's core idea by explicitly describing a complex system using a graph notation. The graph notation is more natural close to the design of a system. This can help users easily to incrementally analyse behaviours of a system via its assertions and invariants. Further, the generated trace can be considered as simulation of a system.

TLA. TLA+ toolbox provides a set of tools allows users to check a specification [6,7]. Among these tools, it uses a model checker to check safety and liveness properties. Though a TLC specification does not explicitly specify a graph, it models a system based on different states, namely a transition system. It may appear that the semantics of a Cyclone specification looks similar to model checking. However, Cyclone's explicit graph notations make it more natural for modelling transition systems. As long as a system can be modelled as a state machine, then users can directly mapped to a Cyclone specification. Further, Cyclone's path conditions allow users to explore a system via graph properties. This could be useful for testing and simulating a particular part of a system.

Uppaal. Uppaal is a tool that allows users to model, simulate and verify real-time systems [26–28]. It is designed for systems that can be modelled as a set of non-deterministic processes. These processes are controlled by real-valued clocks, their communication is done through shared variables. It uses a model checker to perform reachability analysis. Different from Uppaal, Cyclone focus on much more general graph structures rather than specific automata. Cyclone and UPPAAL share different design philosophy. We intentionally designed Cyclone using a general form of graphs such that it can capture structures as long as can be described using a graph. Any specific automata oriented design can be considered as an extension to our existing Cyclone specification language. In this way, our design can be reused and extended to specific context.

Forge. Forge is a educational tool that is built for teaching introductory formal methods and modelling [16]. In fact, Forge is based on Alloy and it adds a number of features that enhance teaching and learning experience of formal modelling. Compare to Forge, Cyclone is an independent language and it simplifies the idea of building a verification task. Cyclone's graphical representation of a specification is particular useful for analysing, exchanging and sharing ideas of a verification task. We have taught Cyclone to 2nd year Computer Science students and they found Cyclone is not only useful for learning formal methods but also understanding other subjects such as theory of computation, testing and graph theories.

ProB. ProB is an animator and model checker for the B method, that is used to check the consistency of a B machine [29,30]. It is based on Prolog and it interprets a specification by using resolution. The simulation with ProB enable users to locate inconsistencies in a specification over finite models. Compare to ProB, the graph representation of an Event-B specification is much simpler and intuitive. The mapping between Event-B elements to Cyclone is quite straightforward. Cyclone is then able to find counter-example of a proposed invariant in Event-B model quickly [18]. Further, Cyclone can also be used for simulation with trace generation (visualisation). This can help users to analyse and understand the cause of errors in a specification.

6.1 Limitations

Cyclone is a very new tool and is particular good at verifying structures that can be explicitly expressed as graphs. This means that mapping from a transition system to a Cyclone specification is very straightforward. The simple graph notations further enable users to explore a system' behaviours via graph properties. Currently, Cyclone has two limitations (1) The initial design of Cyclone focuses on simplicity and usability (using simple graph notations). Hence, it does not support using quantifiers when specifying properties of a system. This may cause users repeatedly writing similar properties multiple times. To balance between expressiveness and simplicity, we plan to introduce a light-weight quantified assertion to free users from such tedious tasks. (2) Cyclone does not explicitly support collection data types such as sets and lists. Though modelling sets and lists can be achieved by using bit-vector in Cyclone, it will be more user friendly to directly support such data types. Based on our experience of using SMT solvers [31,32], encoding collection data types is quite straightforward and the challenge here is to design user friendly notations.

7 Conclusion

In this paper, we present our new specification language Cyclone and highlight some of its features. By combining path conditions with content conditions (assertions and invariants), Cyclone is particularly powerful in verifying models that can be explicitly represented as transition systems. The design philosophy of Cyclone is to make verification accessible to a wide community, through an easy to understand graphical modelling environment. In the future, we plan to integrate Cyclone with multiple SMT solvers and build an ecosystem so that it can be reached by more users.

References

1. Lecomte, T., Servat, T., Pouzancre, G.: Formal methods in safety-critical railway systems. In: 10th Brasilian Symposium on Formal Methods (2007)
2. Ferdinand, C., et al.: Reliable and precise WCET determination for a real-life processor. In: Henzinger, T.A., Kirsch, C.M. (eds.) EMSOFT 2001. LNCS, vol. 2211, pp. 469–485. Springer, Heidelberg (2001). https://doi.org/10.1007/3-540-45449-7_32
3. Cousot, P., et al.: The ASTREÉ analyzer. In Sagiv, M. (ed.) Programming Languages and Systems, Springer, Berlin, pp. 21–30 (2005). https://doi.org/10.1007/978-3-540-31987-0_3
4. Cuoq, P., Kirchner, F., Kosmatov, N., Prevosto, V., Signoles, J., Yakobowski, B.: Frama-C. In: Eleftherakis, G., Hinchey, M., Holcombe, M. (eds.) Software Engineering and Formal Methods, SEFM 2012, LNCS, vol. 7504, pp. 233–247. Springer, Berlin (2012). https://doi.org/10.1007/978-3-642-33826-7_16
5. Abrial, J.R., Butler, M., Hallerstede, S., Hoang, T.S., Mehta, F., Voisin, L.: Rodin: an open toolset for modelling and reasoning in Event-B. Int. J. Softw. Tools Technol. Transfer **12**(6) 447–466 (2010). https://doi.org/10.1007/s10009-010-0145-y
6. Yu, Y., Manolios, P., Lamport, L.: Model checking TLA+ specifications. In: Pierre, L., Kropf, T. (eds.) Correct Hardware Design and Verification Methods, CHARME 1999, LNCS, vol. 1703, pp. 54–66. Springer, Berlin (1999). https://doi.org/10.1007/3-540-48153-2_6
7. Kuppe, M.A., Lamport, L., Ricketts, D.: The TLA+ toolbox. Electron. Proc. Theor. Comput. Sci. **310** 50–62 (2019)
8. Jackson, D.: Alloy: a lightweight object modelling notation. ACM Trans. Softw. Eng. Methodol. **11**(2), 256–290 (2002)
9. Milicevic, A., Near, J.P., Kang, E., Jackson, D.: Alloy*: a general-purpose higher-order relational constraint solver. In: International Conference on Software Engineering, pp. 609–619. IEEE (2015)
10. Bobot, F., Filliâtre, J.C., Marché, C., Paskevich, A.: Why3: shepherd your herd of provers. In: International Workshop on Intermediate Verification Languages, pp. 53–64 (2011)
11. Leino, K.R.M.: Dafny: an automatic program verifier for functional correctness. In: Clarke, E.M., Voronkov, A. (eds.) LPAR 2010. LNCS (LNAI), vol. 6355, pp. 348–370. Springer, Heidelberg (2010). https://doi.org/10.1007/978-3-642-17511-4_20
12. Leuschel, M., Butler, M.: ProB: A model checker for B. In: International symposium of formal methods Europe, Springer, Cham, pp. 855–874 (2003)
13. Paulson, L.C. (ed.): : Zermelo-Fraenkel set theory. In: Isabelle. LNCS, vol. 828, pp. 203–234. Springer, Heidelberg (1994). https://doi.org/10.1007/BFb0030558
14. Bertot, Y., Castéran, P.: Interactive theorem proving and program development: Coq'Art: the calculus of inductive constructions. Springer, Cham (2013)
15. de Moura, L., Kong, S., Avigad, J., van Doorn, F., von Raumer, J.: The lean theorem prover (System description). In: Felty, A.P., Middeldorp, A. (eds.) CADE 2015. LNCS (LNAI), vol. 9195, pp. 378–388. Springer, Cham (2015). https://doi.org/10.1007/978-3-319-21401-6_26

16. Tim Nelson, Ben Greenman, S.P.: Forge: a tool and language for teaching formal methods. In: Object-Oriented Programming, Systems, Languages, and Application (2024)
17. de Moura, L., Bjørner, N.: Z3: An efficient SMT solver. In: Ramakrishnan, C.R., Rehof, J. (eds.): Tools and Algorithms for the Construction and Analysis of Systems, TACAS 2008, LNCS, vol. 4963, pp. 337–340. Springer, Berlin (2008). https://doi.org/10.1007/978-3-540-78800-3_24
18. Wu, H., Cheng, Z.: Verifying event-b hybrid models using cyclone. In: Glässer, U., Creissac Campos, J., Méry, D., Palanque, P. (eds.) ABZ 2023. LNCS, vol. 14010, pp. 179–184. Springer, Cham (2023). https://doi.org/10.1007/978-3-031-33163-3_13
19. Sipser, M.: Introduction to the Theory of Computation. PWS Publishing Company, Boston (1997)
20. Huth, M., Ryan, M.: Logic in Computer Science: Modelling and Reasoning about Systems. Cambridge University Press, USA (2004)
21. Dijkstra, E.W.: Self-stabilizing systems in spite of distributed control. Commun. ACM **17**(11), 643–644 (1974)
22. Quesel, J.D., Mitsch, S., Loos, S., Aréchiga, N., Platzer, A.: How to model and prove hybrid systems with KeYmaera: a tutorial on safety. Int. J. Softw. Tools Technol. Transfer **18**(1), 67–91 (2016)
23. Su, W., Abrial, J.R., Zhu, H.: Formalizing hybrid systems with Event-B and the Rodin platform. Sci. Comput. Program. **94**, 164–202 (2014)
24. Baier, C., Katoen, J.P.: Principles of Model Checking. The MIT Press, Cambridge (2008)
25. Jackson, D.: Alloy: a language and tool for exploring software designs. Commun. ACM **62**(9), 66–76 (2019)
26. Bengtsson, J., Larsen, K., Larsson, F., Pettersson, P., Yi, W.: UPPAAL — a tool suite for automatic verification of real-time systems. In: Alur, R., Henzinger, T.A., Sontag, E.D. (eds.) HS 1995. LNCS, vol. 1066, pp. 232–243. Springer, Heidelberg (1996). https://doi.org/10.1007/BFb0020949
27. Larsen, K.G., Pettersson, P., Yi, W.: UPPAAL in a nutshell. Int. J. Softw. Tools Technol. Transfer **1**(1), 134–152 (1997)
28. Bulychev, P., David, A., Guldstrand Larsen, K., Legay, A., Mikučionis, M., Bøgsted Poulsen, D.: Checking and distributing statistical model checking. In: Goodloe, A.E., Person, S. (eds.) NFM 2012. LNCS, vol. 7226, pp. 449–463. Springer, Heidelberg (2012). https://doi.org/10.1007/978-3-642-28891-3_39
29. Leuschel, M., Butler, M.: Prob: an automated analysis toolset for the b method. Int. J. Softw. Tools Technol. Transfer **10** 185–203 (2008). https://doi.org/10.1007/s10009-007-0063-9
30. Bendisposto, J., et al.: ProB2-UI: a java-based user interface for ProB. In: Lluch Lafuente, A., Mavridou, A. (eds.) FMICS 2021. LNCS, vol. 12863, pp. 193–201. Springer, Cham (2021). https://doi.org/10.1007/978-3-030-85248-1_12
31. Wu, H., Farrell, M.: A formal approach to finding inconsistencies in a metamodel. Softw. Syst. Model. **20**(4), 1271–1298 (2021). https://doi.org/10.1007/s10270-020-00849-8
32. Wu, H.: QMaxUSE: a query-based verification tool for UML class diagrams with OCL invariants. In: FASE 2022. LNCS, vol. 13241, pp. 310–317. Springer, Cham (2022). https://doi.org/10.1007/978-3-030-99429-7_17

Applications of Tests and Proofs

Model-Based Testing of Quantum Computations

Malte Lochau[1(✉)] and Ina Schaefer[2]

[1] University of Siegen, Siegen, Germany
malte.lochau@uni-siegen.de
[2] Karlsruhe Institute of Technology, Karlsruhe, Germany

Abstract. Quantum computers are able to effectively solve certain types of problems being intractable by classical computers, including tasks from linear optimization, machine learning and simulation of natural phenomena. The counter-intuitive behavior of quantum algorithms makes it particularly important to develop practical techniques and tools to support the analysis and quality assurance of quantum programs. For classical programs, software testing is today one of the most effective and easy-to-use quality-assurance techniques. However, many postulates of quantum physics like superposition, entanglement and non-cloneability of qubit states as well as the probabilistic outcome and destructive effects of qubit measurements obstruct any straight-forward adaptation of classical testing techniques to quantum programs. Recent works either treat quantum programs as black-box components with classical interfaces to apply end-to-end testing or shift the focus of quality assurance to formal verification of quantum programs. In this paper, we instead propose a model-based framework for testing quantum computations at the level of execution traces. Our approach is independent of the quantum programming language and hardware used and utilizes probabilistic transition systems as abstract test model for both the specification and implementation to be tested. In our model, we carefully distinguish between controllable and observable as well as between nondeterministic and probabilistic test steps. Our framework makes quantum program testing a partly reactive process that can be complemented by statistical approaches for identifying erroneous qubit states by repeated measurements.

Keywords: Quantum Computing · Testing Relations · Probabilistic Transition Systems

1 Introduction

Quantum computers are able to outperform classical computers in certain types of hard-to-solve problems [17,22,23,41]. The recent advances in this field face developers and researchers with unprecedented challenges [47]. Quantum programming is not yet-another paradigm, but is based on entirely novel concepts

© The Author(s), under exclusive license to Springer Nature Switzerland AG 2025
M. Huisman and F. Howar (Eds.): TAP 2024, LNCS 15153, pp. 127–147, 2025.
https://doi.org/10.1007/978-3-031-72044-4_7

of computational and algorithmic thinking. The counter-intuitive nature of quantum programs and algorithms makes it even more important for developers to have access to practical analysis techniques and tools which support a better understanding of the inner workings of quantum software [14].

In classical software engineering, testing is one of the most popular and effective techniques for quality assurance, although being inherently incomplete [27]. Software testing is easy to learn and use and enjoys rich tool support. In contrast, formal verification techniques which, in theory, produce complete correctness proofs for programs with respect to a specification, are mostly used in safety-critical domains only, due to the high demands on expert skills and lack of scalability. In quantum computing, the state-of-the-art is exactly the opposite: many recent works lift formal verification techniques to quantum programs [10], whereas only few testing approaches exist so far [3]. The goal of formal verification is to prove *logical* correctness of a program abstraction with respect to a specification, whereas the execution environment is usually abstracted away. This is reasonable for classical computers whose reliability reached an almost flawless state (e.g., developers do not have to worry about how program variables are physically stored). In contrast, this assumption is not feasible for quantum computing in the noisy intermediate-scale quantum (NISQ) era [38]: although logically satisfying a specification, a quantum program may, nonetheless, show unexpected behavior when executed on a quantum computer. Hence, it is necessary to also systematically *test* the run-time behavior of a verified quantum program by inspecting the *interaction* with the target environment [5,33,34]. However, lifting classical testing techniques to quantum programs is not straight-forward as many assumptions are obstructed by the postulates of quantum mechanics [36]. This includes the impossibility to observe the state of quantum variables in a non-invasive (read-only) way. Further phenomena like superposition, entanglement and non-cloneability of quantum variables and the probabilistic outcome of measurements further obstruct classical testability of quantum programs. Some recent works therefore treat quantum programs as black-boxes with classical interfaces and apply end-to-end testing thus avoiding interactions with the quantum program itself [1,45].

In this paper, we take a different approach by proposing, to the best of our knowledge, the first model-based testing framework for quantum computations. We argue that model-based testing provides a useful level abstraction for testing quantum computations, by formalizing the interactions between a test process and a quantum program under test at the level of execution traces [13]. This makes our approach independent of the programming language and hardware platform used, yet allows for a fine-grained inspection of quantum computations with respect to a given specification. Our framework utilizes probabilistic transition systems as abstract model for the specification and implementation to be tested [11,39]. We distinguish between controllable and observable, as well as between nondeterministic and probabilistic test steps. We describe the construction and execution of partly reactive test processes based on these models which may be complemented by statistical approaches for identifying erroneous states of quantum variables by repeated measurements [12,16]. We prove soundness of the approach and investigate the distinguishing power of the proposed notions of test processes.

2 Preliminaries

We first provide a brief overview on mathematical foundations of quantum computation. For a comprehensive introduction, we refer to classical text-books [36].

Quantum computations are based on *qubits*. In contrast to classical bits having exactly two possible states (0 and 1), qubits live in the complex vector space.

Complex Numbers. Let $\mathbb{C}$ denote the set of *complex numbers* $z = a+bi$, consisting of pairs of a real number a denoting the *real* part and a real number b denoting the *imaginary* part. The distinguished symbol i denotes the *imaginary unit* for which $i^2 = -1$ holds. Each complex number $z = a + bi$ can be also denoted in polar form $z = |z| \cdot (cos\varphi + i\, sin\varphi)$, where $|z| = \sqrt{a^2 + b^2}$ denotes the *absolute value* and φ denotes the *absolute phase* of z. The *complex conjugate* $z^* = a - bi$ of $z = a + bi$ corresponds to the reflection of z about the real axis.

Hilbert Spaces. An n-dimensional complex vector space is any sub-space of $\mathbb{C}^n$ closed under vector addition and scalar multiplication. Using Dirac's notation, an n-dimensional complex (column) vector ψ is denoted as $|\psi\rangle$ (ket) and the *dual vector* $\langle\psi| = |\psi\rangle^\dagger$ (bra) is the *adjoint* (complex transpose conjugate row vector) of $|\psi\rangle$. The *inner product* $\langle\phi|\psi\rangle$ maps any pair $|\phi\rangle$, $|\psi\rangle$ of vectors from $\mathbb{C}^n$ to some scalar element in $\mathbb{C}$ such that

- $\langle\psi|\psi\rangle \geq 0$ for any $\psi \in \mathbb{C}^n$, where $\langle\psi|\psi\rangle = 0$ iff $|\psi\rangle = 0$,
- $\langle\phi|\psi\rangle = \langle\psi|\phi\rangle^*$, and
- $\langle\phi|\lambda_1\psi_1 + \lambda_2\psi_2\rangle = \lambda_1\langle\phi|\psi_1\rangle + \lambda_2\langle\phi|\psi_2\rangle$

holds. An n-dimensional complex vector space on which the inner product is defined forms an n-dimensional *Hilbert space* $\mathcal{H}^n$. The inner product defines the *length* $||\psi||$ of vector $|\psi\rangle$ as $\sqrt{\langle\psi|\psi\rangle}$. Vector $|\psi\rangle$ is a *unit vector* if $||\psi|| = 1$ holds. Two vectors, $|\psi\rangle$ and $|\phi\rangle$, are *orthogonal* if $\langle\psi|\phi\rangle = 0$ holds. A set of vectors is *orthonormal* if each is a unit vector and all vectors are mutually orthogonal.

Single Qubits. The *state* of a single qubit is a unit vector $|\psi\rangle$ in $\mathcal{H}^2$. Using Dirac's notation, the state of a qubit can be expressed as a linear combination (*superposition*) $|\psi\rangle = \alpha|a\rangle + \beta|b\rangle$, where the two complex vectors $|a\rangle$ and $|b\rangle$ form an orthonormal basis in $\mathbb{C}^2$ and the two complex scalars α and β satisfy $|\alpha|^2 + |\beta|^2 = 1$. The complex numbers α and β define the *amplitudes* of $|\psi\rangle$ with respect to the given basis. If the basis is known, we may simply denote $|\psi\rangle$ as a column vector $|\psi\rangle = \begin{pmatrix}\alpha\\ \beta\end{pmatrix}$ of its amplitudes. In the following, we assume the standard basis: $|0\rangle = \begin{pmatrix}1\\ 0\end{pmatrix}$ for $|a\rangle$ and $|1\rangle = \begin{pmatrix}0\\ 1\end{pmatrix}$ for $|b\rangle$, respectively. In this case, a qubit $|\psi\rangle = \alpha|0\rangle + \beta|1\rangle$ is in state $|0\rangle$ with probability $|\alpha|^2$ and in state $|1\rangle$ with probability $|\beta|^2$.

Multiple Qubits. Quantum algorithms operate on quantum registers containing *multiple* qubits. The composition of the states of two qubits, $|\phi\rangle$ and $|\psi\rangle$, is defined by the *tensor product* $|\phi\rangle \otimes |\psi\rangle$, denoted $|\phi\rangle|\psi\rangle$ in Dirac's notation. Recall that the state of n classical bits can be represented as a vector in the n-dimensional Boolean vector space. In contrast, the state of n qubits is a vector in the 2^n-dimensional Hilbert space $\bigotimes_{i=1}^{n} \mathbb{C}^2$. The standard basis of n qubits can be denoted as column vector containing the binary representation of i, $1 \leq i \leq 2^n$, in n digits. States consisting of multiple qubits which cannot be decomposed into states of the individual qubits using tensor product are called *entangled.*

Example 1. The tensor product of two single qubit states $|\phi_1\rangle = \alpha_1|0\rangle + \beta_1|1\rangle$ and $|\phi_2\rangle = \alpha_2|0\rangle + \beta_2|1\rangle$ in standard basis is $|\phi_1\rangle|\phi_2\rangle = \alpha_1\beta_1|00\rangle + \alpha_1\beta_2|01\rangle + \alpha_2\beta_1|10\rangle + \alpha_2\beta_2|11\rangle$ in $\mathcal{H}^4$. A prominent example is the *Bell* state $|\psi^+\rangle = \frac{1}{\sqrt{2}}(|00\rangle + |11\rangle)$ which is an entangled state as it cannot be decomposed into two single qubit states using tensor product.

We consider *finite* dimensional Hilbert spaces only. A quantum computation operating on a register of n qubits starts in some initial state $|\phi_0\rangle$ in the 2^n-dimensional Hilbert space. We only consider *closed* quantum systems for which the evolution of qubit states is *completely determined* by two kinds of operations: unitary transformations and measurements.

Unitary Transformations. We assume a *discrete* time model where state $|\phi_i\rangle$ reached after i steps is transformed into subsequent state $|\phi_{i+1}\rangle = U|\phi_i\rangle$ by applying a linear operator U. For an n-ary operator U to preserve the Hilbert space, the corresponding $2^n \times 2^n$-matrix must be *unitary* (i.e., $U^\dagger U = I$, where I denotes the 2^n-dimensional unit matrix). Since the inverse of a unitary matrix is also unitary, unitary transformations are *reversible.* The *no-cloning* principle of quantum mechanics postulates that there exists no operator U with $U|\phi\rangle = |\phi\rangle \otimes |\phi\rangle$ (i.e., it is not possible to copy state vectors $|\phi\rangle$ of qubits).

Example 2. The *identity* operator $I = \begin{pmatrix} 1 & 0 \\ 0 & 1 \end{pmatrix}$ preserves the state of a single qubit, whereas the *Pauli* operator $X = \begin{pmatrix} 0 & 1 \\ 1 & 0 \end{pmatrix}$ performs state flip. The *Hadamard* operator $H = \frac{1}{\sqrt{2}}\begin{pmatrix} 1 & 1 \\ 1 & -1 \end{pmatrix}$ transforms a single qubit from state $|0\rangle$ into state $|+\rangle = (|0\rangle + |1\rangle)/\sqrt{2}$ and from state $|1\rangle$ into $|-\rangle = (|0\rangle - |1\rangle)/\sqrt{2}$, thus creating a half-way *superposition* of $|0\rangle$ and $|1\rangle$. Both states have the same magnitude values of amplitude of $1/\sqrt{2}$, but different *relative phases* which might lead to physically observable differences in measurements.

Measurements. To obtain results from a final state of a quantum computation, classical information is extracted from qubits by applying measurements. Measuring a single qubit in state $|\phi\rangle = \alpha|0\rangle + \beta|1\rangle$ in standard basis yields outcome 0 with probability $|\alpha|^2$ and 1 with probability $|\beta|^2$. In addition, the state of $|\phi\rangle$ is transformed into post-measurement state $|\phi'\rangle$ according to the measured outcome m (i.e., either $|0\rangle$ if $m = 0$ or $|1\rangle$ if $m = 1$). Measurements are defined by a collection $\{M_m\}$ (e.g., $\{M_0, M_1\}$) of measurement operators satisfying the *completeness* property $\sum_m M_m^\dagger M_m = I$ (i.e., measurement probabilities $p(m)$ sum up to 1). In contrast to unitary transformations U, measurement operators M_m are not reversible as they collapse the measured state. Using Dirac's notation, measurement operators correspond to *outer products* $|\phi\rangle\langle\psi|$, defined as matrix multiplication of ϕ and transpose ϕ^T. For instance, $M_0 = |0\rangle\langle 0|$ and $M_1 = |1\rangle\langle 1|$, respectively. We limit our considerations to *projective* measurements in which the operators $\{M_m\}$ are *orthogonal.* Projective measurements are *repeatable*: applying them more than once to the same state yields the same result and does not change the state anymore. For instance, measuring the state of the first qubit in an n-ary qubit state $\alpha_0|0\rangle \otimes |\phi_0\rangle + \alpha_1|1\rangle \otimes |\phi_1\rangle$ with ϕ_0 and ϕ_1 being (normalized) $(n-1)$-ary qubit states leads to state $|0\rangle \otimes |\phi_0'\rangle$ if the outcome is 0 and state $|1\rangle \otimes |\phi_1'\rangle$ if the outcome is 1, respectively.

Example 3. Quantum computations are often represented as quantum circuits which are composed of quantum gates. For instance, in the circuit:

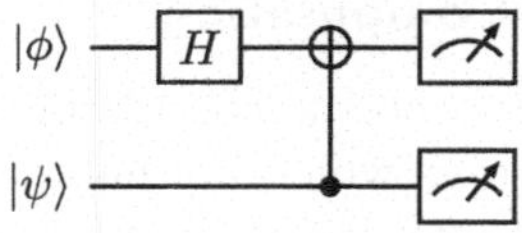

each row (wire) is dedicated to one qubit to which the given sequence of operators along the wire is applied from left to right using matrix multiplication. The parallel composition of the states of multiple qubits along a circuit is obtained using tensor product. In the example, the initial states of the two qubits, $|\phi\rangle$ and $|\psi\rangle$, are first prepared independently, for instance using classical input bits, either as $|0\rangle = \begin{pmatrix}1\\0\end{pmatrix}$ or as $|1\rangle = \begin{pmatrix}0\\1\end{pmatrix}$, respectively. Combining both by $|\phi\rangle \otimes |\psi\rangle$ yields one of $|00\rangle = \begin{pmatrix}1\\0\\0\\0\end{pmatrix}$, $|01\rangle = \begin{pmatrix}0\\1\\0\\0\end{pmatrix}$, $|10\rangle = \begin{pmatrix}0\\0\\1\\0\end{pmatrix}$, or $|11\rangle = \begin{pmatrix}0\\0\\0\\1\end{pmatrix}$.

In the next step, the Hadarmard gate H (see Example 2) is applied to the first qubit, whereas no gate (i.e., identity I) is applied to the second qubit:

$$H \otimes I = \frac{1}{\sqrt{2}}\begin{pmatrix}1 & 1\\1 & -1\end{pmatrix} \otimes \begin{pmatrix}1 & 0\\0 & 1\end{pmatrix} = \frac{1}{\sqrt{2}}\begin{pmatrix}1 & 0 & 1 & 0\\0 & 1 & 0 & 1\\1 & 0 & -1 & 0\\0 & 1 & 0 & -1\end{pmatrix}$$

The following gate is the quantum version of controlled not (CNOT), where the qubit marked by $\oplus$ controls the qubit marked by $\bullet$. Hence, the matrix representation of the whole circuit is:

$$(H \otimes I) \cdot CNOT = \frac{1}{\sqrt{2}}\begin{pmatrix}1 & 0 & 1 & 0\\0 & 1 & 0 & 1\\0 & 1 & 0 & -1\\1 & 0 & -1 & 0\end{pmatrix}$$

Finally, the states of both qubits are measured independently. If the input vector is $|00\rangle$, we obtain the Bell state $|\psi^+\rangle$ from Example 1 on which measurement either yields $|00\rangle$ or $|11\rangle$ both with probability $\frac{1}{2}$ due to the *entangled* states of both qubits. This agreement of both qubits on the measurement outcomes is due to the (strongest possible) statistical correlation between their states rather than due to some hidden communication. Thus, we may also use composed measurement operators, M_{00} and M_{11}, to measure both qubit simultaneously instead of applying cascaded measurements on single qubits. Then, both would be measured with probability $\frac{1}{2}$, whereas M_{10} and M_{01} both would have probability 0.

3 Test Models for Quantum Computations

We now describe process models serving as a formal foundation for model-based testing of quantum computations.

3.1 Models of Quantum Computation

Today's quantum algorithms rely on the *QRAM* model in which the control-flow is guided by a classical computer which delegates sub-tasks to a quantum co-processor operating on a quantum register [29,40]. These sub-tasks are performed in three stages: (1) prepare an initial qubit state vector from classical input data, (2) apply sequences of operators to transform the input state vector to an output state vector, and (3) apply a final measurement to extract classical output data from the output state vector. The circuit in Example 3 follows this schema. To be more precise, a quantum circuit constitutes one *instance* of a quantum computation with a fixed number of gates (steps). In general, quantum programs describe *families* of circuit instances, where the input data determines the shape of the circuit instance [29]. Prominent quantum algorithms like Shor [41] and Grover [22] are *static* as the circuit instances are determined while preparing the input parameters. In *dynamic* algorithms such as variational quantum algorithms, circuit instances may be updated 'on-the-fly' after every circuit execution step [9]. Measurement-based quantum algorithms generate the tail of a circuit execution based on intermediate measurements using quantum versions of classical control structures (e.g., probabilistic conditionals and loops with constant bounds [6]). In any case, the resulting computation corresponds to a finite quantum circuit.

From a functional point of view, an implementation **Imp** of a quantum program defines, similar to a classical program, a mapping $\mathbf{Imp} : \mathcal{I} \to \mathcal{O}$ from an input data domain $\mathcal{I}$ to an output data domain $\mathcal{O}$. The two key differences to classical programs are that a quantum computation is always *finite* and that computational steps may be inherently *non-deterministic* due to probabilistic measurement outcomes. From a process-oriented point of view, a generalized quantum program together with the given input data determines a quantum computation (circuit instance) as a finite sequence of alternating steps of *deterministic* applications of operators U and *non-deterministic* (probabilistic) measurement outcomes M_m.

Reasoning about the correctness of an implementation of a program **Imp** requires a separate specification **Spec**. In addition to functional correctness requirements, given as a mapping **Spec** : $\mathcal{I} \rightarrow \mathcal{O}$ from inputs to *expected* outputs, a specification of a quantum program includes guarantees in terms of (1) minimum success probability of measuring the correct outputs, and (2) complexity bounds including the maximum number of qubits and steps performed for inputs (i.e., maximum width and depth of circuit instances) [10]. The purpose of (2) is to ensure that **Imp** is indeed a quantum program that exploits the advantages of quantum computations [17,23] instead of simply calling a classical implementation solving the specified behavior in a presumably inefficient, yet functionally correct way. Various notions of equivalences **Imp** $\simeq$ **Spec** have been proposed to denote that a quantum computation **Imp** satisfies a specification **Spec** (see Sect. 5). These works vastly differ in the representation of quantum programs **Imp** and specifications **Spec** and the relation $\simeq$ between both. In the following, we describe process models for both **Imp** and **Spec** as a formal basis for the testing relations for quantum computations to be defined in Sect. 4.

3.2 Process Models for Testing Quantum Computations

Our quantum test model formalism is based on labeled transition systems. We distinguish between models for nondeterministic and probabilistic processes.

Nondeterministic Processes. Labeled transition systems represent operational semantics of computational processes as branching sequences of discrete computational steps. Labeled transition systems consist of a set S of *states* and a set of *transitions* $s \xrightarrow{a} s'$ between states $s, s' \in S$. Transitions are labeled over a set Act of *actions* performed in a step, causing state s to evolve to state s'.

Definition 1 (Labeled Transition System). A *labeled transition system* is a tuple $(S, Act, \longrightarrow)$, where S is a set of *states*, Act is a finite set of *actions*, and $\longrightarrow \subseteq S \times Act \times S$ is a set of *action-labeled transitions.*

We write $s \xrightarrow{a} s'$ for $(s, a, s') \in \longrightarrow$ and by $s \not\xrightarrow{a}$ we express that there is no $s' \in S$ such that $(s, a, s') \in \longrightarrow$ holds. State $s \in S$ is a *termination state* if $s \not\xrightarrow{a}$ for all $a \in Act$ and by $S_{term} \subseteq S$ we refer to the subset of all termination states.

A finite *process* (run) of a labeled transition system is defined with respect to an initial state $s_0 \in S$ as an alternating sequence (*path*) $s_0 \xrightarrow{a_1} s_1 \xrightarrow{a_2} \cdots \xrightarrow{a_k} s_k$ of states and transitions of length k. The *trace* $a_1 a_2 \cdots a_k \in Act^*$ of a path is the projection onto the sequence of actions. A trace is *completed* if $s_k \in S_{term}$ holds for the last state of the corresponding path. A labeled transition system is *deterministic* if for all pairs of states $s \in S$ and actions $a \in Act$ there exist *at most one* state $s' \in S$ such that $s \xrightarrow{a} s'$ holds. A labeled transition system is *finitely branching* if for each state s, the set of states s' reachable by some transition $s \xrightarrow{a} s'$ is finite. Finally, we call a labeled transition system *finite* if for any initial state $s_0 \in S$, every trace is finite.

We use labeled transition systems as process models for quantum computations operating on an n-dimensional qubit register. Hence, the set of states S corresponds to the 2^n-dimensional Hilbert space $\mathcal{H}^{2^n}$ and the set of actions *Act* includes a set $\mathcal{U}$ of unitary operators U and a set $\mathcal{M}$ of ensembles $\{M_m\}$ of measurement operators. A step $s \xrightarrow{U} s'$ denotes an application of operator U to state s which yields the transformed state $s' = U(s)$. To keep the notation simple, we also write $s \xrightarrow{M_m} s'$ to denote that measurement operator M_m, if applied to state s, yields post-measurement state s' for outcome m.

Example 4. Considering the circuit in Example 3 with $Act = \{H \otimes I, CNOT\} \cup \{M_{00}, M_{11}, M_{01}, M_{10}\}$, initial state $|00\rangle$ has two completed paths: $|00\rangle \xrightarrow{H\otimes I} \cdots \xrightarrow{CNOT} |\psi^+\rangle \xrightarrow{M_{00}} |00\rangle$ and $|00\rangle \xrightarrow{H\otimes I} \cdots \xrightarrow{CNOT} |\psi^+\rangle \xrightarrow{M_{11}} |11\rangle$.

The initial state $s_0 \in S$ corresponds to the preparation of the input qubit state of a quantum computation. In this sense, a labeled transition system represents a *family* of quantum computations (e.g., circuit instances) as described by a quantum program. This representation is *finitely branching* and *deterministic* as the sets $\mathcal{U}$ and $\mathcal{M}$ are, by definition, finite and their applications completely determine the subsequent states. The labeled transition system is also *finite* as the corresponding circuit instances are finite. From a testing point of view, it is indeed feasible to assume that applications of operators U, although being determined by the circuit layout, pose deterministic steps whose releases may be *externally controlled* in a step-wise manner by a tester during testing/debugging [34]. In contrast, steps labeled by measurements M_m actually consists of two sub-steps: (1) choose measurement ensemble $\{M_m\} \in \mathcal{M}$ and (2) apply the operator M_m to transform the current state to the post-measurement state corresponding to the measurement outcome m. Sub-step (1) is, similar to steps labeled U, externally controllable, whereas the outcome m guiding sub-step (2) is neither externally controllable nor deterministic, but internally probabilistic.

Probabilistic Processes. Probabilistic transition systems extend labeled transition systems by adding as a second component to transition labels a real number $p \in [0, 1]$ denoting the *probability* of the transition to happen in a run.

Definition 2 (Probabilistic Transition System). A *probabilistic transition system* is a tuple $(S, Act, \Longrightarrow)$, where S and *Act* are defined as in Definition 1, whereas $\Longrightarrow \subseteq S \times Act \times [0, 1] \times S$ such that for all $s \in S$ it holds that

$$\sum_{(s,a,p,s') \in \Longrightarrow} p \in \{0, 1\}.$$

We write $s \overset{a}{\Longrightarrow}_p s'$ if $(s, a, p, s') \in \Longrightarrow$ holds. The definition ensures that for every state s the sum of probabilities p of all outgoing transitions $s \overset{a}{\Longrightarrow}_p s'$ either equals to 1 or to 0 (if $s \in S_{term}$ holds). The notions of finite *paths* and *traces* are similar to labeled transition systems. The *path probability* of a path $\pi = s_0 \overset{a_1}{\Longrightarrow}_{p_1} s_1 \overset{a_2}{\Longrightarrow}_{p_2} \cdots \overset{a_n}{\Longrightarrow}_{p_n} s_n$ starting in state s_0 is inductively defined as:

- $Pr(s_0) = 1$, and

- $Pr(\pi' \xrightarrow{a_k}_{p_k} s_k) = Pr(\pi') \cdot p_k$.

The *trace probability* $Pr(w)$ of a trace $w = a_1 a_2 \cdot a_n \in Act^*$ is given by the sum of probabilities $Pr(\pi)$ of all paths π having w as action sequence.

Example 5 Reconsidering Example 4, we have two completed probabilistic paths: $|00\rangle \xrightarrow{H\otimes I}_1 \cdots \xrightarrow{CNOT}_1 |\psi^+\rangle \xrightarrow{M_{00}}_{0.5} |00\rangle$ as well as $|00\rangle \xrightarrow{H\otimes I}_1 \cdots \xrightarrow{CNOT}_1 |\psi^+\rangle \xrightarrow{M_{11}}_{0.5} |11\rangle$, respectively, both with probability 0.5.

Although the steps denoting measurement outcomes are internally probabilistic, the sequential application of operators U and measurement ensembles $\{M_m\}$ are, again, deterministic following the *implemented* behavior of the circuit. However, if a model is used as a test model to specify the *expected* behavior of candidate implementations, it is often necessary to permit externally controllable nondeterministic choices which are later resolved by a tester [13,42]. We thus combine nondeterministic and probabilistic steps into one process model [39].

Nondeterministic Probabilistic Processes. Nondeterministic probabilistic processes generalize probabilistic processes by nondeterministic choices between probability distributions over transitions. A (discrete) probability distribution over a countable set X is a function $\mu : X \to [0,1]$ for which $\sum_{x\in X} \mu(x) = 1$ holds. Probability distribution μ has *finite support* if the support set $supp(\mu) = \{x \in X \mid \mu(x) > 0\}$ is finite and we refer to the set of all such distributions over X by $\mathcal{D}(X)$. Moreover, distribution μ is *simple* if $\mu(x) = 1$ holds for some $x \in X$.

Definition 3 (Nondeterministic Probabilistic Transition System). A *nondeterministic probabilistic transition system* is a tuple $(S, Act, \Longrightarrow)$, where S and Act are defined as in Definition 1, whereas $\Longrightarrow \subseteq S \times \mathcal{D}(Act \times S)$ holds.

We use the same transition arrows as in Definition 2 to avoid bloating notation. We write $s \xrightarrow{a}_{\mu,p} s'$ to denote that $(s,\mu) \in \Longrightarrow$ holds with $\mu(a,s') = p$. If, for instance, $(s,\mu) \in \Longrightarrow$ and $(s,\mu') \in \Longrightarrow$ hold, then in state s the probability distribution assigning transition probabilities to all supported pairs of actions and target states is chosen nondeterministically to be either μ or μ'.

Example 6. Concerning Example 4, we may want to leave open for the tester if the ensemble $\{M_0, M_1\}$ is applied to both qubits individually in some ordering or if $\{M_{00}, M_{11}\}$ is used in the final measurement step.

The notions of path probability and trace probability cannot be directly adapted to this model as this requires resolution of nondeterminism first (see Sect. 4).

4 Test Processes for Quantum Computations

We next develop a model-based testing theory for quantum computations based on the process models from Sect. 3.

4.1 Test Processes and Tested Processes

Testing an implementation **Imp** (tested process) against a specification **Spec** is done by deriving test cases (test processes) **Test** from **Spec** which run in parallel to **Imp** to simulate the environment of the tested process. In a model-based setting, we assume **Spec**, **Imp** and **Test** all to be represented using the same modeling formalism, where the model for **Spec** is available to derive **Test** models. In contrast, the model of **Imp** is unknown, but it is only assumed that such a model exists and acts as a proper process that exposes its external behavior when interacting with a test process **Test**. This assumption is known as testing hypothesis [4].

External Actions vs. Internal Actions. Another important principle of model-based testing is that the specification **Spec** (test model) may describe the expected behavior of a candidate implementation **Imp** in a way that abstracts from internal implementation details. We distinguish the set of externally exposed actions *Act*, on which both the specification and implementation agree to synchronize during test executions, from a set of internal operations Ω hidden in the implementation to realize those actions. In case of quantum computations, Ω comprises the sets $\mathcal{U}$ and $\mathcal{M}$ and we assume the existence of a mapping $\lambda : Act \rightarrow \Omega$ such that $s \xrightarrow{a} s'$ implies that state s' results from applying operator $\lambda(a)$ to state s. This assumption permits different realizations of the same action a in **Imp** and **Spec** as long as the externally exposed sequences of actions from *Act* of **Imp** match those expected by **Spec**. We may further generalize mapping λ to a relation to permit different implementations of the same action $a \in Act$ within the same **Imp**. As any composition of quantum gates can be aggregated into a single matrix [2], different mappings λ allow us to reason about steps of quantum computations at arbitrary levels of granularity (i.e., from single gates to complete circuits).

Example 7. We consider different examples of quantum coin flips. The labeled transition system in Fig. 1 on the left represents the state of a coin by a single qubit, where $|0\rangle$ denotes *head* and $|1\rangle$ denotes *tail*. Mapping λ maps action *flip* to the operator X (see Example 2) which causes a coin flip with exactly one turnover. The actions *head* and *tail* are mapped to the measurement operators M_0 and M_1, respectively (where probabilities are attached in brackets).

The previous example does not represent an actually implemented quantum computation **Imp** as it includes nondeterministic choices between operator applications and measurements and it is not finite. Instead, this model may serve as a specification **Spec** to derive test processes **Test** interacting with **Imp**.

4.2 Non-probabilistic Test Processes

We first consider the more abstract case in which **Spec** and **Imp** are both represented as non-probabilistic labeled transition systems (see Definition 1).

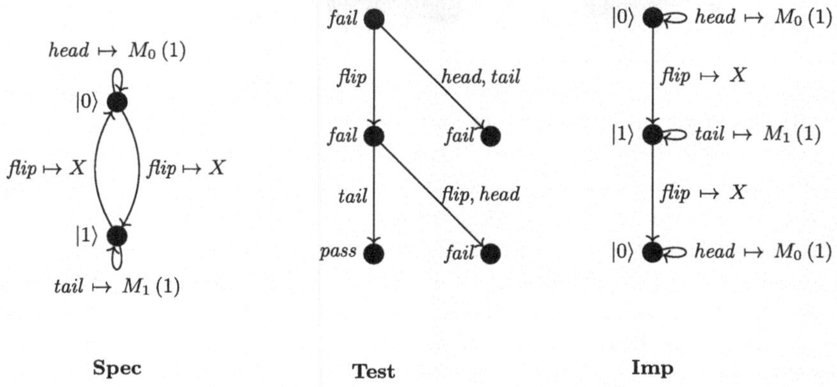

Fig. 1. Example of a Non-Probabilistic Test Process for a Quantum Coin Flip.

Construction of Test Processes. A non-probabilistic test process **Test** is a labeled transition system $(T, Act, \longrightarrow_T)$ that is derived from the labeled transition system $(S, Act, \longrightarrow_S)$ of **Spec**. The set of states T is partitioned into two subsets, T_{pass} and T_{fail}. We recursively construct the set T of states t of **Test** and the transition relation $\longrightarrow_T$ by traversing states $s \in S$ of **Spec** using the recursive procedure $\texttt{con}(s, t)$. The procedure is initialized by adding an initial state t_0 to T_{fail} and by calling $\texttt{con}(s_0, t_0)$, where s_0 is the initial state of **Spec**. Every call of $\texttt{con}(s, t)$ leads to a nondeterministic choice between the following three cases, depending on the current states s and t.

- Case *(Operator)*: if $s \xrightarrow{a}_S s'$ with $\lambda(a) \in \mathcal{U}$, then
  - add $t' \in T_{fail}$ and $t \xrightarrow{a}_T t'$;
  - add $t'' \in T_{fail}$ and for all $a' \in Act \setminus \{a\}$ add $t \xrightarrow{a'}_T t''$;
  - call $\texttt{con}(s', t')$;
- Case *(Measure)*: if $s \xrightarrow{a_1}_S s'_1, \ldots, s \xrightarrow{a_k}_S s'_k$ with $\{\lambda(a_1), \ldots \lambda(a_k)\} \subseteq \{M_m\} \in \mathcal{M}$, then
  - add $t'_i \in T_{pass}$ and $t \xrightarrow{a_i}_T t'_i$ for all $1 \leq i \leq k$;
  - add $t'' \in T_{fail}$ and for all $a' \in Act \setminus \{a_1, \ldots, a_k\}$ add $t \xrightarrow{a'}_T t''$;
  - call $\texttt{con}(s'_1, t'_1)$, ..., $\texttt{con}(s'_k, t'_k)$;
- Case *(Term)*: if $t \in T_{pass}$, then terminate;

Case *Operator* adds a test step that triggers an application of operator U in **Imp** if this is specified as a possible next step of the current state s in **Spec**. The application of U is enforced as all other possible steps of **Imp** lead to a fresh terminating *fail* state t'' in **Test**. Note that the fresh state t' reached in **Test** after successfully applying U is also a *fail* state as it seems reasonable that a test process should only terminate after a final measurement step. Hence, con is called at least one more time on (s', t'). Case *Measure* introduces a measurement step into the test process by means of a nondeterministic choice between all those operators M_m expected as possible measurement outcomes m in **Spec**. The choice only includes those operators M_m from the ensemble $\{M_m\}$ for which the current state s in **Spec** contains a transition (i.e., outcome m has an expected probability > 0). All other outcomes m' with probability 0 lead to a terminating *fail* state, whereas all expected outcomes m lead to a *pass* state in which the test process might terminate (case *Term*) or further steps are recursively added by calling `con`. Note that we do not impose any further restrictions on **Spec** (e.g., it may contain cycles and nondeterministic choices between measurements and operator applications). However, to ensure termination of the construction, we at least require that from every state $s \in S$ a measurement step is reachable and we bound the number of recursive calls to some k to ensure that **Test** is finite. Moreover, as **Test** is *acyclic* by construction, it ensures finite test process executions.

Execution of Test Processes. The interaction between a test process and a tested process can be described by the synchronous product of the labeled transition systems of **Test** and **Imp**.

Definition 4 (Synchronous Product). Let $P_1 = (S_1, Act, \longrightarrow_1)$ and $P_2 = (S_2, Act, \longrightarrow_2)$ be two labeled transition systems over the same set *Act*. The *synchronous product* of P_1 and P_2 is a labeled transition system $P_1||P_2 = (P_1 \times P_2, Act, \longrightarrow_{1||2})$ where $\longrightarrow_{1||2}$ is the least relation such that $(s_1, s_2) \xrightarrow{a}_{1||2} (s_1', s_2')$ if $s_1 \xrightarrow{a}_1 s_1'$ and $s_2 \xrightarrow{a}_2 s_2'$ holds.

Every completed trace of **Imp** || **Test** of length $k > 0$ is a possible execution of test process **Test** on the tested process **Imp**. The tested process **Imp** *passes* an execution of **Test** if for the final state (i_k, t_k) of the completed path it holds that $t_k \in T_{pass}$, and **Imp** fails **Test**, otherwise. Note that $t_k \in T_{term}$ holds in any case, whereas i_k is not necessarily a terminating state of **Imp** as **Test** may terminate earlier. In addition, for **Imp** to properly interact with *all* derivable test processes **Test**, we may assume *measurement-completion* of **Imp** which means that *all* measurements in $\mathcal{M}$ are potentially applicable in *every* state of **Imp**. In other words, a tester interacting with **Imp** is able to introduce additional measurements into **Imp** for testing purposes. This assumption ensures that **Imp** never blocks measurement requests in **Test** which is common in model-based testing (e.g., called input-enabledness in [42]).

Example 8. Fig. 1 shows an implementation **Imp** (right) as well as a test process **Test** (center) derived from **Spec** (left) for the quantum coin flip example. Process **Imp** performs exactly two consecutive *flips* and then terminates. It satisfies *measurement-completion* as the current state of the coin can be measured in all states. Process **Test** performs one *flip* and then measures whether the coin is in state *tail*. Hence, **Imp** passes **Test** which is reasonable as **Imp** is a two-wise unfolding of **Spec** with deterministic measurement outcomes in every state.

To generalize, we write [**Imp** *passes* **Test**] if *every* completed path of **Imp** || **Test** terminates in a *pass*-state, and [**Imp** *fails* **Test**], otherwise.

Theorem 1 (Soundness). *For every test process* **Test** *constructed from* **Spec** *it holds that* [**Spec** *passes* **Test**].

Proof. Let us assume that [**Spec** *passes* **Test**] holds. Moreover, by $P = (S \times T, Act, \longrightarrow_{S||T})$, we denote the labeled transition system corresponding to the synchronous product **Spec** || **Test** of the labeled transition system $(S, Act, \longrightarrow_S)$ of specification **Spec** and the labeled transition system $(T, Act, \longrightarrow_T)$ of test process **Test** constructed from **Spec** using procedure con. Then, by assumption, for every path

$$(s_0, t_0) \xrightarrow{a_0}_{S||T} (s_1, t_1) \xrightarrow{a_1}_{S||T} \cdots \xrightarrow{a_k}_{S||T} (s_k, t_k)$$

corresponding to a *completed* trace $a_0\, a_1 \cdots a_k \in Act^*$ of length $k > 0$ of P, it holds that $t_k \in T_{pass}$. We prove this by induction over the path length i.

- Case $i = 0$. For $(s_0, t_0) \in S \times T$ it holds, by construction, that $k_0 \in T_{fail}$. However, as we only consider completed paths of length $k > 0$, the path under consideration contains at least one more step (see next case).
- Case $i \to i+1$, $0 < i < k$. For $(s_i, t_i) \in S \times T$, $0 < i < k$, it holds that $(s_i, t_i) \notin (S \times T)_{term}$. From this it follows that $t_i \notin T_{term}$ as well as $s_i \notin T_{term}$. The latter holds because the path contains at least one more transition $(s_i, t_i) \xrightarrow{a_{i+1}}_{S||T} (s_{i+1}, t_{i+1})$ labeled by some action a_{i+1}. The corresponding transition $t_i \xrightarrow{a_{i+1}} t_{i+1}$ in **Test** has been constructed by traversing some transition $s_i \xrightarrow{a_{i+1}} s_{i+1}$ in **Spec**, thus $s_i \notin S_{term}$ holds. Depending on the type of action $a_{i+1} \in Act$, either case *Operator* or case *Measure* has been applied for adding transition $t_i \xrightarrow{a_{i+1}} t_{i+1}$ to **Test**. In case of *Operator*, it holds that $t_{i+1} \in T_{fail}$ and also that the path contains at least one more step $(s_{i+1}, t_{i+1}) \xrightarrow{a_{i+2}} (s_{i+2}, t_{i+2}))$ afterwards as case *Term* is not applicable for t_{i+1}. In case of *Measure*, it holds that $t_{i+1} \in T_{pass}$ as there exists a corresponding transition $s_i \xrightarrow{a_{i+1}} s_{i+1}$ for the same measurement outcome in **Spec**. Then, either case *Term* is applied thus confirming our initial assumption, or the path contains at least one more step $(s_{i+1}, t_{i+1}) \xrightarrow{a_{i+2}} (s_{i+2}, t_{i+2}))$ which yields another application of case $i \to i+1$.
- Case $i = k$. If $i = k$ holds, then it follows that $t_i \in T_{term}$ as **Test** is constructed by synchronously traversing a path of **Spec**. As shown for case $i \to i+1$, the preceding step $(s_{i-1}, t_{i-1}) \xrightarrow{a_i} (s_i, t_i)$ must be a successful measurement-step such that $t_i \in T_{pass}$ holds. □

As we abstract from probabilities of measurement outcomes, *completeness* does, in general, not hold as illustrated by the next examples.

Example 9. Figure 2 shows two examples, P_1 and P_2, using two qubits to represent coins. In both examples, action *ht* (first coin *head*, second *tail*) refers to measurement M_{01}, *th* to M_{10}, *tt* to M_{11} and *hh* to M_{00}. Action *flip*$_0$ (flipping first coin) refers to operator $X \otimes I$ and *flip*$_1$ to $I \otimes X$, respectively. In P_1, both coins are flipped independently, whereas P_2 contains two additional states in which both coins are entangled in two possible ways: either both have the same symbol on top, or both have different symbols on top. After measurement, the entangled state collapses, and the afterwards both coins behave as in P_1. If we

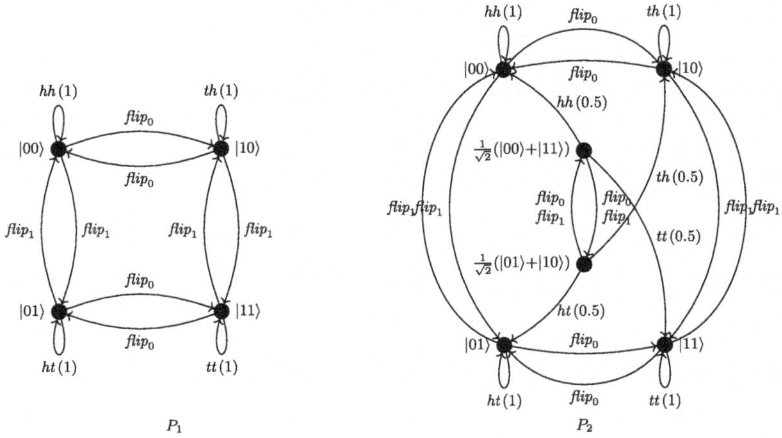

Fig. 2. Examples of Flipping Two Quantum Coins.

use P_2 as **Spec** and P_1 as **Imp**, we can construct a **Test** that distinguishes an entangled initial state of P_2 from the non-entangled initial states in P_1 (if **Test** starts with a measurement and observes an outcome in P_1 which is not expected due to the initial entanglement in P_2). In contrast, if we use P_1 as **Spec** and P_2 as **Imp**, we are not able to construct a **Test** that distinguishes both models as P_1 initially permits more measurement outcomes than P_2.

The two examples, P_3 and P_4, in Fig. 3 represent single coin flips, where in both models *head* is mapped to M_0 and *tail* to M_1. In contrast, we use X for *flip* in P_3, but H in P_4. In P_3, we may have as initial state an arbitrary superposition of *head* and *tail* depending on the parameters $\alpha > 0$ and $\beta > 0$, whereas in P_4 we initially have a half-way superposition. These possibly different initial superpositions are not distinguishable by a **Test** that only measures in the initial state as the outcome appears to behave nondeterministically if we do not take the different probabilities into account. However, if **Test** performs another *flip* afterwards both models *may* be distinguished as P_3 then behaves deterministically, whereas P_4 creates another half-way entanglement.

4.3 Probabilistic Test Processes

We now assume both **Spec** and **Imp** to expose probabilistic behavior. To be more precise, in **Imp** measurement outcomes follow *deterministic* probability distributions (see Definition 2) determined by the current state, whereas **Spec**, may in each step contain *nondeterministic* choices between different measurements with different probability distributions (see Definition 3). To derive deterministic probabilistic test processes **Test** from **Spec** applicable to **Imp**, we first have to resolve all these nondeterministic choices in **Spec**.

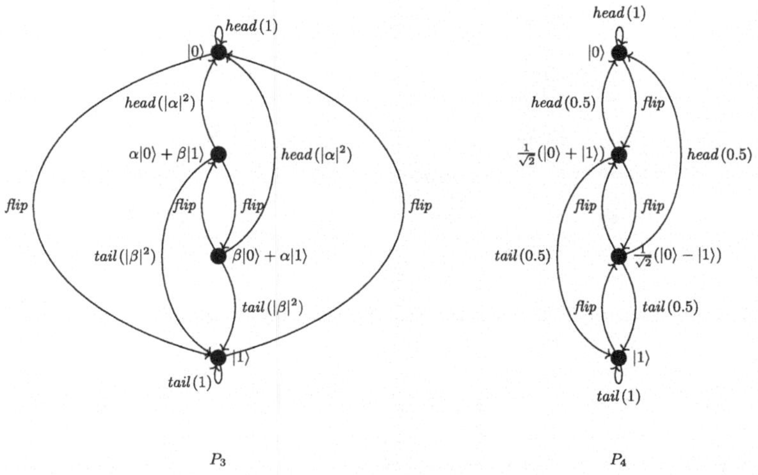

Fig. 3. Examples of Flipping a Single Quantum Coin in Superposition.

Resolving Nondeterminism. Given a nondeterministic probabilistic transition system $(S, Act, \Longrightarrow)$, a *scheduler* is a function $\sigma : (\Longrightarrow) \rightarrow [0,1]$ such that $\sum_{(s,\mu)\in\Longrightarrow} \sigma(s,\mu) = 1$ holds for each state $s \in S$. A scheduler assigns to each pair $(s,\mu) \in\Longrightarrow$ a probability which allows us to construct a deterministic probabilistic transition system $(S, Act, \Longrightarrow')_\sigma$ from $(S, Act, \Longrightarrow)$ in which $s \overset{a}{\Longrightarrow}'_p s'$ holds with $p = \sigma(s,\mu) \cdot \sum_{(s,\mu)\in\Longrightarrow} \mu(a, s')$. In the following, we limit our considerations to *deterministic schedulers* $\sigma : (\Longrightarrow) \rightarrow \{0,1\}$ with simple distributions (i.e., assigning either probability 0 or 1 to each transition).

Construction and Execution of Probabilistic Test Processes. The construction of probabilistic processes **Test** from deterministic probabilistic specifications **Spec** can be performed by slightly adapting procedure `con` described above. We therefore simply adopt the probabilities p of transitions $s \overset{a}{\Longrightarrow}_p s'$ traversed in **Spec** for the corresponding transitions $t \overset{a}{\Longrightarrow}_p t'$ constructed in **Test**. Note that in case of deterministic schedulers σ, the probabilities of unexpected transitions to *fail* states t'' (second bullet of case *Operator* and *Measure*) are, by construction, equal to 0. The interaction between **Test** and **Imp** can be described by adapting the synchronous product from Definition 4 as follows.

Definition 5 (Probabilistic Synchronous Product). Given two probabilistic transition systems, $P_1 = (S_1, Act, \Longrightarrow_1)$ and $P_2 = (S_2, Act, \Longrightarrow_2)$, over Act, the *probabilistic synchronous product* of P_1 and P_2 is a probabilistic labeled transition system $P_1||P_2 = (P_1 \times P_2, Act, \Longrightarrow_{1||2})$ where $\Longrightarrow_{1||2}$ is the least relation such that $(s_1, s_2) \overset{a}{\Longrightarrow}_{1||2,p_{1,2}} (s_1', s_2')$ if $s_1 \overset{a}{\Longrightarrow}_{1,p_1} s_1'$ and $s_2 \overset{a}{\Longrightarrow}_{2,p_2} s_2'$ with $p_{1,2} = \frac{p_1 \cdot p_2}{\nu(s_1,s_2)}$, where $\nu(s_1, s_2) = \sum_{a\in Act} Pr_{s_1}(a) \cdot Pr_{s_2}(a)$ holds.

Note that $\nu(s_1, s_2)$ serves as a normalization factor in which $Pr_{s_1}(a)$ and $Pr_{s_2}(a)$ denote the probabilities for trace a starting in state s_1 and s_2, respectively.

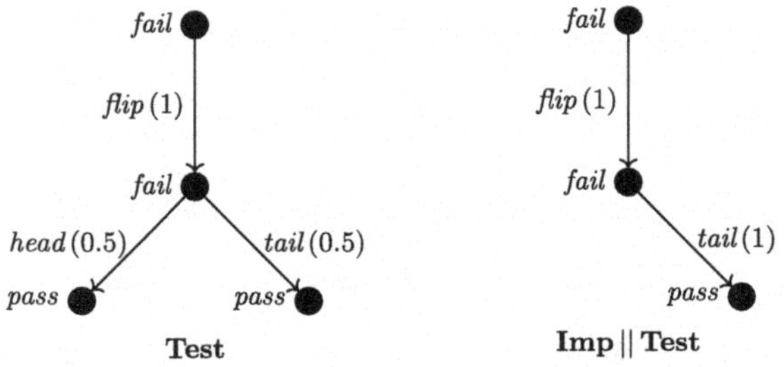

Fig. 4. Example of a Probabilistic Test Process for Single Quantum Coin Flip.

Every completed trace w of **Imp** || **Test** is a possible execution of **Test** on **Imp**. Let $Ct_P \subseteq Act^*$ denote the set of completed traces w of process P with trace probability $Pr_P(w)$. By $[\,\mathbf{Imp}\ passes_p\ \mathbf{Test}\,]$ we denote that **Imp** passes **Test** with probability p. We define

$$p = \frac{1}{|Ct_{\mathbf{Test}}|} \sum_{w \in Ct_{\mathbf{Test}}} 1 - |Pr_{\mathbf{Test}}(w) - Pr_{\mathbf{Imp}\,||\,\mathbf{Test}}(w)|$$

to denote the normalized sum of deviations of probabilities of completed traces $w \in Ct_{\mathbf{Test}}$ of **Test** observed in **Imp** || **Test**. Note that for a final state t_k reached in **Test** after a completed trace w of **Imp** || **Test** to be a proper *pass*-state, we now not only require $t_k \in T_{pass}$ but also $t_k \in T_{term}$ as **Imp** might get stuck before **Test** is terminated.

Example 10 Let us assume that **Imp** in Fig. 1 should now be tested against P_4 in Fig. 3 serving as **Spec**. The test process **Test** shown in Fig. 4 (left) is derived from **Spec** by a deterministic scheduler σ. The scheduler applies one *flip* in the initial state $|0\rangle$ and then measures the coin in the subsequent state $\frac{1}{\sqrt{2}}(|0\rangle + |1\rangle)$ which yields both possible outcomes, *head* and *tail*, with probability 0.5 each. In the probabilistic synchronous product **Imp** || **Test** shown in Fig. 1 on the right, only the outcome *tail* can be observed with a normalized probability of 1 as outcome *head* has probability 0 in **Imp** after one *flip*. The set $Ct_{\mathbf{Test}} = \{flip \cdot head, flip \cdot tail\}$ of completed traces of **Test** contains two possible executions with probabilities $Pr_{\mathbf{Test}}(flip \cdot head) = Pr_{\mathbf{Test}}(flip \cdot tail) = 0.5$. In contrast, if applied to **Imp**, we have $Pr_{\mathbf{Imp}\,||\,\mathbf{Test}}(flip \cdot head) = 0$ corresponding to a failing execution of **Test** on **Imp**, whereas $Pr_{\mathbf{Imp}\,||\,\mathbf{Test}}(flip \cdot tail) = 1$ corresponds to a passing execution. Hence, normalization yields $[\,\mathbf{Imp}\ passes_{0.5}\ \mathbf{Test}\,]$.

We now prove soundness of the probabilistic test process construction.

Theorem 2 (Soundness). *For every test process* **Test** *constructed from* **Spec** *using scheduler* σ *it holds that* $[\,\mathbf{Imp}\ passes_1\ \mathbf{Test}\,]$.

Proof. After applying scheduler σ, the construction of probabilistic test processes **Test** from probabilistic specifications **Spec** is performed in a similar way as in the non-probabilistic case, using procedure `con` (see Theorem 2). Hence, we also have $t_k \in T_{term}$ for the final state (s_k, t_k) of any path corresponding to a completed trace of the probabilistic synchronous product **Spec** || **Test**. In addition, the probability p_{i+1} of each transition $s_i \xRightarrow{a_{i+1}}_{p_{i+1}} s_{i+1}$, $0 < i < k$, traversed in **Spec** during the construction of **Test** is copied one-by-one to become the probability for the transition $t_i \xRightarrow{a_{i+1}}_{p_{i+1}} t_{i+1}$ added into **Test**. Thus, in each step

$$(s_i, t_i) \xRightarrow{a_{i+1}}_{s||t,p_{1,2}} (s_{i+1}, t_{i+1})$$

of the probabilistic synchronous product, it holds for the corresponding steps $s_i \xRightarrow{a_{i+1}}_{p_{s_{i+1}}} s_{i+1}$ in **Spec** and $t_i \xRightarrow{a_{i+1}}_{p_{t_{i+1}}} t_{i+1}$ in **Test** that $p_{s_{i+1}} = p_{t_{i+1}}$. After multiplication of $p_{s_{i+1}}$ and $p_{t_{i+1}}$ and normalization, the probability $p_{1,2}$ of the corresponding transition of **Spec** ||**Test** in step $i+1$ is equal to $p_{s_{i+1}}$ of **Spec** and $p_{t_{i+1}}$ of **Test**, respectively. As a consequence, the probability of any (completed) trace of **Spec** || **Test** is also equal to the probability of that trace in **Spec** as well as in **Test**. Thus, it holds that [**Spec** $passes_1$ **Test**]. □

Discussion. The construction of **Imp** || **Test** and the calculation of probability p in [**Imp** $passes_p$ **Test**] presumes exact knowledge about transition probabilities of **Imp** which is not possible due to the postulates of quantum mechanics. In fact, it is impossible to fully distinguish non-orthogonal states by single measurements only, such as the two superposition states in P_4 in Fig. 3. Using repeated measurements (i.e., repeated executions of the same test process), we are, however, able to statistically approximate the states of qubits [15,16,21]. Finally, the developed framework gives rise to the definition of *testing equivalences* on quantum processes, where $P \simeq_{te} P'$ holds, if the two processes P and P' are not distinguishable by any test process **Test** [13].

5 Related Work

We discuss related work on testing quantum programs, notions of equivalence of quantum computations as well as model-based testing of probabilistic processes.

Testing Quantum Programs. The challenges in testing quantum computations has been first pointed out by Biamonte and Perkowski [5]. A comprehensive overview on the state-of-the-art in quantum software testing is provided by two recent surveys [3]. The authors observe two trends: (1) statistical approaches for identifying (erroneous) states using repeated measurements, and (2) using Hoare-style program verification [10] and model-checking techniques [46] instead of classical testing to prove correctness of quantum programs. Apart from that, most works on quantum testing either operate at circuit level [33,34,43] or take a black-box perspective to apply classical combinatorial testing [1,45]. Some works propose to fuse testing and verification techniques by adding run-time assertions to quantum programs [24,26,30]. Further works assess effectiveness of quantum testing techniques including quantum circuit mutation [32], taxonomies for quantum bugs [25] and collections of reproducible quantum bugs [8]. However, no approach exists so far lifting model-based testing to quantum computations at the level of execution traces as proposed in this paper.

Equivalence of Quantum Programs. Various works have been proposed to reason about equivalence of quantum programs for different purposes, such as (1) model-based verification of behavioral correctness and (2) correctness of compiler transformations. Concerning (1), different formalisms and equivalence notions have been used, including language equivalence of quantum automata [35] and quantum finite-state machines [44] and probabilistic bisimulation of quantum processes [18,19]. Concerning (2), techniques for proving functional equivalence at circuit level often use the ZX-calculus [37] which employs graph isomorphisms as equivalence notion, whereas other works use decision diagrams [7]. None of these works define equivalence notions for quantum computations based on model-based testing processes being independent of the programming language.

Model-Based Testing of Probabilistic Processes. Based on the seminal work by DeNicola and Hennessy on model-based testing equivalences for nondeterministic processes [13], various extensions also handle probabilistic behavior during testing. Most closely related to our approach are the works by Christoff [11] on testing deterministic probabilistic systems as well as by Segala et al. [39] on testing nondeterministic probabilistic systems. Also, probabilistic extensions of I/O conformance testing introduced by Tretmans [42] have been proposed [20,21]. Our work may be seen as the first instantiation of these concepts specifically tailored to the characteristics of quantum computations.

6 Conclusion

We proposed a model-based testing framework for quantum computations. The framework is independent of the programming language used and instead employs various extensions of labeled transition systems as abstract test modeling formalism for specification, implementation as well as for the test processes.

The framework builds a conceptual basis for a wide range of future work. The construction of sound test processes can be combined with algorithms for automated test-case generation [42], where different notions of coverage may be defined beyond black-box criteria [1]. This includes metrics to quantify precision of probabilistic outcomes with respect to the number of repeated test executions [16,21]. Another notion of coverage would be to quantify the precision of test equivalence depending on the number of complementary measurement steps to be added to a circuit for testing purposes. Based on these considerations, tool support can be developed for test modeling and test-case generation integrated in quantum programming environments like qiskit [28].

Conceptually, the step from closed to open quantum systems involves the relationship between (non-)compositional testing and entanglement of sub components [31] as well as realistic fault models for quantum computations [32]. Moreover, the framework can be adapted to other formalisms like the density-operator notation [36] which corresponds to fully probabilistic processes [11]. Finally, our notion of *measurement-completion* seems related to measurement-based quantum computation [6].

References

1. Ali, S., Arcaini, P., Wang, X., Yue, T.: Assessing the effectiveness of input and output coverage criteria for testing quantum programs. In: 2021 14th IEEE Conference on Software Testing, Verification and Validation (ICST), pp. 13–23 (2021). https://doi.org/10.1109/ICST49551.2021.00014
2. Amy, M.: Towards large-scale functional verification of universal quantum circuits. Electron. Proc. Theor. Comput. Sci. **287**, 1–21 (2019). https://doi.org/10.4204/EPTCS.287.1
3. García de la Barrera, A., García-Rodríguez de Guzmán, I., Polo, M., Piattini, M.: Quantum software testing: State of the art. J. Softw. Evol. Process **35**(4), e2419 (2023). https://doi.org/10.1002/smr.2419
4. Bernot, G., Gaudel, M.C., Marre, B.: Software testing based on formal specifications: a theory and a tool. Softw. Eng. J. (1991). https://doi.org/10.1049/sej.1991.0040
5. Biamonte, J., Perkowski, M.: Testing a quantum computer, October 2004. https://doi.org/10.48550/arXiv.quant-ph/0409023
6. Briegel, H.J., Browne, D.E., Dür, W., Raussendorf, R., Van den Nest, M.: Measurement-based quantum computation. Nat. Phys. **5**(1), 19–26 (2009). https://doi.org/10.1038/nphys1157
7. Burgholzer, L., Wille, R.: Advanced equivalence checking for quantum circuits. IEEE Trans. Comput. Aided Des. Integr. Circuits Syst. **40**(9), 1810–1824 (2021). https://doi.org/10.1109/TCAD.2020.3032630
8. Campos, J., Souto, A.: QBugs: a collection of reproducible bugs in quantum algorithms and a supporting infrastructure to enable controlled quantum software testing and debugging experiments (2021). https://doi.org/10.48550/arXiv.2103.16968
9. Cerezo, M., et al.: Variational quantum algorithms. Nat. Rev. Phys. **3**(9), 625–644 (2021). https://doi.org/10.1038/s42254-021-00348-9
10. Chareton, C., Bardin, S., Lee, D., Valiron, B., Vilmart, R., Xu, Z.: Formal methods for quantum programs: a survey (2021). https://arxiv.org/abs/2109.06493
11. Christoff, I.: Testing equivalences and fully abstract models for probabilistic processes. In: Baeten, J.C.M., Klop, J.W. (eds.) CONCUR 1990. LNCS, vol. 458, pp. 126–138. Springer, Heidelberg (1990). https://doi.org/10.1007/BFb0039056
12. Cramer, M., et al.: Efficient quantum state tomography. Nat. Commun. **1**(1) (2010). https://doi.org/10.1038/ncomms1147
13. De Nicola, R., Hennessy, M.: Testing equivalences for processes. Theoret. Comput. Sci. **34**(1), 83–133 (1984). https://doi.org/10.1016/0304-3975(84)90113-0
14. Dey, N., Ghosh, M., kundu, S.S., Chakrabarti, A.: QDLC – the quantum development life Cycle (2020). https://doi.org/10.48550/arXiv.2010.08053
15. Eisert, J., et al.: Quantum certification and benchmarking. Nat. Rev. Phys. **2**(7), 382–390 (2020). https://doi.org/10.1038/s42254-020-0186-4
16. Elben, A., et al.: The Randomized Measurement Toolbox. Nat. Rev. Phys. **5**(1), 9–24 (2022). https://doi.org/10.1038/s42254-022-00535-2
17. Farhi, E., Harrow, A.W.: Quantum supremacy through the quantum approximate optimization algorithm (2019). https://doi.org/10.48550/arXiv.1602.07674
18. Feng, Y., Duan, R., Ji, Z., Ying, M.: Probabilistic bisimulations for quantum processes. Inf. Comput. **205**(11), 1608–1639 (2007). https://doi.org/10.1016/j.ic.2007.08.001
19. Feng, Y., Duan, R., Ying, M.: Bisimulation for Quantum processes. ACM Trans. Program. Lang. Syst. **34**(4) (2012). https://doi.org/10.1145/2400676.2400680

20. Gerhold, M., Stoelinga, M.: IOCO theory for probabilistic automata. Electron. Proc. Theor. Comput. Sci. **180**, 23–40 (2015). https://doi.org/10.4204/EPTCS.180.2
21. Gerhold, M., Stoelinga, M.: Model-based testing of probabilistic systems. In: Stevens, P., Wasowski, A. (eds.) Fundamental Approaches to Software Engineering. pp. 251–268. Springer, Berlin (2016). https://doi.org/10.1007/978-3-662-49665-7_15
22. Grover, L.K.: A fast quantum mechanical algorithm for database search. In: Proceedings of the Twenty-Eighth Annual ACM Symposium on Theory of Computing, STOC 1996, pp. 212-219. ACM, New York, NY, USA (1996). https://doi.org/10.1145/237814.237866
23. Harrow, A.W., Hassidim, A., Lloyd, S.: Quantum algorithm for linear systems of equations. Phys. Rev. Lett. **103**, 150502 (2009). https://doi.org/10.1103/PhysRevLett.103.150502
24. Honarvar, S., Mousavi, M.R., Nagarajan, R.: Property-based testing of quantum programs in Q#. In: Proceedings of the IEEE/ACM 42nd International Conference on Software Engineering Workshops, ICSEW 2020, pp. 430-435. ACM, New York, NY, USA (2020). https://doi.org/10.1145/3387940.3391459
25. Huang, Y., Martonosi, M.: QDB: from quantum algorithms towards correct quantum programs. In: Barik, T., Sunshine, J., Chasins, S. (eds.) 9th Workshop on Evaluation and Usability of Programming Languages and Tools (PLATEAU 2018), vol. 67, pp. 4:1–4:14. Schloss Dagstuhl – Leibniz-Zentrum für Informatik (2019). https://doi.org/10.4230/OASIcs.PLATEAU.2018.4
26. Huang, Y., Martonosi, M.: Statistical assertions for validating patterns and finding bugs in quantum programs. In: Proceedings of the 46th International Symposium on Computer Architecture, pp. 541-553. ACM, New York, NY, USA (2019). https://doi.org/10.1145/3307650.3322213
27. Hynninen, T., Kasurinen, J., Knutas, A., Taipale, O.: Software testing: survey of the industry practices. In: 2018 41st International Convention on Information and Communication Technology, Electronics and Microelectronics (MIPRO), pp. 1449–1454 (2018). https://doi.org/10.23919/MIPRO.2018.8400261
28. Javadi-Abhari, A., et al.: Quantum computing with Qiskit (2024). https://doi.org/10.48550/arXiv.2405.08810
29. Knill, E.: Conventions for quantum pseudocode (2022). https://doi.org/10.48550/arXiv.2211.02559
30. Liu, J., Byrd, G.T., Zhou, H.: Quantum circuits for dynamic runtime assertions in quantum computation. In: Proceedings of the Twenty-Fifth International Conference on Architectural Support for Programming Languages and Operating Systems, ASPLOS 2020, pp 1017-1030. ACM, New York, NY, USA (2020). https://doi.org/10.36227/techrxiv.11319929
31. Luthmann, L., Mennicke, S., Lochau, M.: Compositionality, decompositionality and refinement in input/output conformance testing. In: Kouchnarenko, O., Khosravi, R. (eds.) FACS 2016. LNCS, vol. 10231, pp. 54–72. Springer, Cham (2017). https://doi.org/10.1007/978-3-319-57666-4_5
32. Mendiluze, E., Ali, S., Arcaini, P., Yue, T.: Muskit: a mutation analysis tool for quantum software testing. In: 2021 36th IEEE/ACM International Conference on Automated Software Engineering (ASE), pp. 1266–1270 (2021). https://doi.org/10.1109/ASE51524.2021.967856

33. Miranskyy, A., Zhang, L.: On Testing quantum programs. In: 2019 IEEE/ACM 41st International Conference on Software Engineering: New Ideas and Emerging Results (ICSE-NIER), pp. 57–60 (2019). https://doi.org/10.1109/ICSE-NIER.2019.00023
34. Miranskyy, A., Zhang, L., Doliskani, J.: On testing and debugging quantum software (2021). https://doi.org/10.48550/arXiv.2103.09172
35. Moore, C., Crutchfield, J.P.: Quantum automata and quantum grammars. Theoret. Comput. Sci. **237**(1), 275–306 (2000). https://doi.org/10.1016/S0304-3975(98)00191-1
36. Nielsen, M.A., Chuang, I.L.: Quantum Computation and Quantum Information. Cambridge University Press, Cambridge (2010)
37. Peham, T., Burgholzer, L., Wille, R.: Equivalence checking of quantum circuits with the ZX-calculus. IEEE J. Emerg. Sel. Top. Circ. Syst. **12**(3), 662–675 (2022). https://doi.org/10.1109/JETCAS.2022.3202204
38. Preskill, J.: Quantum computing in the NISQ era and beyond. Quantum **2**, 79 (2018). https://doi.org/10.22331/q-2018-08-06-79
39. Segala, R.: Testing probabilistic automata. In: Montanari, U., Sassone, V. (eds.) CONCUR 1996. LNCS, vol. 1119, pp. 299–314. Springer, Heidelberg (1996). https://doi.org/10.1007/3-540-61604-7_62
40. Selinger, P., Valiron, B.: A lambda calculus for quantum computation with classical control. In: Urzyczyn, P. (ed.) TLCA 2005. LNCS, vol. 3461, pp. 354–368. Springer, Heidelberg (2005). https://doi.org/10.1007/11417170_26
41. Shor, P.: Algorithms for quantum computation: discrete logarithms and factoring. In: Proceedings 35th Annual Symposium on Foundations of Computer Science, pp. 124–134 (1994). https://doi.org/10.1109/SFCS.1994.365700
42. Tretmans, J.: Test generation with inputs, outputs and repetitive quiescence. Softw. Concepts Tools **17**(3), 103–120 (1996), https://api.semanticscholar.org/CorpusID:8056400
43. Wang, J., Gao, M., Jiang, Y., Lou, J., Gao, Y., Zhang, D., Sun, J.: QuanFuzz: fuzz testing of quantum program (2018). https://doi.org/10.48550/arXiv.1810.10310
44. Wang, Q., Liu, J., Ying, M.: Equivalence checking of quantum finite-state machines. J. Comput. Syst. Sci. **116**, 1–21 (2021). https://doi.org/10.1016/j.jcss.2020.08.004
45. Wang, X., Arcaini, P., Yue, T., Ali, S.: Application of combinatorial testing to quantum programs. In: 2021 IEEE 21st International Conference on Software Quality, Reliability and Security (QRS), pp. 179–188 (2021). https://doi.org/10.1109/QRS54544.2021.00029
46. Ying, M., Feng, Y.: Model checking quantum systems — a survey (2018). https://doi.org/10.48550/arXiv.1807.09466
47. Zhao, J.: Quantum software engineering: landscapes and horizons. CoRR **abs/2007.07047** (2020)

AFFINITREE: A Compositional Framework for Formal Analysis and Explanation of Deep Neural Networks

Maximilian Schlüter(✉) and Bernhard Steffen

TU Dortmund University, Dortmund, Germany
maximilian.schlueter@tu-dortmund.de

Abstract. We present AFFINITREE, a compositional framework for analyzing Deep Neural Networks (DNNs) based on three elementary principles: (1) symbolic execution, (2) infeasible path elimination, and (3) abstraction. The combination of these principles allows one to elegantly solve a number of interesting analysis and verification tasks, like traditional verification problems with pre- and post-conditions, model explanations in terms of semantically equivalent decision trees, concolic execution for slice-oriented testing, and visual verification of two-dimensional slices. The paper illustrates the flexibility of AFFINITREE over three different use cases covering fairness evaluation, adversarial examples, and counterfactuals. AFFINITREE is available as a modular open source library for replication, experimentation, and extension.

Keywords: Deep Learning · Explainable Artificial Intelligence · Activation Pattern Decomposition · Symbolic Execution · Rule Extraction · Interpretable Surrogate Model · Input Space Partition · Continuous Piece-wise Linear · Tool

1 Introduction and Motivation

Deep Neural Networks (DNNs) have become an essential machine learning (ML) model based on their impressive performance on various historically challenging tasks [29]. Despite their success, the learned functions of DNNs exhibit counter-intuitive behaviors, such as susceptibility to adversarial attacks [16]. Their high number of parameters and inherent functional complexity render them typically beyond human comprehension and control, leading to their characterization as *opaque* or *black-box models* [6,12,60]. Consequently, there is a pressing need for algorithms and tools to help us understand and validate DNNs, which are grouped under the name *explainable AI*. Recent publications [10,23,28,36] indicate that existing explanation methods are insufficient to achieve, e.g., safety goals, therefore the authors propose a shift to formal and rigorous explanations for DNNs.

To assess the appropriateness of the learned function, a growing body of mathematical notions has been introduced to DNNs. For example, the Lipschitz constant provides information on how susceptible the DNN is to changes in

© The Author(s), under exclusive license to Springer Nature Switzerland AG 2025
M. Huisman and F. Howar (Eds.): TAP 2024, LNCS 15153, pp. 148–167, 2025.
https://doi.org/10.1007/978-3-031-72044-4_8

the input [26]. Robustness is used to prove the absence of adversarial examples for small neighborhoods. When the DNN is piece-wise linear, its number of linear regions is used to measure the complexity of the learned function [40]. Counterfactuals [57] and visualizations of the preimage partition [22] can be used to explore how individual decisions are made.

In this paper, we present AFFINITREE[1], an open-source Rust library with Python bindings that tackles the opaqueness of piece-wise linear DNNs through formal methods. A key feature of AFFINITREE is a transformation based on symbolic execution that preserves the semantic properties of the original DNN by re-encoding them in a format inherently more comprehensible: a decision tree. As this transformation on its own can be computationally involved, AFFINITREE applies established techniques from program analysis to speed up the process without sacrificing correctness. In particular, AFFINITREE features a modular system that is built on top of the following techniques:

- **Symbolic Execution** performs a correct and complete decomposition of the DNN's parallel data flow, addressing its inherent sources of opaqueness like distributivity and non-linearity.
- **Infeasible Path Elimination** uses LP solvers to prune paths that cannot influence the decision-making process of the DNN, reducing the average case running time from exponential to polynomial in the number of neurons.
- **Composition** allows the application of continuous or non-continuous piece-wise linear functions to existing trees, enabling straightforward applications of pre-conditions, post-conditions, abstractions, and concolic execution.

To our knowledge, AFFINITREE is the first framework that implements these techniques specifically tailored to DNNs. In contrast to other tools, all methods in AFFINITREE are implemented in a compiled, system language for maximal performance. When using our thin Python wrapper one can orchestrate these techniques conveniently without incurring noticeable overhead. Based on its modularity, AFFINITREE is the first tool that can provide all of the following forms of explanations (based on the same underlying model):

- **Model Explanation:** A decision tree can be computed as a complete and correct surrogate model of the DNN.
- **Outcome Explanation:** Path(s) in the tree provide a set of necessary and/or sufficient predicates inputs must satisfy for a given classification.
- **Counterfactual Explanation:** Based on the decision tree, one can compute what attributes must change in the input to reach another class.
- **Preimage Partition:** By looking at the exact decision boundaries of the classifier, one can judge if the learned model is reasonable.

After a brief overview of the theoretical background (Sect. 2) and related work (Sect. 3), we sketch the features of AFFINITREE in Sect. 4. The main part of the paper is Sect. 5, which presents the design and algorithms of AFFINITREE. We demonstrate AFFINITREE's modular nature in different scenarios in Sect. 6 and conclude with Sect. 7.

[1] https://github.com/Conturing/affinitree-py.

2 Theoretical Background

After training has completed, most deep neural networks $h\colon \mathbb{R}^{n_0} \to \mathbb{R}^{n_L}$ can be expressed as fully-connected, feed-forward neural networks [18]:

$$h : \boldsymbol{x} \mapsto \big(h_L \circ \sigma_{L-1} \circ \cdots \circ \sigma_1 \circ h_1\big)(\boldsymbol{x}) \tag{1}$$

where L is the number of layers, n_ℓ the number of neurons in the ℓ-th layer, $h_\ell(\boldsymbol{x}) = \boldsymbol{W}_\ell \boldsymbol{x} + \boldsymbol{b}_\ell\colon \mathbb{R}^{n_{\ell-1}} \to \mathbb{R}^{n_\ell}$ are linear functions, and σ_i are non-linear, (almost everywhere) differentiable activation functions ($1 \leq \ell \leq L$). This holds true for, e.g., convolutions, pooling, residual connections, batch-normalization, attention, and memory cells. When specified in this form, it is easy to see that the semantic complexity of the DNN arises through application of the non-linear activation functions $\sigma_1, \ldots, \sigma_{L-1}$ in Eq. (1). Many popular activation functions are (continuous) piece-wise linear (CPWL), allowing a precise mathematical analysis of the DNN. Examples include $\mathrm{ReLU}(x){:=}\max\{x, 0\}$ [14], $\mathrm{LeakyReLU}(x){:=}\max\{x, 0\} + \min\{\alpha x, 0\}$ [35], $\mathrm{Maxout}(\boldsymbol{x}){:=}\max_k\{\boldsymbol{w_k}^\top \boldsymbol{x} + b_k\}$ [15], Max Pooling [30], and Argmax.

When all activation functions are CPWL, then so is the entire DNN h and one can decompose it into finitely many input regions $Q_1, \ldots, Q_r \subseteq \mathbb{R}^{n_0}$ such that h is linear when restricted to each region. The linear regions with corresponding functions can be stated constructively using *activation patterns*. For the case of ReLU, we say that a neuron $h_{\ell,i}$ is active if it falls into the identity case of ReLU ($h_{\ell,i} \geq 0$), and inactive otherwise ($h_{\ell,i} < 0$). We define an activation pattern $a \in \prod_{\ell=1}^{L-1}\{0,1\}^{n_\ell}$ that encodes for each hidden neuron $h_{\ell,i}$ the active case as $a_{\ell,i} = 1$ and the inactive as $a_{\ell,i} = 0$. The ReLU of layer ℓ can then be written as the diagonal matrix $\sigma_\ell = \mathrm{diag}(\boldsymbol{a}_\ell)$. Thus, for each activation pattern a every layer $1 \leq \ell \leq L$ of the network h simplifies to a single linear function $\boldsymbol{V}_\ell^a \boldsymbol{x} + \boldsymbol{c}_\ell^a$:

$$\boldsymbol{V}_\ell^a{:=}\begin{cases} \boldsymbol{W}_\ell \,\mathrm{diag}(\boldsymbol{a}_{\ell-1})\, \boldsymbol{V}_{\ell-1}^a & \text{if } \ell > 1 \\ \boldsymbol{W}_1 & \text{if } \ell = 1 \end{cases}$$

$$\boldsymbol{c}_\ell^a{:=}\begin{cases} \boldsymbol{W}_\ell \,\mathrm{diag}(\boldsymbol{a}_{\ell-1})\, \boldsymbol{c}_{\ell-1}^a + \boldsymbol{b}_\ell & \text{if } \ell > 1 \\ \boldsymbol{b}_1 & \text{if } \ell = 1 \end{cases}$$

As the activation pattern a assumes that the inputs to ReLU fall into certain regions, it implies restrictions onto the input. These define the boundary (linear region) in which h corresponds to the respective linear function of a:

$$Q_\ell^a(\boldsymbol{x}){:=}\begin{cases} \bigwedge\{\, \boldsymbol{V}_\ell^a[i,\bullet]\, \boldsymbol{x} + c_\ell^a[i] \geq 0 \,\big|\, a_\ell[i] = 1 \,\} \wedge & \text{if } \ell > 0 \\ \bigwedge\{\, \boldsymbol{V}_\ell^a[i,\bullet]\, \boldsymbol{x} + c_\ell^a[i] < 0 \,\big|\, a_\ell[i] = 0 \,\} \wedge Q_{\ell-1}^a(\boldsymbol{x}) & \\ \top & \text{if } \ell = 0 \end{cases}$$

The points $\boldsymbol{x}$ satisfying $Q_\ell^a(\boldsymbol{x})$ form a convex polyhedral set. If this set is empty, we say that Q_ℓ^a is infeasible. Combining these one can decompose h accordingly into linear pieces [9,52]:

$$h(\boldsymbol{x}) = \sum_a \left(\boldsymbol{V}_L^a\, \boldsymbol{x} + \boldsymbol{c}_L^a\right) Q_L^a(\boldsymbol{x}) \tag{2}$$

This representation can, in principle, be easily analyzed for many semantic properties φ of h, like *robustness*, by checking φ for each of the $r \leq 2^n$ linear regions (where $n = n_1 + \cdots + n_{L-1}$ is the number of hidden neurons in h):

$$\forall a \in \prod_{\ell=1}^{L-1} \{0,1\}^{n_\ell}, \forall x \in \mathbb{R}^{n_0}:\ Q_L^a(\boldsymbol{x}) \implies \varphi(\boldsymbol{V}_L^a\, \boldsymbol{x} + \boldsymbol{c}_L^a; \boldsymbol{x})$$

When φ is a linear property, this expression can be encoded into a linear program for each a. In other cases, one can use MILP or SMT solvers or neural network verification tools to test the truth value of the formula.

As such, this decomposition was proposed multiple times in the literature, e.g., in the context of symbolic and concolic execution [17,43,48,52,53,56], neural network verification [3,8,13,50,55], explainability through surrogate models [2,9,24,25,31,42,45,51], bounding and counting linear regions to measure expressiveness [1,18,20,21,39,40,49,58], visualization of decision boundaries [22], extracting compact trees of controllers [33], reverse engineering of DNN parameters [46], and connections to other fields of mathematics [4]. Additionally, MILP formulations are used for calculating the Lipschitz constant [26].

3 Related Work

The tool DeepConcolic [53] uses symbolic and concrete analysis to derive a finite set of inputs $\mathcal{T}$, called a test suite, that maximize the satisfaction of previously defined coverage metrics $\mathfrak{R}$. These metrics can be stated in a logic called *DR*, which is based on Quantified Linear Logic over Rationals. Example formulas are given for Lipschitz Continuity, Neuron Coverage, Sign Sign Coverage, and Neuron Boundary Coverage. Based on an initial test point t_0, the test suite $\mathcal{T}$ is iteratively extended by first solving an optimization problem that returns one of the metrics $r \in \mathfrak{R}$ which is likely to be satisfied based on concrete execution of test cases in $\mathcal{T}$. Then, symbolic execution is used (based on Eq. (2)) to find a new input that satisfies r. If no such input can be found after a given computational budget, the metric is said to have failed and is removed from $\mathfrak{R}$.

The tool NeuroSPF [56] translates a DNN (FNN or CNN) into an equivalent Java program by a straightforward encoding of the network's data flow. The resulting program is analyzed with the Symbolic (Java) PathFinder, which supports concolic execution of Java bytecode. SPF allows specifying which solver should be used to check the feasibility of program paths, like Z3. In their paper [56], the authors demonstrate how the tool can be used to check robustness

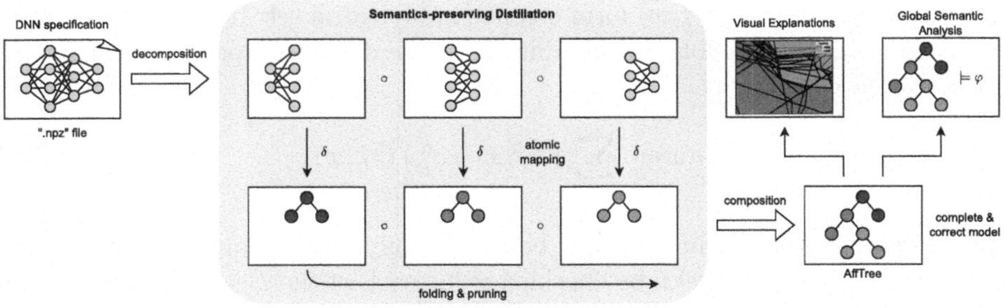

Fig. 1. Illustration of AFFINITREE's divide and conquer approach to distillation. Starting with a DNN (top left), we first decompose the network into its individual layers (top middle). Then, each layer is transformed into an equivalent `AffTree` instance (bottom middle). These are then composed in the same order to construct the final `AffTree` that represents the complete network (bottom right). For efficiency, we apply infeasible path elimination in-between each composition application.

where all but a central pixel in an MNIST image are fixed. By treating this central pixel symbolically, they found an adversarial example.

The tool SplineCam [22] provides 2D visualizations of the decision boundaries of DNNs (FNN or CNN) with ReLU or Leaky ReLU activation. For that it combines the decomposition of Eq. (2) with a graph-based approach to calculate the intersection of the surface $S \subseteq \mathbb{R}^{n_0 \cdot n_L}$ of the continuous function $h\colon \mathbb{R}^{n_0} \to \mathbb{R}^{n_L}$ of the neural network with a given 2D slice defined by a hyperplane $H = \{\boldsymbol{x} \in \mathbb{R}^{n_0 \cdot n_L} \mid \boldsymbol{w}^\top \boldsymbol{x} = 0\}$. They report that their algorithm has an average case complexity of $\mathcal{O}(n^2)$ where n is the number of input hyperplanes. By computing the preimage partition, SplineCam can create plots, but also calculate measures over the polytopes like volume and eccentricity.

4 Overview and Features

The central process of AFFINITREE is to *distill* a neural network into a decision tree (c.f. Fig. 1). This decision tree then fulfills the role of a *faithful surrogate model*. As a *surrogate model*, it encodes the semantic properties of the underlying opaque neural network (*black-box model*) using an alternative data structure that is by its nature more comprehensible (*white-box model*)[2]. It is *faithful*,[3] meaning that it represents exactly the same mathematical function as the DNN.

From the viewpoint of explainability, only a few ML models are eligible as surrogate models. Based on interdisciplinary research, the following three ML models can be considered humanly comprehensible: decision trees, rule based models, and sometimes linear systems [19,32,38]. From the technical side, we found that—out of these three—decision trees lend themselves best for high-fidelity explanations. This is because many neural networks are piece-wise linear

[2] Alternative terms are *glass*, *transparent*, or *ante-hoc interpretable model*.
[3] Also called *fidelitous*, *semantics-preserving*, or *functionally equivalent*.

(PWL) functions and PWL functions can be stored exactly in decision trees similar to BSP trees [47,48]. Based on this fact, we developed a semantics-preserving transformation from piece-wise linear networks into decision trees (Sect. 2). The resulting trees can capture the intricate structure of DNNs in a way that enables rigorous analysis.

On the technical side, AFFINITREE is an open source library written in Rust building on top of the performant 'slab' library for memory management, 'ndarray' for linear algebra, and external LP solvers for determining infeasible paths (with built-in support for 'highs' and 'minilp'). We also provide Python bindings that closely match the Rust API while integrating into the existing Python data-science landscape. AFFINITREE provides a central data structure, called `AffTree`, to store a piece-wise linear function in form of a decision tree, as well as many methods operating on this tree. Its key features are:

- semantics-preserving distillation of any piece-wise linear DNN into an `AffTree`
- application of any (continuous or non-continuous) piece-wise linear precondition
- concolic mode that fixes inputs to specified values
- pruning of infeasible paths and other redundancies
- efficient iteration over the linear regions of an `AffTree`
- visualizations built on top of Graphviz and matplotlib
- built-in support for commonly used functions in deep learning such as ReLU, LeakyReLU, Hard Hyperbolic Tangent, Hard Sigmoid, Threshold, and Argmax

During the implementation of the library, we focused on performance, memory efficiency, and extendability: Rust's ecosystem provides many tools—from the compiler, over static analysis, to performance benchmark tools—to ensure an efficient implementation. To achieve extendability, we designed a modular API that makes use of the algebraic features of decision trees as presented in [48]:

All higher-level functions of AFFINITREE *boil down to an application of the composition operator.*

Composition is used for the semantics-preserving distillation process, to apply pre- and post-conditions to an `AffTree`, to fix inputs for concolic execution, and for visualizations (e.g., to apply geometric transformations).

5 Design of AFFINITREE

In this section, we take a look into the technical details of AFFINITREE. Starting with the data structure in Sect. 5.1, we continue with a general description of the distillation process in Sect. 5.2, followed by the design and implementation of the composition operator in Sect. 5.3. Finally, we introduce the pruning methods and preconditions that are essential for the performance of AFFINITREE in Sect. 5.4 and Sect. 5.5, respectively.

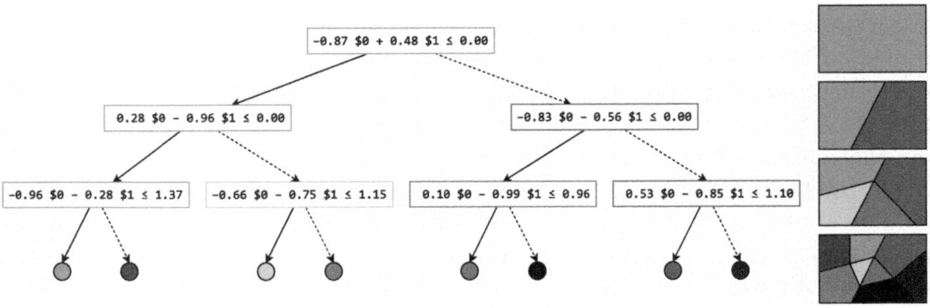

Fig. 2. Illustration of an `AffTree` (left) and its corresponding space partition (right). Based on the decision nodes in each layer of the tree, the input space (preimage) is partitioned into regions. Each decision node introduces a binary split, and with that split divides the input space into two new subregions. Here one can see the similarity to BSP trees [54].

5.1 Core Data Structure

The core data structure of AFFINITREE is the `AffTree` struct (Rust's class type). It is based on the theory presented in [47]. An `AffTree` is a full binary tree, that is, every node in the graph has either two or zero children. We call the nodes with two children *inner nodes* and the nodes with zero children *terminals*. Inner nodes are equipped with a linear predicate of the form $\boldsymbol{q}^\top \boldsymbol{x} \leq b$ where $\boldsymbol{q} \in \mathbb{R}^{n_0}$ and $b \in \mathbb{R}$ are fixed values, $\boldsymbol{x}$ is a symbolic representation of the input vector, and n_0 is the input dimension. Terminals store a linear function $\boldsymbol{W}\boldsymbol{x} + \boldsymbol{b}$ where again $\boldsymbol{W} \in \mathbb{R}^{n_L \times n_0}$, $\boldsymbol{b} \in \mathbb{R}^{n_L}$ are fixed, $\boldsymbol{x}$ is symbolic, and n_L is the output dimension. An example of an `AffTree` is given in Fig. 2.

The tree structure of `AffTrees` allows an efficient sharing of predicates along multiple paths in the tree. To enumerate all linear regions of the stored PWL function in an `AffTree`, we provide an efficient iterator based on depth-first traversal. This operation is frequently used, e.g., when removing infeasible paths or in the context of neural network verification. The tree structure is also useful for storing and propagating additional information originating from concrete use cases.

To ensure memory efficiency and to avoid fragmentation, the tree is stored in a continuous array, an *arena*, managed by the slab library. Each node contains the array index of its parent and of its two children, as well as information about the linear decision or linear function associated with the node. The tree supports many forms of traversal (e.g., depth-first, memory-order). Nodes can be added, updated, and removed. Removing nodes also cascades to their descendants, as these would be otherwise unreachable 'dead weight'.

5.2 Distillation Process

To start of the distillation process, one first needs to specify the desired DNN in a compatible format. Inside AFFINITREE, a DNN is currently expressed as a sequence of `Layers`, where each `Layer` represents one piece-wise linear function. Technically, a `Layer` is an enum (Rust's sum type) with cases for common components of DNNs like linear layers and different activation functions. AFFINITREE has built-in support for converting PyTorch models and specially formatted numpy files into such sequences. AFFINITREE provides a convenience function to distill an `AffTree` from this sequence (Fig. 1). Under the hood, each `Layer` instance is converted to a small, semantically equivalent `AffTree` instance using predefined schemas. Then, the resulting `AffTrees` are composed in the given order. After each composition step an important optimization technique is applied, which removes redundancy (Sect. 5.4).

Based on these optimizations, the distillation of a DNN with input dimension n_0 and a total of h partial ReLUs attaining r different activation patterns (see [49]) has a worst case running time of $\mathcal{O}(rf(n_0, h))$ where f is the running time of the chosen LP solver when solving an LP with n_0 variables and h inequalities. The parameter $r \leq 2^h$ is uniquely determined by the given DNN and can be further upper bounded by its architecture (*bottlenecks*) and input dimension n_0 [49]. In the average case, r is polynomial in the depth of the DNN but still exponential in its input dimension [21]. When using concolic execution, n_0 decrease by the amount of fixed inputs and h by the amount of partial ReLUs which are fixed to one activation pattern as a consequence of the reduced input patterns.

5.3 Modular Composition

Modularity is a well-established design pattern in software construction. It is an essential tool to reduce complexity, to provide a simple yet powerful API, and to allow easy extension. In AFFINITREE, this pattern is implemented based on the eponymous (function) composition operator of (algebraic) decision trees [47]. This operator allows a modular construction of complex `AffTrees` from simpler building blocks. Concretely, this operator corresponds to a sequential function application:

$$(t_2 \circ t_1)(\boldsymbol{x}) = t_2(t_1(\boldsymbol{x})) \;\; \forall \boldsymbol{x}$$

where t_1, t_2, and $t_2 \circ t_1$ are `AffTree` instances and $\circ$ denotes composition.

Composition is implemented using classic graph algorithms. Here, we essentially copy the tree of the second argument t_2 once for each terminal of the first tree t_1. Each such terminal of t_1 is used to update its copy of t_2, where the terminal essentially acts as a precondition that transforms the input space of the second tree t_2. The resulting tree is added to t_1 in place of the respective terminal.

5.4 Semantics-Preserving Pruning

The number of possible activation patterns/linear regions in a DNN can increase exponentially in the number of neurons in the worst case, as was shown in [40] using a carefully constructed DNN. However, even in the worst case the number

Algorithm 1 Infeasible Path Elimination

```
for all (v, P) ∈ enum(G) do                    ▷ v is a node and P its path condition
    if v = root(G) then
        continue
    p ← parent(G, v)
    if p.witness ∈ solution_space(P) then
        v.witness ← p.witness
        continue
    s ← solve_lp(constraints = P, costs = x ↦ 0)
    if s.infeasible then
        remove_subtree(G, v)
    else
        v.witness ← s.optimal_point
```

of feasible linear regions can be less than 2^r when including the architecture of the DNN [1]. Further, the average case grows only polynomial in the number of neurons [21]. The infeasible path elimination removes unattainable patterns from the tree, which can be up to 40% for each layer. Thus, this optimization is essential for the performance of the distillation. On the other hand, determining if a path is feasible is also costly. As a result, the runtime of the whole distillation process is dominated by this operation. Therefore, an efficient implementation is key.

Infeasible Path Elimination. The technique of eliminating infeasible paths was established for algebraic decision structures (ADDs) with dependent predicates [41]. Sketched briefly, this optimization discovers paths along which the path conditions are not satisfiable by any possible input, thus they are *infeasible*. Thus, infeasible nodes contribute no value to the semantics of the structure while taking up resources.[4] The number of nodes that can be pruned are considerable: If a node is infeasible, then so are all its descendants. Thus, the entire subtree can be pruned, or even better, not be constructed in the first place. Current empirical data suggests that at deeper layers of the tree a node has on average just 1.2 feasible children.

To check the satisfiability of the path conditions, which all are linear predicates, we use linear program (LP) solvers. However, at the scale of `AffTree` solving an LP for every possible path becomes quickly unmaintainable. Therefore, AFFINITREE includes several improvements that reduce the number of LPs that have to be solved to detect infeasible paths. For one, we explore the tree in a depth first manner, which allows us to reuse many of the computations done for previously visited nodes. Further, we store this information in the tree for future invocations of this optimization. A simple but effective example for this is that we store a witness for the feasibility of a node, which ensures that for each feasible linear region of the DNN only one LP is solved (indifferent of when the user calls infeasible elimination).

[4] In a tree one can identify paths from the root to a node with the node itself.

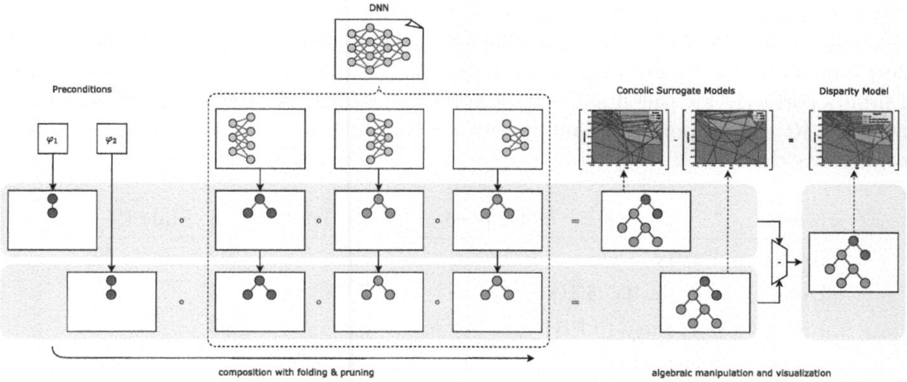

Fig. 3. Illustration of a concolic execution based on two preconditions.

Our implementation has an algorithmic complexity of at most $\mathcal{O}(nf(n_0, h))$ where n is the number of nodes, h the height, and n_0 the input dimension of the tree; and $f(n_0, h)$ is the runtime of the LP solver given a linear program of h inequalities and n_0 variables. A simplified algorithmic description can be found in Algorithm 1), for readability edge cases are intentionally left out.

Redundant Predicate Elimination. Another optimization from ADDs is redundancy elimination. In its most broad term, redundancy in a decision tree is whenever all subtrees of a decision node compute the same function. In [5] a technique was introduced that detects redundancy through graph isomorphism. However, this algorithm requires a fixed variable ordering, which is too expensive for `AffTrees`. Besides that, the probability that a distilled `AffTree` from a DNN contains two equal predicates is a zero volume in the parameter space.

Despite that, terminals can easily be equal when using certain post-conditions such as argmax or class characterization for classification tasks. In these cases, a simpler variant of [5] is sufficient: in a bottom-up fashion, whenever all children of a decision are syntactically equal terminals, replace the decision by either of its children.

5.5 Preconditions

Many considered properties in the context of neural networks (e.g. in verification settings) are (piece-wise) linear. Thus, they can be integrated directly into AFFINITREE using again its compositional structure. Conceptually, this is based on [43]. In our tool, preconditions are just another `AffTree` instance. Thus, they subsume all (continuous and non-continuous) piece-wise linear functions such as the established polyhedral sets and star sets in verification settings [55]. In contrast to these, `AffTrees` can also transform the input space, e.g., in form of geometric transformations like scaling, shearing, rotation, reflection, projection,

Table 1. Fairness metrics for the considered DNN over the test set with respect to the sensitive feature sex. A consistent disparity can be observed across all metrics. PR: the proportion of all inputs classified as positive by the DNN; TPR: the proportion of inputs correctly identified as positive among those actually exceeding an income of \$50K; FPR: the proportion of inputs erroneously identified as positive among those earning less than \$50K.

Metric	Disparity ($\|\Delta\%\|$)	Female (%)	Male (%)
Accuracy Parity	13	92	79
Demographic Parity (PR)	20	3	23
Equal Opportunity (TPR)	21	23	54
Equalized Odds (FPR)	9	1	10

and slicing. The latter, which corresponds also to a concolic execution, is particularly useful when fixing all but two dimensions to generate *visual explanations*, an example of which is shown in Fig. 3. We will explore this further in Sect. 6.

6 Demonstration

All experiments in this section were performed with AFFINITREE version 0.22.0 on an AMD EPYC 7763 with 256 cores à 2.450GHz and 2TB of RAM. Execution times of the experiments of each figure range from a few seconds up to an hour on a single core. For DNN training, PyTorch was used powered by an NVIDIA GeForce RTX 3090. For more details, see our accompanying artifact.

6.1 Fairness Analysis

First, we demonstrate multiple aspects of AFFINITREE in a setting for analyzing *fairness*. The concept of algorithmic fairness has recently received much attention. Put briefly, it involves addressing systematic disparities in error rates (or other conditional probabilities) across demographics differing in a sensitive attribute [37,44]. DNNs are particularly susceptible to bias (i.e., unfairness) due to their chaotic nature and reliance on good training data. Achieving fairness in DNNs remains an open issue, yet it is deemed necessary for their widespread adoption in sensitive applications. Existing strategies to mitigate bias in DNNs include (i) regularization, (ii) data pre-processing, and (iii) retraining with extended datasets [34]. AFFINITREE offers a framework that facilitates the identification and visual exploration of *individual fairness* violations [11].

As a running example, we selected a DNN trained on the UCI adult dataset [27], a prominent dataset in the field of algorithmic fairness. It consists of 14 attributes (6 numeric, 8 categorical), including sensitive attributes like sex, race, and age. For clarity, we excluded all categorical variables except for sex, but all results are also valid when including them. This results in an input dimension of $n_0 = 8$. The model aims to predict whether an individual's income surpasses

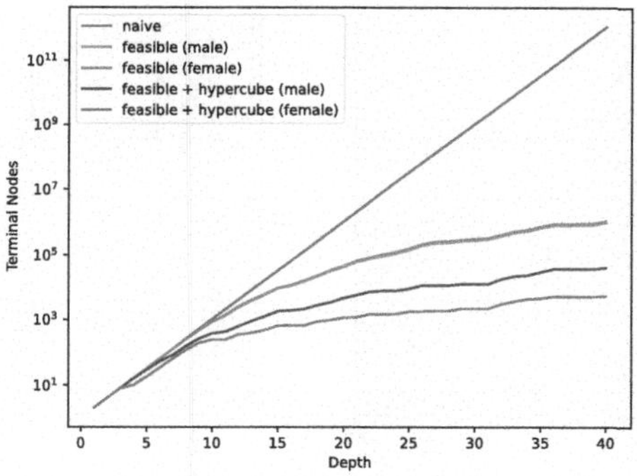

Fig. 4. Comparison of the number of terminal nodes of the discussed `AffTrees` in Eqs. (4) and (5) and their theoretical worst case. As can be seen, the different optimization strategies successfully reduce the number of nodes without compromising correctness.

\$50,000 ($n_L = 2$). Our DNN consists of four hidden layers à 10 neurons with ReLU activation. It was trained for 20 epochs with fairness regularization from fairret [7] (KL projection of true positive rate), resulting in a test set accuracy of 83.50%. A summary of popular fairness metrics for this DNN with respect to sex is provided in Table 1. As can be seen, the DNN exhibits a clear disparity against the female demographic. However, this summary is insufficient for *understanding* it.

With AFFINITREE, we can highlight specific instances of possible bias or unfair treatment within the model's decision-making process. For applying it, let us formalize violations of individual fairness for our case, which states that similar inputs differing in the sensitive attribute sex are treated differently by the DNN h:

$$h(\boldsymbol{x}[S \mapsto \mathit{male}]) \neq h(\boldsymbol{x}[S \mapsto \mathit{female}]) \tag{3}$$

where S denotes the sensitive feature, and $\boldsymbol{x}[S \mapsto s]$ sets attribute S of $\boldsymbol{x}$ to the value s. We directly extended this notion to input regions. A *region of disparity* $Q \subseteq \mathbb{R}^{n_L}$ is an inclusion-maximal set such that all points in that set satisfy Eq. (3). Now, the regions of disparity of h are exactly the connected components of the inputs that satisfy the algebraic formula:

$$\left| h \circ \varphi(S \mapsto \mathit{male}) - h \circ \varphi(S \mapsto \mathit{female}) \right| \geq \epsilon \tag{4}$$

where $\varphi(S \mapsto s)(\boldsymbol{x}) := \boldsymbol{x}[S \mapsto s]$ is a function that sets attribute S of inputs $\boldsymbol{x}$ to value s, and ϵ is a small number greater than zero. Such a representation is especially amenable for lifting to decision trees. Indeed, every operation in this term is piece-wise linear. Further, when expressed in this form the term has the benefit of numerical stability for floating point numbers. Thus, the term can already be computed with AFFINITREE (c.f. Fig. 3).

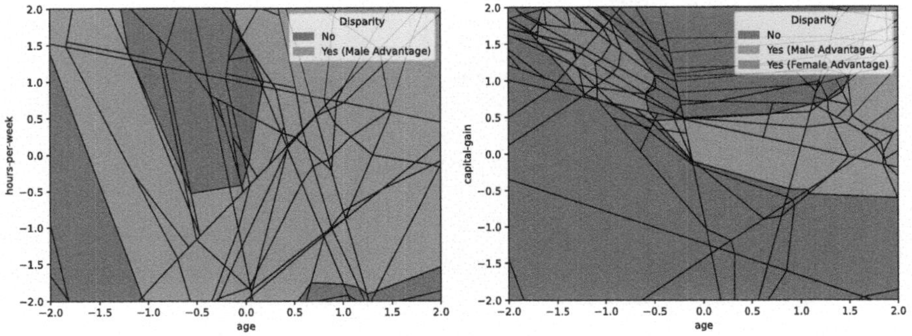

(a) Test sample 5053

(b) Test sample 94

Fig. 5. Visualization of extreme cases of disparity in two-dimensional slices aligned with coordinate axes and test samples.

In the context of DNNs, it is best to restrict the analysis to probable inputs, as DNNs are unreliable on out-of-distribution data. To accomplish this, we can simply prepend a convex precondition. As the data was already standardized before training (scaled to have unit variance and a mean of zero), we can choose the hypercube $P = [-1.0, 1.0]^6 \times [0.0, 1.0]^2$:

$$\left| h \circ \mathbb{I}(P) \circ \varphi(S \mapsto m) - h \circ \mathbb{I}(P) \circ \varphi(S \mapsto f) \right| \geq \epsilon \tag{5}$$

where $\mathbb{I}(X)$ is a variation of the characteristic function of set X:

$$\mathbb{I}(X)(\boldsymbol{x}) := \begin{cases} \boldsymbol{x} & \text{if } \boldsymbol{x} \in X \\ \textit{undefined} & \text{otherwise} \end{cases}$$

This term can be encoded and executed in AFFINITREE producing a tree that exactly characterizes all regions of disparity. AFFINITREE's optimizations—infeasible path elimination and redundancy elimination—considerably reduce the computational resources required to calculate these trees (Fig. 4). In the case of the considered DNN, the left tree (male precondition) has 81803 nodes and the right (female precondition) 10789 nodes. Already one can see that the actual number of nodes in the distilled `AffTrees` is significantly lower than the theoretic worst case of $2^{40} \approx 10^{12}$. The final tree after taking the difference has 808713 nodes, which is another three orders of magnitude lower than the worst case, which is the product of both tree sizes.

For application in the realm of explainability, much more interesting are concrete cases. Given some input $\boldsymbol{z}$, we may ask: How does the region of disparity look around $\boldsymbol{z}$ (if it exists)? As such regions are situated in the input space, their high-dimensionality makes them hard to visualize. With AFFINITREE, we can generate two-dimensional slices into these regions making them easy to comprehend by humans. In contrast to projections, the slices are accurate depictions of a specific subspace. Given a sample $\boldsymbol{z}$ and a set of two axes I with $S \notin I$,

$|I| = 2$, one can define a piece-wise linear function $t(\boldsymbol{z}, I)$ that enables us to find regions of disparity in the two-dimensional slice I containing $\boldsymbol{z}$:

$$t(\boldsymbol{z}, I) := \left| h \circ \mathbb{I}(P) \circ \psi_I(\boldsymbol{z}[S \mapsto m]) - h \circ \mathbb{I}(P) \circ \psi_I(\boldsymbol{z}[S \mapsto f]) \right|$$

where $t(\boldsymbol{z}, I)(\boldsymbol{x}) \geq \epsilon$ gives the desired regions of disparity and

$$\big(\psi_I(\boldsymbol{z})(\boldsymbol{x})\big)_i := \begin{cases} x_i & \text{if } i \in I \\ z_i & \text{otherwise} \end{cases}$$

Based on the term $t(\boldsymbol{z}, I)$ one can define multiple new metrics, however, defining them here formally would be out of the scope of this demonstration. We found that roughly 10% of samples from the training set and 13% from the test set violate individual fairness according to Eq. (3). For the 1314 samples from the test set that violate individual fairness and all axis combinations $I \in \{(i, j) \mid 0 \leq i < j \leq 6 \wedge i, j \neq 1\}$ (excluding the attribute 'fnlwgt'), we distilled the `AffTree` of $t(\boldsymbol{z}, I)$. Based on the resulting trees, we computed the ratio between the areas of disparity to the overall area (which is bounded by P). The highest ratio of 72% was found for sample number 5053 with axis 'age' and 'hours-per-week' (Fig. 5a). Although the DNN was regularized to improve fairness, we saw a considerable disparity between the areas that favored females to the ones that favored males, the latter being considerably higher. The highest female advantage (6.85%) was found for sample number 94 with axis 'age' and 'capital-gain', which is visualized in Fig. 5b.

6.2 Decision Boundaries Near Adversarial Examples

In this scenario, we use AFFINITREE to visually explore decision boundaries near adversarial examples. For that we distill decision trees of a fixed DNN using preconditions that are built around adversarial examples. We show that despite reasonable accuracy scores on the test set, there exists directions $\boldsymbol{v}$ in the input space where adversarials occur, e.g., $h(\boldsymbol{x} + \lambda \boldsymbol{v}) \neq h(\boldsymbol{x})$ for a large range of λ. Such directions highlight systematical vulnerabilities of the DNN.

Adversarial examples are a puzzling phenomenon of DNNs that are often cited to highlight the chaotic nature of DNNs. For a given point $\boldsymbol{x} \in \mathbb{R}^{n_0}$ belonging to class c_1, an adversarial example is a point $\boldsymbol{x}_{\mathbf{adv}}$ that lies very close to the original $\|\boldsymbol{x} - \boldsymbol{x}_{\mathbf{adv}}\|_p \leq \epsilon$ but which is incorrectly classified as belonging to a different class $h(\boldsymbol{x}_{\mathbf{adv}}) \neq c_1$ by the DNN. For this example, we consider the Fashion MNIST dataset [59], which consists of 28×28 pixel grayscale images ($n_0 = 784$) representing ten categories of fashion articles ($n_L = 10$). We train a DNN consisting of three hidden layers with 15 neurons and ReLU activations on the dataset. After 20 epochs the network achieves an accuracy of 84.9% on the test set.

For the generation of adversarial examples we apply the well-know Fast Gradient Sign Attack (FGSA) [16] to this DNN. The attack uses the loss function J to guide the search to regions where the DNN performs worse:

$$\boldsymbol{x}_{\mathbf{adv}} = \boldsymbol{x} + \epsilon \cdot \text{mask} \cdot \text{sign}(\nabla_x J(\theta, \boldsymbol{x}, y))$$

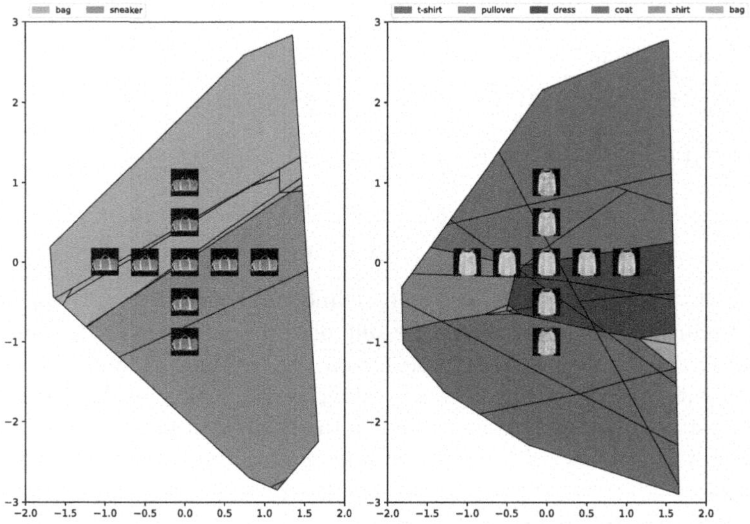

(a) Training sample 4798 (b) Training sample 25617

Fig. 6. Decision boundaries given by AFFINITREE for a DNN trained on Fashion MNIST. Using the stated sample as anchor point, two orthogonal axes of the input space are explored: from top to bottom is the adversarial attack direction and from left to right the first principal component. For reference the adversarial at (0, 0) and eight other points are visualized, which illustrate that the DNN is clearly wrong in its classification. Further, one can see that the adversarials are not localized but continue along a spacial axis. (Color figure online)

Even when using a very small $\epsilon = 0.0005$ the attack finds for 153 out of the 50000 training samples adversarial examples. For each adversarial example $\boldsymbol{x}_{\mathbf{adv}}$, we first constructed a suitable two-dimensional subspace $S(\boldsymbol{x}_{\mathbf{adv}}) \subset \mathbb{R}^{784}$, which is likely to contain interesting points. To achieve this, the subspace is spanned by (i) the first principal component of the data set and (ii) the axis between the original point $\boldsymbol{x}$ and its adversarial $\boldsymbol{x}_{\mathbf{adv}}$ (which also works for other adversarial attacks). The (affine) subspace is then shifted so that it is centered at the adversarial:

$$S(\boldsymbol{x}_{\mathbf{adv}}) = \boldsymbol{x}_{\mathbf{adv}} + \mathrm{span}\{\boldsymbol{pc}_1, \boldsymbol{x} - \boldsymbol{x}_{\mathbf{adv}}\}$$

By construction $\boldsymbol{x}, \boldsymbol{x}_{\mathbf{adv}} \in S(\boldsymbol{x}_{\mathbf{adv}})$. Using standard linear algebra techniques one can define a distance-preserving, linear mapping $\varphi(\boldsymbol{x}_{\mathbf{adv}})\colon \mathbb{R}^2 \to S(\boldsymbol{x}_{\mathbf{adv}})$, which is the desired precondition for our distillation. Further, we add again a constraint that bounds inputs to plausible values inside $[0, 1]^{784}$, leading to the piece-wise linear function

$$t(\boldsymbol{x}_{\mathbf{adv}}) := h \circ \mathbb{I}([0, 1]^{784}) \circ \varphi(\boldsymbol{x}_{\mathbf{adv}}) \; : \mathbb{R}^2 \to \{0, \ldots, 9\}$$

Notice that this precondition corresponds to concolic execution over the values of $\boldsymbol{x}_{\mathbf{adv}}$ with two degrees of freedom, which improves the running time considerably.

By applying φ first the box-shape of $[0,1]^{784}$ is also transformed into a convex polyhedral boundary.

Following the same steps as in Fig. 1, we created a plot of the preimage partition located at the adversarial example (Fig. 6). The shown plot is a slice of the input space that corresponds one-to-one to $S(\boldsymbol{x}_{\mathbf{adv}}) \cap [0,1]^{784}$. First, we may look at the reference images, which also correspond to the exact point where they are placed. One can see that all images are similar enough that one would assume that they are classified consistently. However, the bag depicted in sample 4798 in Fig. 6a is also seen as a sneaker ■ by the model. The coat depicted by sample 25617 in Fig. 6b is also seen as a pullover ■, dress ■, and t-shirt ■. To see this in more detail, we may now look at the decision boundaries calculated by AFFINITREE. Contrary to intuition, the adversarials belong not to small regions of outliers, but continue in entire spacial directions. Further, note that the input images are not degenerate edge cases (e.g., out-of-distribution data or random noise), but actually depict completely valid clothing items.

6.3 Counterfactual Explanations

(a) MNIST image 137

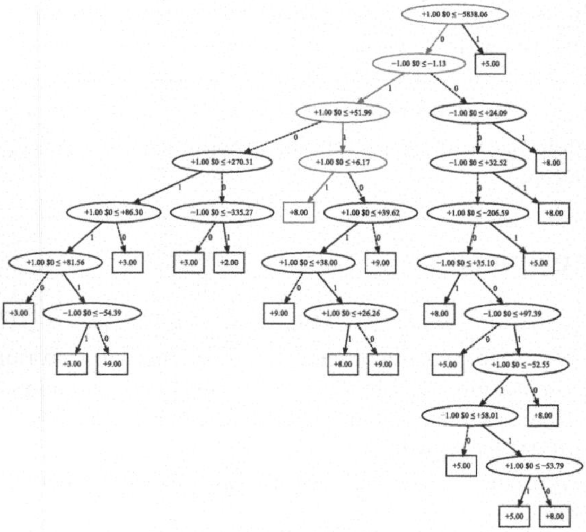

(b) `AffTree`

Fig. 7. On the left: MNIST image of an '8' with pixel $(15, 15)$ highlighted in red. On the right: `AffTree` that describes how the input is classified depending on the value of pixel $(15, 15)$. (Color figure online)

Finally, we conclude our demonstration section with a scenario proposed in [56] for the tool NeuroSPF. In this case, an MNIST sample is taken from the training set (Fig. 7a), which is the basis for a concolic execution: The pixel located at position $(15, 15)$ is made symbolically while all others stay fixed. Through a concolic execution one can then determine how much this pixel must change in order to influence the decision. This corresponds to a counterfactual explanation. Further, when the change is small enough (l_∞ distance less than ϵ), the modified image serves also as an adversarial example.

For classification, we constructed a fully connected DNN with one hidden layer of 15 and one of 10 neurons and ReLU activation (12010 parameters). Fixing all but pixel $(15, 15)$, AFFINITREE computed the decision tree shown in Fig. 7b. The path that is taken by the original MNIST image is highlighted in red.

7 Conclusion

We presented AFFINITREE, a novel open source library to tackle the opaque nature of DNNs by transforming them into interpretable decision trees based on symbolic and concolic execution. AFFINITREE provides effective optimization techniques to prune infeasible paths and redundant decisions for providing concise, faithful explanations. Using concolic execution, these explanations can be tailored to focus on interesting slices of the domain, to obtain surrogate models which can nicely be visualized in cases where all but two dimensions are provided with concrete values. The result is a novel visual approach to explanation based on preimage partitions and concolic slicing, which counteracts the exponential costs of increased input dimensions by focusing on the dimensions that matter. We are convinced that images like the ones shown for bias and adversarial example detection are a promising means for increasing the trust and understanding of DNNs.

References

1. Arora, R., Basu, A., Mianjy, P., Mukherjee, A.: Understanding deep neural networks with rectified linear units. In: 6th International Conference on Learning Representations, ICLR 2018, Vancouver, BC, Canada, 30 April–3 May 2018, Conference Track Proceedings. OpenReview.net (2018). https://openreview.net/forum?id=B1J_rgWRW
2. Aytekin, C.: Neural networks are decision trees. arXiv preprint arXiv:2210.05189 (2022)
3. Bak, S.: nnenum: verification of ReLU neural networks with optimized abstraction refinement. In: Dutle, A., Moscato, M.M., Titolo, L., Muñoz, C.A., Perez, I. (eds.) NFM 2021. LNCS, vol. 12673, pp. 19–36. Springer, Cham (2021). https://doi.org/10.1007/978-3-030-76384-8_2
4. Balestriero, R., Baraniuk, R.G.: Mad max: affine spline insights into deep learning. Proc. IEEE **109**(5), 704–727 (2020)
5. Bryant, R.E.: Graph-based algorithms for Boolean function manipulation. IEEE Trans. Comput. **100**(8), 677–691 (1986)
6. Burrell, J.: How the machine 'thinks': understanding opacity in machine learning algorithms. Big Data Soc. **3**(1), 2053951715622512 (2016)
7. Buyl, M., Defrance, M., De Bie, T.: FAIRRET: a framework for differentiable fairness regularization terms. arXiv preprint arXiv:2310.17256 (2023)

8. Böing, B., Müller, E.: On training and verifying robust autoencoders. In: 2022 IEEE 9th International Conference on Data Science and Advanced Analytics (DSAA), pp. 1–10 (2022). https://doi.org/10.1109/DSAA54385.2022.10032334
9. Chu, L., Hu, X., Hu, J., Wang, L., Pei, J.: Exact and consistent interpretation for piecewise linear neural networks: a closed form solution. In: Proceedings of the 24th ACM SIGKDD International Conference on Knowledge Discovery & Data Mining, pp. 1244–1253 (2018)
10. Dimanov, B., Bhatt, U., Jamnik, M., Weller, A.: You shouldn't trust me: learning models which conceal unfairness from multiple explanation methods (2020)
11. Dwork, C., Hardt, M., Pitassi, T., Reingold, O., Zemel, R.: Fairness through awareness. In: Proceedings of the 3rd Innovations in Theoretical Computer Science Conference, pp. 214–226 (2012)
12. Facchini, A., Termine, A.: Towards a taxonomy for the opacity of AI systems. In: Müller, V.C. (ed.) PTAI 2021. Studies in Applied Philosophy, Epistemology and Rational Ethics, vol. 63, pp. 73–89. Springer, Cham (2021). https://doi.org/10.1007/978-3-031-09153-7_7
13. Gehr, T., Mirman, M., Drachsler-Cohen, D., Tsankov, P., Chaudhuri, S., Vechev, M.: Ai2: safety and robustness certification of neural networks with abstract interpretation. In: 2018 IEEE symposium on security and privacy (SP), pp. 3–18. IEEE (2018)
14. Glorot, X., Bordes, A., Bengio, Y.: Deep sparse rectifier neural networks. In: Proceedings of the Fourteenth International Conference on Artificial Intelligence and Statistics, pp. 315–323. JMLR Workshop and Conference Proceedings (2011)
15. Goodfellow, I., Warde-Farley, D., Mirza, M., Courville, A., Bengio, Y.: Maxout networks. In: International Conference on Machine Learning, pp. 1319–1327. PMLR (2013)
16. Goodfellow, I.J., Shlens, J., Szegedy, C.: Explaining and harnessing adversarial examples. arXiv preprint arXiv:1412.6572 (2014)
17. Gopinath, D., Wang, K., Zhang, M., Pasareanu, C.S., Khurshid, S.: Symbolic execution for deep neural networks. arXiv preprint arXiv:1807.10439 (2018)
18. Goujon, A., Etemadi, A., Unser, M.: On the number of regions of piecewise linear neural networks. J. Comput. Appl. Math. **441**, 115667 (2024)
19. Guidotti, R., Monreale, A., Ruggieri, S., Turini, F., Giannotti, F., Pedreschi, D.: A survey of methods for explaining black box models. ACM Comput. Surv. **51**(5) (2018https://doi.org/10.1145/3236009
20. Hanin, B., Rolnick, D.: Complexity of linear regions in deep networks. In: Chaudhuri, K., Salakhutdinov, R. (eds.) Proceedings of the 36th International Conference on Machine Learning. Proceedings of Machine Learning Research, vol. 97, pp. 2596–2604. PMLR (2019). https://proceedings.mlr.press/v97/hanin19a.html
21. Hanin, B., Rolnick, D.: Deep ReLU networks have surprisingly few activation patterns. Adv. Neural. Inf. Process. Syst. **32** (2019)
22. Humayun, A.I., Balestriero, R., Balakrishnan, G., Baraniuk, R.G.: SplineCam: Exact visualization and characterization of deep network geometry and decision boundaries. In: Proceedings of the IEEE/CVF Conference on Computer Vision and Pattern Recognition, pp. 3789–3798 (2023)
23. Ignatiev, A., Narodytska, N., Marques-Silva, J.: On validating, repairing and refining heuristic ml explanations. arXiv preprint arXiv:1907.02509 (2019)
24. İrsoy, O., Alpaydın, E.: PathFinder: discovering decision pathways in deep neural networks. arXiv preprint arXiv:2210.00319 (2022)
25. Jia, S., Lin, P., Li, Z., Zhang, J., Liu, S.: Visualizing surrogate decision trees of convolutional neural networks. J. Vis. **23**, 141–156 (2020)

26. Jordan, M., Dimakis, A.G.: Exactly computing the local Lipschitz constant of ReLU networks. Adv. Neural. Inf. Process. Syst. **33**, 7344–7353 (2020)
27. Kohavi, R., Becker, B.: UCI adult data set. UCI Meach. Learn. Repository **5** (1996)
28. Lakkaraju, H., Bastani, O.: "How do i fool you?" manipulating user trust via misleading black box explanations. In: Proceedings of the AAAI/ACM Conference on AI, Ethics, and Society, pp. 79–85 (2020)
29. LeCun, Y., Bengio, Y., Hinton, G.: Deep learning. Nature **521**(7553), 436–444 (2015)
30. LeCun, Y., Bottou, L., Bengio, Y., Haffner, P.: Gradient-based learning applied to document recognition. Proc. IEEE **86**(11), 2278–2324 (1998)
31. Lee, G.H., Jaakkola, T.S.: Oblique decision trees from derivatives of ReLU networks. In: International Conference on Learning Representations (2020). https://openreview.net/forum?id=Bke8UR4FPB
32. Lipton, Z.C.: The mythos of model interpretability: in machine learning, the concept of interpretability is both important and slippery. Queue **16**(3), 31–57 (2018)
33. Logemann, T., Veith, E.M.: NN2EQCDT: equivalent transformation of feed-forward neural networks as DRL policies into compressed decision trees, vol. 15, pp. 94–100 (2023)
34. Lohaus, M., Kleindessner, M., Kenthapadi, K., Locatello, F., Russell, C.: Are two heads the same as one? Identifying disparate treatment in fair neural networks. Adv. Neural. Inf. Process. Syst. **35**, 16548–16562 (2022)
35. Maas, A.L., Hannun, A.Y., Ng, A.Y., et al.: Rectifier nonlinearities improve neural network acoustic models. In: Proceedings of the ICML, Atlanta, GA, vol. 30, p. 3 (2013)
36. Marques-Silva, J., Ignatiev, A.: Delivering trustworthy AI through formal XAI. In: Proceedings of the AAAI Conference on Artificial Intelligence, vol. 36, pp. 12342–12350 (2022)
37. Mehrabi, N., Morstatter, F., Saxena, N., Lerman, K., Galstyan, A.: A survey on bias and fairness in machine learning. ACM Comput. Surv. (CSUR) **54**(6), 1–35 (2021)
38. Molnar, C.: Interpretable machine learning (2020). Lulu.com
39. Montúfar, G.: Notes on the number of linear regions of deep neural networks (2017)
40. Montufar, G.F., Pascanu, R., Cho, K., Bengio, Y.: On the number of linear regions of deep neural networks. Adv. Neural Inf. Process. Syst. **27** (2014)
41. Murtovi, A., Bainczyk, A., Nolte, G., Schlüter, M., Steffen, B.: Forest gump: a tool for verification and explanation. Int. J. Softw. Tools Technol. Transf. (2023). https://doi.org/10.1007/s10009-023-00702-5
42. Nguyen, T.D., Kasmarik, K.E., Abbass, H.A.: An exact transformation from deep neural networks to multi-class multivariate decision trees. arXiv preprint arXiv:2003.04675 (2020)
43. Nolte, G., Schlüter, M., Murtovi, A., Steffen, B.: The power of typed affine decision structures: a case study. Int. J. Softw. Tools Technol. Transf. (2023). https://doi.org/10.1007/s10009-023-00701-6
44. Olteanu, A., Castillo, C., Diaz, F., Kıcıman, E.: Social data: Biases, methodological pitfalls, and ethical boundaries. Front. Big Data **2**, 13 (2019)
45. Parimbelli, E., Buonocore, T.M., Nicora, G., Michalowski, W., Wilk, S., Bellazzi, R.: Why did AI get this one wrong?-tree-based explanations of machine learning model predictions. Artif. Intell. Med. **135**, 102471 (2023)
46. Rolnick, D., Kording, K.: Reverse-engineering deep ReLU networks. In: International Conference on Machine Learning, pp. 8178–8187. PMLR (2020)

47. Schlüter, M., Nolte, G.: Introduction to symbolic execution of neural networks-towards faithful and explainable surrogate models. Electron. Commun. EASST **82** (2023)
48. Schlüter, M., Nolte, G., Murtovi, A., Steffen, B.: Towards rigorous understanding of neural networks via semantics-preserving transformations. Int. J. Softw. Tools Technol. Transf. (2023). https://doi.org/10.1007/s10009-023-00700-7
49. Serra, T., Tjandraatmadja, C., Ramalingam, S.: Bounding and counting linear regions of deep neural networks. In: International Conference on Machine Learning, pp. 4558–4566. PMLR (2018)
50. Singh, G., Gehr, T., Püschel, M., Vechev, M.: An abstract domain for certifying neural networks. Proc. ACM Program. Lang. **3**(POPL), 1–30 (2019)
51. Sudjianto, A., Knauth, W., Singh, R., Yang, Z., Zhang, A.: Unwrapping the black box of deep ReLU networks: interpretability, diagnostics, and simplification. ArXiv abs/2011.04041 (2020)
52. Sun, Y., Huang, X., Kroening, D., Sharp, J., Hill, M., Ashmore, R.: Testing deep neural networks. arXiv preprint arXiv:1803.04792 (2018)
53. Sun, Y., Wu, M., Ruan, W., Huang, X., Kwiatkowska, M., Kroening, D.: Concolic testing for deep neural networks. In: Proceedings of the 33rd ACM/IEEE International Conference on Automated Software Engineering, pp. 109–119 (2018)
54. Thibault, W.C., Naylor, B.F.: Set operations on polyhedra using binary space partitioning trees. In: Proceedings of the 14th annual conference on Computer Graphics and Interactive Techniques, pp. 153–162 (1987)
55. Tran, H.-D., et al.: Star-based reachability analysis of deep neural networks. In: ter Beek, M.H., McIver, A., Oliveira, J.N. (eds.) FM 2019. LNCS, vol. 11800, pp. 670–686. Springer, Cham (2019). https://doi.org/10.1007/978-3-030-30942-8_39
56. Usman, M., Noller, Y., Păsăreanu, C.S., Sun, Y., Gopinath, D.: NeuroSPF: a tool for the symbolic analysis of neural networks. In: 2021 IEEE/ACM 43rd International Conference on Software Engineering: Companion Proceedings (ICSE-Companion), pp. 25–28. IEEE (2021)
57. Verma, S., Dickerson, J., Hines, K.: Counterfactual explanations for machine learning: a review. arXiv preprint arXiv:2010.10596 **2** (2020)
58. Wang, Y.: Estimation and comparison of linear regions for ReLU networks. In: IJCAI, pp. 3544–3550 (2022)
59. Xiao, H., Rasul, K., Vollgraf, R.: Fashion-MNIST: a novel image dataset for benchmarking machine learning algorithms (2017)
60. Zednik, C.: Solving the black box problem: a normative framework for explainable artificial intelligence. Philos. Technol. **34**(2), 265–288 (2021)

Exploring Loose Coupling of Slicing with Dynamic Symbolic Execution on the JVM

Malte Mues(✉), Julian Rüschoff, and Ben Hermann

TU Dortmund University, Dortmund, Germany
{malte.mues,julian.rueschoff,ben.hermann}@tu-dortmund.de

Abstract. Dynamic symbolic execution is an effective technique for fuzzing programs with application to software verification as well if the search terminates during symbolic execution. However, the state space explosion problem often prevents the symbolic search from exploring the entire state space. As static analysis operates on the whole program rather than single execution paths, it can cut out parts of the program that are irrelevant for verifying a property. In this paper, we explore how slicing can be used before dynamic symbolic execution for analyzing assertion reachability in `Java` programs. We report on our first experience using state-of-the-art open-source `Java` slicers on the SV-COMP `Java` benchmark before applying `GDart`, a dynamic symbolic execution engine for `Java`. Currently, this experiment has not been successful, as the slicers are not mature enough to reliably produce correct slices of a task in the SV-COMP benchmark. However, in a few examples, the approach delivered promising results that motivate the future development of slicers for `Java`.

Keywords: Java Verification · Java Slicing · Dynamic Symbolic Execution · Tool Combination

1 Introduction

Formal methods are made to prove functional or security properties of systems. Despite their theoretical efficiency they are still not established as today's standard in day-to-day software engineering (except for special domains such as, e.g., railways [9], avionics [7], and security-critical embedded systems [8]). There are single projects conducted by large software companies with (semi-)formal methods that had remarkable success on standard commercial software (e.g., Zelkova and Tiros by Backes et al. [3] at AWS, or `SAGE` by Godefroid et al. [14] and its application for bug finding at Microsoft [13]). Garavel et al. [11] conducted an expert survey on formal methods in 2020 for the 25th anniversary of FMICS. While the experts agreed on the potential impact formal methods might have on software development in general, they also agreed with the main criticism

© The Author(s), under exclusive license to Springer Nature Switzerland AG 2025
M. Huisman and F. Howar (Eds.): TAP 2024, LNCS 15153, pp. 168–175, 2025.
https://doi.org/10.1007/978-3-031-72044-4_9

that research invests too little in the consolidation of existing results and building robust tools. In addition, 70% of the respondents agreed that researchers should focus on scalability and applicability rather than the next fundamental breakthroughs.

Dynamic symbolic execution (cf. DART by Godefroid et al. [12]) is a technique that executes a program concretely and collects constraints on branching points to build a constraint tree. This constraint tree is unrolled similar to program unrolling in traditional symbolic execution [16]. Whitebox fuzzing as conducted in SAGE tries to unroll as much as possible of the constraint tree. If dynamic symbolic execution should be used for verification rather than fuzzing, it is required to unroll the complete constraint tree. The *state space explosion* problem prevents this in the general case. Unbounded loops or heap data structures always allow one additional execution in the symbolic constraint tree.

In previous work, Mues and Howar [17] have shown that dynamic symbolic execution can be implemented robustly on an industrial-grade JVM. The resulting tool is called GDart. Thanks to the modular design of GDart, the symbolic execution is independent of the concrete execution. The symbolic unrolling is encapsulated in the DSE component. The concrete executor is encapsulated in a component called SPouT [18] and is powered by the GraalVM [22]. For scaling the approach, integrating static analysis either in the DSE component or as an independent tool before GDart seems promising. There are various examples, of how this is beneficial for C analysis [2,3,19]. To the best of our knowledge, there is no tool available that follows these ideas for the JVM.

In this paper, we report our first experience in consolidating different ideas for Java slicing as a static analysis tool before dynamic symbolic execution aiming for better scalability and applicability of formal methods in cooperation. Assertion reachability is used as a property for the Java track at SV-COMP [4]. State-of-the-art slicing tools for Java are applied to slice the program for each assertion encountered in the program used as a verification task. GDart is run on each slice produced and the results from all slices are integrated into the final verdict. Our main finding so far is, that JavaSlicer [10] is the only available tool that successfully performs slicing on the SV-COMP Java benchmark. We found single examples where the approach can improve on the benchmark compared with GDart alone. However, to the best of our knowledge, there is no current Java slicer available that could be reliably used as a preprocessor for Java programs before applying dynamic symbolic execution.

Related Work. Static and dynamic analysis of Java programs has been researched for many decades now. For this paper, we cannot cover all trends and tools that have been proposed in the past. Instead, we will focus on either ideas around slicing, or available slicing tools. Tripp et al. [21] demonstrated thin slicing proposed by Sridharan et al. [20] as an efficient static analysis algorithm for taint analysis of Java web-applications. While the implementation in the evaluation is built on the IBM T.J. Watson Libraries for Analysis (WALA), we could not find an open-source version of thin slicing to include in the experi-

```java
public static void main(String[]
↪  args) {
  int x = Verifier.nondetInt();
  if (x > 0) return;
  test(x);
}
public static void test(int x) {
x = x + 1;
switch (x) {
  case 2:
    System.out.println("Foo2");
    assert false;
    break;
  case 3000:
    System.out.println("Foo3000");
    break;
  default:
    System.out.println("def 2");
    break;
}
}
```

(a) The original task.

```java
public static void main(String[]
↪  args) {
  int x = Verifier.nondetInt();
  if (x > 0)
    return;
  test(x);
}

public static void test(int x) {
  x = x + 1;
  switch(x) {
    case 2:
      {
        boolean assertRep1 =
        ↪  false;
        assert assertRep1;
      }
  }
}
```

(b) The slicing result.

Fig. 1. An example of slicing the jpf-regression/ExSymExeSwitch_true example from the SV-COMP Java benchmarks.

ments. However, there is still some slicing code in WALA that has not been adapted to modern Java.

Apart from WALA there are very few open-source implementations of slicers for Java. In 2008, Hammacher [15] implemented the JavaSlicer in his bachelor thesis. For a long time, it used to be the only open-source implementation for slicing Java. Recently, Slice4J by Ahmed et al. [1] and JavaSlicer by Galindo et al. [10] aimed to fill this void in the Java tooling landscape. Unfortunately, Galindo et al. and Hammacher use the same name for their respective tool. In this paper, we use the name JavaSlicer to refer to the implementation by Galindo et al.

Outline. Section 2 gives an example of successful application of Java slicing. The general tooling is described in Sect. 3. The remaining sections describe the results and conclude the paper.

2 Motivating Example

Figure 1a shows an example task from the SV-COMP Java benchmark[1] [5]. It is a simple task aiming at specific language features rather than complex system

[1] https://gitlab.com/sosy-lab/benchmarking/sv-benchmarks/-/blob/main/java.

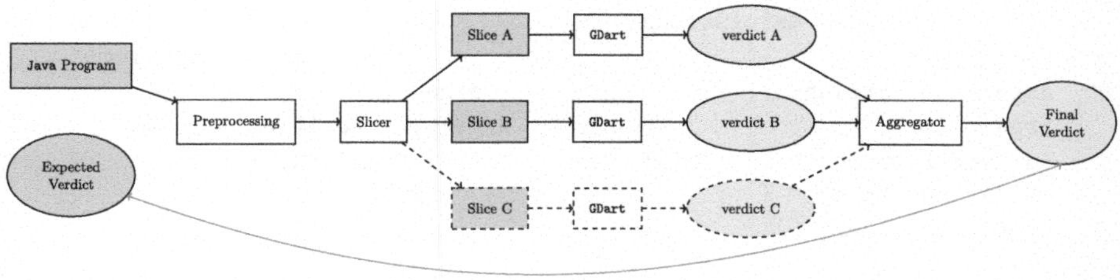

Fig. 2. The analysis pipeline for applying a slicer before `GDart`. The colored rectangles are `Java` programs, and the colored ellipses are verdicts. The white boxes are tools or scripts that work on the input. The intermediate program between preprocessing and the slicer is not shown. The final verdict can be compared with the expected verdict.

behavior. Here, a switch statement is examined. SV-COMP `Java` tasks currently verify exclusively for assertion reachability. The tasks use calls to the *Verifier* class to inform the verifier about a nondeterministic value introduced a this point. It is a way to simulate random inputs of a certain type to the program and offers the verifier control over the inputs for verification purposes. The verification task is to prove that the assertion holds for any value potentially returned by the *Verifier* class. In this task, there is only one *assert false* statement. The verification goal is to determine whether this assert statement is reachable or not. In general, arbitrary amounts of asserts are allowed in the benchmarks.

The switch statement branches in three ways. However, the assert is only present in one of them. For a successful verification, it is sufficient to evaluate whether the assert holds on this path. The idea of using slicing is that the slicer extracts the single path with all relevant program behavior and `GDart` is then run on the slice. In this example, it worked well. Figure 1b shows the slicer's output.

The slice has significantly less code. The print statements have been sliced away as well. As slicing for statements is not supported by the used slicers, the asserted condition has been assigned to the boolean variable *assertRep1* that is checked in the *assert* later. The fewer branching points make dynamic symbolic execution significantly easier.

3 Analysis Pipeline

Applying a slicer before `GDart` is not a linear process, as the slicer aims in each slice for one assertion statement in the verification task. If a verification task has more than one assert statement (e.g., the MinePump tasks in the SV-COMP `Java` benchmark) slicing generates one verification task per assert statement in the benchmark. Figure 2 shows the effect of this behavior. The multiple slices require multiple runs of `GDart`. As described in the motivating example in Sect. 2, a preprocessor is needed that assigns the assertion condition to a boolean intermediate variable to allow slicing. Lines 13 and 14 of Subfig. 1b shows the result

```java
public static void main(String[] args) {
  args = new String[1];
  args[0] = Verifier.nondetString();
  char[] charArray = {
    args[0].charAt(0),
    ...
```

(a) Excerpt of the original task

```java
public static void main(String[] args) {
  args[0] = Verifier.nondetString();
  char[] charArray = { args[0].charAt(0),
  ...
```

(b) The slice of the same lines

Fig. 3. The SV-COMP `Java` task StringValue03 in the jbmc-regression folder.

of this rewrite. Apart from this change, the program is unchanged in the preprocessing step. After preprocessing, the slicer generates different slices and `GDart` runs on each slice. An aggregator component compiles the final verdict. If one of the `GDart` runs returns *false*, this implies that the assertion is reachable in this slice and therefore the assertion in the original program should be reachable. The aggregator verdict is *false* in this case independent of the results of all other slices. If none of the slices returns *false* and one of the slices returns *unknown* or *error* due to crashes or reaching the resource limit, the overall verdict is *unknown*. Only if all slices of a program are verified to have unreachable assertions, the aggregator returns *true* to signal that none of the assertions in the program is reachable. These return values follow the SV-COMP standards for task specification. The overall result is then compared with the predefined expected verdict.

SV-COMP requires verification witnesses together with the verdict. At the moment, there is no community agreement for verifying correctness witnesses. For violation witnesses, `GDart` would have to be rerun on the original program with the concrete values leading to an assertion violation in the slice to produce a violation witness in the SV-COMP format that is valid with the original program. However, generating witnesses is not the main focus of this study and might be resolved more efficiently in the future.

4 Results

We evaluate the analysis pipeline described in the previous section on the `Java` SV-COMP benchmark. The benchmark contains 587 tasks and specifies an expected verdict for all of them. Our baseline is pure `GDart`, which solves currently 474 of the 587 tasks correctly and none incorrectly. We used the SV-COMP resource limits of 8 vCores, 15 GB of RAM, and 900 s CPU time. `GDart` runs on the local version of the verifier cloud[2] at TU Dortmund. The verifier cloud allows running tasks with the `BenchExec` framework by Beyer et al. [6] across multiple machines and is also used for running SV-COMP.

[2] https://vcloud.sosy-lab.org.

```
public static void main(String[] args)
↪ {
  int N = Verifier.nondetInt();
  Verifier.assume(N > 0);

  int a[] = new int[N];
  for (int i = 0; i < N; i++) {
    a[i] = N - i;
  }
  sort(a);
  assert (N < 2 || a[0] < a[1]);
}
```

(a) Excerpt of the original task

```
public static void main(String[]
↪  args) {
  int N = Verifier.nondetInt();
  int[] a = new int[N];
  for (int i = 0; i < N; i++) {
    a[i] = N - i;
  }
  {boolean assertReplacement515 =
       (N < 2 || a[0] < a[1]);
    assert assertReplacement515;}
}
```

(b) The slice of the same lines

Fig. 4. The SV-COMP Java task InsertionSort-FunSat01 in the algorithms folder.

As described in Sect. 1, only Slice4J[3] and JavaSlicer[4] are feasible state-of-the-art Java slicer. Both tools have been published with papers within the last five years and target at least Java 11. For Slice4J, we could not reproduce the results from the paper, nor could we get it to slice our benchmarks. It is a dynamic slicer that instruments the Java program first and then gathers information for slicing while running the instrumented jar. We provided a runnable jar, but after the instrumentation step, the Slice4J was no longer able to run the jar. The script for running the shipped benchmarks also failed. Therefore, we disregarded Slice4J for this experiment.

JavaSlicer worked out of the box as described in the repository README. For the 587 tasks, it produced 1632 slices. We packaged all slices as verification tasks in the verifier cloud format and have run GDart on them. For 879 of 1632 tasks (roughly 54%), the runner script of GDart could not compile the resulting slice as the slicer produced invalid code. 538 could not be executed after compilation, because JavaSlicer removed the main class entirely with the main method during slicing. These numbers alone demonstrate that there is a large gap between slicing theory and making it applicable on Java programs.

Of the tasks that have been sliced successfully and could be solved, 60 reachable assertions have been found. 48 tasks have been classified correctly for unreachable assertions. For 39 tasks that have a reachable assertion, GDart proved it unreachable on the slice. Figure 3 shows one of these task. While the original task in Subfig. 3a ensures that the *args* array is initialized to a String array with one element, the slice in Subfig. 3b sliced this away incorrectly. As the function is invoked without arguments to the Java program in GDart, GDart claims the assertion in the slice unreachable as the access to *args[0]* fails as *args* is always an empty array. JavaSlicer deliberately changes the program semantics in this case and the GDart concrete driver used for SV-COMP limits

[3] https://github.com/resess/Slicer4J.

[4] https://github.com/mistupv/JavaSlicer.

the execution space in a way that does not compensate for this change. In 3 cases, unreachable assertions become reachable in the slice. Figure 4 shows one of these three examples. The slicer cut the *Verifier.assume(N > 0)* in Line 3 of Subfig. 4a. This call is used in the verification task to bound N to a number greater than 0. In addition, the *sort(a)* call in Line 9 of Subfig. 4a is sliced away. For the verification, the *sort(a)* call is essential. It is a general pattern that dataflow leading to parameters that are passed to a method as parameters and are changed in place are neglected by the `JavaSlicer`. However, the assertion in Line 10 of Subfigure 4b indeed becomes reachable while it holds on the original program.

5 Conclusion

In this paper, we evaluated the idea of using a state-of-the-art program slicer for reducing the state space in `Java` software verification tasks to apply dynamic symbolic execution in continuation on the obtained slices. While this technique is well established for analyzing other programming languages, there are currently no sufficient state-of-the-art slicers for `Java` available for this task. Providing a robust `Java` slicer that does not change the program semantic of the variables influencing the slicing target is currently an open research challenge. `JavaSlicer` [10] has shown promising performance in some cases, however, the experiments pointed out problems with implicit dataflow in parameters passed to methods, constructors, and across exception handling. The loose coupling of the two techniques shipwreck on the slicer's performance and shows that slicing `Java` program requires further consolidation before a tighter integration with dynamic symbolic execution is possible. However, we think it is worth exploring this idea further and laying the groundwork for an analysis pipeline that couples the two techniques in this contribution.

References

1. Ahmed, K., Lis, M., Rubin, J.: Slicer4J: a dynamic slicer for Java. In: ESEC/FSE 2021, pp. 1570–1574. Association for Computing Machinery, New York (2021). https://doi.org/10.1145/3468264.3473123
2. Avgerinos, T., Rebert, A., Cha, S.K., Brumley, D.: Enhancing symbolic execution with veritesting. In: ICSE 2014, pp. 1083–1094 (2014). https://doi.org/10.1145/2568225.2568293
3. Backes, J., et al.: One-click formal methods. IEEE Softw. **36**(6), 61–65 (2019). https://doi.org/10.1109/MS.2019.2930609
4. Beyer, D.: State of the art in software verification and witness validation: SV-COMP 2024. In: Finkbeiner, B., Kovács, L. (eds.) TACAS 2024. LNCS, vol. 14572, pp. 299–329. Springer, Cham (2024). https://doi.org/10.1007/978-3-031-57256-2_15
5. Beyer, D.: SV-benchmarks: benchmark set for software verification (SV-COMP 2024) (2024). https://doi.org/10.5281/zenodo.10669723, https://doi.org/10.5281/zenodo.10669723

6. Beyer, D., Löwe, S., Wendler, P.: Reliable benchmarking: requirements and solutions. STTT **21**(1), 1–29 (2019). https://doi.org/10.1007/s10009-017-0469-y
7. Brahmi, A., et al.: Industrial use of a safe and efficient formal method based software engineering process in avionics. In: ERTS 2020 (2020)
8. Djoudi, A., et al.: A bottom-up formal verification approach for common criteria certification: application to JavaCard virtual machine. In: ERTS 2022 (2022)
9. Ferrari, A., Beek, M.H.T.: Formal methods in railways: a systematic mapping study. ACM Comput. Surv. **55**(4) (2022). https://doi.org/10.1145/3520480
10. Galindo, C., Perez, S., Silva, J.: A program slicer for Java (tool paper). In: Schlingloff, B.H., Chai, M. (eds.) SEFM 2022. LNCS, vol. 13550, pp. 146–151. Springer, Cham (2022). https://doi.org/10.1007/978-3-031-17108-6_9
11. Garavel, H., Beek, M.H., Pol, J.: The 2020 expert survey on formal methods. In: ter Beek, M.H., Ničković, D. (eds.) FMICS 2020. LNCS, vol. 12327, pp. 3–69. Springer, Cham (2020). https://doi.org/10.1007/978-3-030-58298-2_1
12. Godefroid, P., Klarlund, N., Sen, K.: DART: directed automated random testing. In: PLDI 2005, pp. 213–223. ACM (2005). https://doi.org/10.1007/978-3-642-19237-1_4
13. Godefroid, P., Levin, M.Y., Molnar, D.: SAGE: whitebox fuzzing for security testing: SAGE has had a remarkable impact at Microsoft. Queue **10**(1), 20–27 (2012). https://doi.org/10.1145/2090147.2094081
14. Godefroid, P., Levin, M.Y., Molnar, D.A., et al.: Automated whitebox fuzz testing. In: NDSS 2008, vol. 8, pp. 151–166 (2008)
15. Hammacher, C.: Design and implementation of an efficient dynamic slicer for Java. Bachelor's thesis (2008)
16. King, J.C.: Symbolic execution and program testing. Commun. ACM **19**(7), 385–394 (1976). https://doi.org/10.1145/360248.360252
17. Mues, M., Howar, F.: GDart: an ensemble of tools for dynamic symbolic execution on the java virtual machine (competition contribution). In: TACAS 2022. LNCS, vol. 13244, pp. 435–439. Springer, Cham (2022). https://doi.org/10.1007/978-3-030-99527-0_27
18. Mues, M., Howar, F., Dierl, S.: SPouT: symbolic path recording during testing - a concolic executor for the JVM. In: Schlingloff, B.H., Chai, M. (eds.) SEFM 2022. LNCS, vol. 13550, pp. 91–107. Springer, Cham (2022). https://doi.org/10.1007/978-3-031-17108-6_6
19. Slabý, J., Strejček, J., Trtík, M.: Checking properties described by state machines: on synergy of instrumentation, slicing, and symbolic execution. In: Stoelinga, M., Pinger, R. (eds.) FMICS 2012. LNCS, vol. 7437, pp. 207–221. Springer, Heidelberg (2012). https://doi.org/10.1007/978-3-642-32469-7_14
20. Sridharan, M., Fink, S.J., Bodik, R.: Thin slicing. In: SPLASH 2007, pp. 112–122 (2007). https://doi.org/10.1145/1250734.1250748
21. Tripp, O., Pistoia, M., Fink, S.J., Sridharan, M., Weisman, O.: TAJ: effective taint analysis of web applications. ACM Sigplan Not. **44**(6), 87–97 (2009). https://doi.org/10.1145/1543135.1542486
22. Würthinger, T., et al.: One VM to rule them all. In: SPLASH 2013, pp. 187–204. Association for Computing Machinery, New York (2013). https://doi.org/10.1145/2509578.2509581

Author Index

B
Barth, Max 45
Blanchard, Allan 65

C
Correnson, Loïc 65

D
Djoudi, Adel 65

E
Ehlers, Rüdiger 3

F
Flinkow, Thomas 107

H
Hermann, Ben 168
Huang, Li 25

J
Jakobs, Marie-Christine 45

K
Kosmatov, Nikolai 65, 87

L
Lochau, Malte 127
Loulergue, Frédéric 87

M
Méry, Dominique 107
Meyer, Bertrand 25
Mues, Malte 168

O
Oriol, Manuel 25

P
Pérez, Daniel Gracia 87

R
Rüschoff, Julian 168

S
Schaefer, Ina 127
Schlüter, Maximilian 148
Steffen, Bernhard 148

W
Wu, Hao 107

Z
Ziani, Yani 87

© The Editor(s) (if applicable) and The Author(s), under exclusive license
to Springer Nature Switzerland AG 2025

M. Huisman and F. Howar (Eds.): TAP 2024, LNCS 15153, p. 177, 2025.
https://doi.org/10.1007/978-3-031-72044-4

SPRINGER NATURE

GPSR Compliance

The European Union's (EU) General Product Safety Regulation (GPSR) is a set of rules that requires consumer products to be safe and our obligations to ensure this.

If you have any concerns about our products, you can contact us on ProductSafety@springernature.com

In case Publisher is established outside the EU, the EU authorized representative is:

Springer Nature Customer Service Center GmbH
Europaplatz 3
69115 Heidelberg, Germany

The manufacturer's authorised representative in the EU is Springer
Nature Customer Service Centre GmbH, Europaplatz 3, 69115 Heidelberg,
Germany. If you have any concerns regarding our products, please
contact ProductSafety@springernature.com

Printed and bound by CPI Group (UK) Ltd, Croydon, CR0 4YY
01/10/2026
02225952-0006